LANGUAGE AND LITERACY SERIES

Dorothy S. Strickland, FOUNDING EDITOR
Celia Genishi and Donna E. Alvermann, SERIES EDITORS
ADVISORY BOARD: *Richard Allington, Kathryn Au, Bernice Cullinan, Colette Daiute,*
Anne Haas Dyson, Carole Edelsky, Mary Juzwik, Susan Lytle, Django Paris, Timothy Shanahan

Reading, Writing, and Talk: Inclusive Teaching Strategies
for Diverse Learners, K–2
MARIANA SOUTO-MANNING & JESSICA MARTELL

Go Be a Writer!: Expanding the Curricular Boundaries of
Literacy Learning with Children
CANDACE R. KUBY & TARA GUTSHALL RUCKER

Partnering with Immigrant Communities:
Action Through Literacy
GERALD CAMPANO, MARÍA PAULA GHISO, & BETHANY J. WELCH

Teaching Outside the Box but Inside the Standards:
Making Room for Dialogue
BOB FECHO, MICHELLE FALTER, & XIAOLI HONG, EDS.

Literacy Leadership in Changing Schools:
10 Keys to Successful Professional Development
SHELLEY B. WEPNER, DIANE W. GÓMEZ, KATIE EGAN CUNNINGHAM,
KRISTIN N. RAINVILLE, & COURTNEY KELLY

Literacy Theory as Practice:
Connecting Theory and Instruction in K–12 Classrooms
LARA J. HANDSFIELD

Literacy and History in Action: Immersive Approaches to
Disciplinary Thinking, Grades 5–12
THOMAS M. MCCANN, REBECCA D'ANGELO, NANCY GALAS, & MARY
GRESKA

Pose, Wobble, Flow:
A Culturally Proactive Approach to Literacy Instruction
ANTERO GARCIA & CINDY O'DONNELL-ALLEN

Newsworthy—Cultivating Critical Thinkers, Readers, and
Writers in Language Arts Classrooms
ED MADISON

Engaging Writers with Multigenre Research Projects:
A Teacher's Guide
NANCY MACK

Teaching Transnational Youth—
Literacy and Education in a Changing World
ALLISON SKERRETT

Uncommonly Good Ideas—
Teaching Writing in the Common Core Era
SANDRA MURPHY & MARY ANN SMITH

The One-on-One Reading and Writing Conference:
Working with Students on Complex Texts
JENNIFER BERNE & SOPHIE C. DEGENER

Critical Encounters in Secondary English:
Teaching Literary Theory to Adolescents, Third Edition
DEBORAH APPLEMAN

Transforming Talk into Text—Argument Writing, Inquiry,
and Discussion, Grades 6–12
THOMAS M. MCCANN

Reading and Representing Across the Content Areas:
A Classroom Guide
AMY ALEXANDRA WILSON & KATHRYN J. CHAVEZ

Writing and Teaching to Change the World:
Connecting with Our Most Vulnerable Students
STEPHANIE JONES, ED.

Educating Literacy Teachers Online:
Tools, Techniques, and Transformations
LANE W. CLARKE & SUSAN WATTS-TAFFEE

Other People's English: Code-Meshing,
Code-Switching, and African American Literacy
VERSHAWN ASHANTI YOUNG, RUSTY BARRETT,
Y'SHANDA YOUNG-RIVERA, & KIM BRIAN LOVEJOY

WHAM! Teaching with Graphic Novels Across
the Curriculum
WILLIAM G. BROZO, GARY MOORMAN, & CARLA K. MEYER

The Administration and Supervision of Reading Programs,
5th Edition
SHELLEY B. WEPNER, DOROTHY S. STRICKLAND,
& DIANA J. QUATROCHE, EDS.

Critical Literacy in the Early Childhood Classroom:
Unpacking Histories, Unlearning Privilege
CANDACE R. KUBY

Inspiring Dialogue:
Talking to Learn in the English Classroom
MARY M. JUZWIK, CARLIN BORSHEIM-BLACK,
SAMANTHA CAUGHLAN, & ANNE HEINTZ

Reading the Visual:
An Introduction to Teaching Multimodal Literacy
FRANK SERAFINI

Race, Community, and Urban Schools:
Partnering with African American Families
STUART GREENE

ReWRITING the Basics:
Literacy Learning in Children's Cultures
ANNE HAAS DYSON

Writing Instruction That Works:
Proven Methods for Middle and High School Classrooms
ARTHUR N. APPLEBEE & JUDITH A. LANGER, WITH KRISTEN CAMPBELL
WILCOX, MARC NACHOWITZ, MICHAEL P. MASTROIANNI, &
CHRISTINE DAWSON

Literacy Playshop: New Literacies, Popular Media, and
Play in the Early Childhood Classroom
KAREN E. WOHLWEND

Critical Media Pedagogy:
Teaching for Achievement in City Schools
ERNEST MORRELL, RUDY DUEÑAS, VERONICA GARCIA,
& JORGE LOPEZA

A Search Past Silence: The Literacy of Young Black Men
DAVID E. KIRKLAND

The ELL Writer:
Moving Beyond Basics in the Secondary Classroom
CHRISTINA ORTMEIER-HOOPER

Reading in a Participatory Culture:
Remixing *Moby-Dick* in the English Classroom
HENRY JENKINS & WYN KELLEY, WITH KATIE CLINTON, JENNA
MCWILLIAMS, RICARDO PITTS-WILEY, & ERIN REILLY, EDS.

Summer Reading:
Closing the Rich/Poor Achievement Gap
RICHARD L. ALLINGTON & ANNE MCGILL-FRANZEN, EDS.

continued

For volumes in the NCRLL Collection (edited by JoBeth Allen and Donna E. Alvermann) and the Practitioners Bookshelf Series
(edited by Celia Genishi and Donna E. Alvermann), as well as other titles in this series, please visit www.tcpress.com.

Language and Literacy Series, *continued*

Real World Writing for Secondary Students:
Teaching the College Admission Essay and
Other Gate-Openers for Higher Education
JESSICA SINGER EARLY & MEREDITH DECOSTA

Teaching Vocabulary to English Language Learners
MICHAEL F. GRAVES, DIANE AUGUST, &
JEANETTE MANCILLA-MARTINEZ

Literacy for a Better World:
LAURA SCHNEIDER VANDERPLOEG

Socially Responsible Literacy
PAULA M. SELVESTER & DEBORAH G. SUMMERS

Learning from Culturally and Linguistically Diverse
Classrooms: Using Inquiry to Inform Practice
JOAN C. FINGON & SHARON H. ULANOFF, EDS.

Bridging Literacy and Equity
ALTHIER M. LAZAR ET AL.

"Trust Me! I Can Read"
SALLY LAMPING & DEAN WOODRING BLASE

Reading Girls
HADAR DUBROWSKY MA'AYAN

Reading Time
CATHERINE COMPTON-LILLY

A Call to Creativity
LUKE REYNOLDS

Literacy and Justice Through Photography
WENDY EWALD, KATHARINE HYDE, & LISA LORD

The Successful High School Writing Center
DAWN FELS & JENNIFER WELLS, EDS.

Interrupting Hate
MOLLIE V. BLACKBURN

Playing Their Way into Literacies
KAREN E. WOHLWEND

Teaching Literacy for Love and Wisdom
JEFFREY D. WILHELM & BRUCE NOVAK

Overtested
JESSICA ZACHER PANDYA

Restructuring Schools for Linguistic Diversity,
Second Edition
OFELIA B. MIRAMONTES, ADEL NADEAU, & NANCY L. COMMINS

Words Were All We Had
MARÍA DE LA LUZ REYES, ED.

Urban Literacies
VALERIE KINLOCH, ED.

Bedtime Stories and Book Reports
CATHERINE COMPTON-LILLY & STUART GREENE, EDS.

Envisioning Knowledge
JUDITH A. LANGER

Envisioning Literature, Second Edition
JUDITH A. LANGER

Writing Assessment and the Revolution in Digital Texts
and Technologies
MICHAEL R. NEAL

Artifactual Literacies
KATE PAHL & JENNIFER ROWSELL

Educating Emergent Bilinguals
OFELIA GARCÍA & JO ANNE KLEIFGEN

(Re)Imagining Content-Area Literacy Instruction
RONI JO DRAPER, ED.

Change Is Gonna Come
PATRICIA A. EDWARDS ET AL.

When Commas Meet Kryptonite
MICHAEL BITZ

Literacy Tools in the Classroom
RICHARD BEACH ET AL.

Harlem on Our Minds
VALERIE KINLOCH

Teaching the New Writing
ANNE HERRINGTON, KEVIN HODGSON, & CHARLES MORAN, EDS.

Children, Language, and Literacy
CELIA GENISHI & ANNE HAAS DYSON

Children's Language
JUDITH WELLS LINDFORS

"You Gotta BE the Book," Second Edition
JEFFREY D. WILHELM

Children's Literature and Learning
BARBARA A. LEHMAN

Storytime
LAWRENCE R. SIPE

Effective Instruction for Struggling Readers, K–6
BARBARA M. TAYLOR & JAMES E. YSSELDYKE, EDS.

The Effective Literacy Coach
ADRIAN RODGERS & EMILY M. RODGERS

Writing in Rhythm
MAISHA T. FISHER

Reading the Media
RENEE HOBBS

teaching**media***literacy*.com
RICHARD BEACH

What Was It Like?
LINDA J. RICE

Research on Composition
PETER SMAGORINSKY, ED.

The Vocabulary Book
MICHAEL F. GRAVES

New Literacies in Action
WILLIAM KIST

READING
WRITING
AND TALK

Inclusive Teaching Strategies for Diverse Learners, K–2

Mariana Souto-Manning
Jessica Martell

Foreword by Gloria Ladson-Billings

TEACHERS COLLEGE PRESS

TEACHERS COLLEGE | COLUMBIA UNIVERSITY
NEW YORK AND LONDON

Published by Teachers College Press, 1234 Amsterdam Avenue, New York, NY 10027

Library of Congress Cataloging-in-Publication Data

Names: Souto-Manning, Mariana, author. | Martell, Jessica, author.
Title: Reading, writing, and talk : inclusive teaching strategies for diverse
   learners, K–2 / Mariana Souto-Manning, Jessica Martell ; foreword by
   Gloria Ladson-Billings.
Description: New York, NY : Teachers College Press, [2016] | Series: Language
   and literacy series | Includes bibliographical references and index.
Identifiers: LCCN 2015047579| ISBN 9780807757574 (pbk.) | ISBN
9780807757581
   (hardcover) | ISBN 9780807774717 (ebook)
Subjects: LCSH: Language arts (Primary) | English language—Study and
   teaching—Foreign speakers. | Culturally relevant pedagogy.
Classification: LCC LB1528.S64 2016 | DDC 372.6—dc23
LC record available at http://lccn.loc.gov/2015047579

ISBN 978-0-8077-5757-4 (paper)
ISBN 978-0-8077-5758-1 (hardcover)
ISBN 978-0-8077-7471-7 (ebook)

Printed on acid-free paper
Manufactured in the United States of America

23 22 21 20 19 18   8 7 6 5 4 3

We dedicate this book to our spouses and partners in life,

Dwight C. Manning
and
Boy Andre Martell

Thank you for believing in us and in the work we do.
Thank you for your ongoing support, encouragement, and love.
Most of all, thank you for reminding us each and every day:
"If you don't like something, change it."
—Maya Angelou

Contents

Foreword   *Gloria Ladson-Billings*   ix

Acknowledgments   xiii

1. **Reading, Writing, and Talk with Diverse Children**   1

   On the Breathtaking Diversity of Children in K–2 Classrooms   1

   Homogeneity as an Unreal Norm   4

   Moving Away from the Standardization of Teaching   6

   A Story of Valuing Many Languages and Multiple Literacies   8

   Teaching "English Language Learners"—and We Are ALL Language Learners   15

2. **Understanding the Diversity of Children's Language and Literacy Practices**   17

   Observing and Documenting Children's Language and Literacy Practices   18

   Recognizing Sociocultural Knowledge and Experiences   22

   Talk   26

   Print   27

   Reading   30

   Listening to and Valuing the Stories Children Tell   31

   Reflecting on Diverse Literacies and Looking Ahead . . .   38

3. **Building a Learning Community That Honors Diversities**   39

   Looking Around:
   What Story Your Classroom Tells and How You Can Rewrite It   40

   Valuing Children's Literate Lives   45

   Inviting Families into the Classroom to Share Expertise   47

   Focusing on Authenticity and Interest in Reading, Writing, and Talk   54

   Play, Language, and Literacy   57

   Reflecting on Building Learning Communities and Looking Ahead . . .   58

4. **On Oral Language: Considering Meaningful Possibilities and Learning Authentically from Diverse Children in K–2 Classrooms**   **59**

Oral Language   60

Storying in the Earliest Years   61

Role of Play in Literacy Development   67

Examining Classroom Talk   73

Oral Language and Friendships, Fairness, and Fantasy   75

Oral Language and Culturally Relevant Teaching   77

Reflecting on Oral Language and Looking Ahead . . .   79

5. **On Reading Words and Worlds: Considering Diverse Possibilities, Perspectives, and Points of View in K–2 Classrooms**   **81**

Reading   82

Understanding Early Literacy and Young Children's Reading   85

Engaging in Read-Alouds   93

Sharing Shared Reading   96

Re-Envisioning Reading Workshop   97

Assessment as Documenting Children's Literacy Practices   103

Reflecting on Reading and Looking Ahead . . .   110

6. **On Writing Diverse Words and Worlds: Writing a Curriculum That Honors the Brilliance of Diverse Children**   **111**

Early Writing   112

Writing with Purpose   113

Interactive Writing   116

Making Writing Workshop Relevant for Your Setting   121

Teaching Spelling: When? How? Why?   132

Motivating and Inspiring Writers   135

Documenting Growth   139

Reflecting on Writing and Looking Ahead . . .   140

Conclusion: Negotiating Beliefs, Standards, and Practices to Create Classrooms Where Diverse Learners Are Valued   **141**

Children's Book List   **144**

References   **146**

Index   **154**

About the Authors   **160**

Foreword

I confess that I am like a fish out of water in the world of early childhood education. Certainly as a parent and grandparent, I have had the joy of interacting with young children. But those interactions were deeply grounded in the love I have for those particular children. My role in those interactions was to keep them happy and safe; communication often revolved around avoiding danger and keeping them laughing. And almost all of those interactions were one-on-one. When my middle son and his wife had twins I found caring for them—even for small stretches of time—daunting. I cannot imagine how a teacher with a classroom full of little ones finds the wherewithal to cope with so many different personalities who have little or no motivation to be compliant with what a teacher desires.

I learned of the challenge of early childhood teaching quite by accident. When it was time for my youngest child to enroll in preschool, I had not done the preparation of getting her on the "right" preschool waiting lists as soon as I learned I was pregnant. My inquiry regarding enrollment at the preschool of my choice the summer before we wanted her to start was met with incredulity. "Oh no," the director exclaimed. "You should have placed her on the list 2 years ago!" (Mind you, my child was 3 years old.) Then I learned that the *only* way my daughter could be considered for this preschool was if I were willing to serve as a "participating parent" and spend one day a week at the preschool from 9:00 A.M. to noon assisting the teachers. Desperate and running out of options, I agreed to be a participating parent. My job was to "play" with the kids, read to anyone who wanted to hear a story, help with bathroom emergencies, supervise "nutrition" (i.e., snack) time, and encourage children to participate in daily clean-up.

While the duties seemed doable, I learned quickly that young children are deeply curious and brutally frank about a number of things that adults would rather avoid. Children want to know about the differences in the world they inhabit. "Why is that lady fat?" "Where is that man's leg?" "Why are those people begging for money?" These are the kinds of questions that children may ask, only to have the adults around them respond, "Shhhh— that's not nice!" Although psychologists tell us that children recognize racial and ethnic differences by the time they are about 2 years old, racial, ethnic, linguistic, and other forms of difference are among the things we as educators are rarely ready to confront.

Unfortunately, too many early childhood teachers want to shy away from the realities that children seem ready to confront. I once did a professional development session on using children's and young adult literature to deal with uncomfortable truths in our history and culture. One of the books I shared is an illustrated text called *Nettie's Trip South* by Ann Turner. The author wrote the book based on the diary of a great-great aunt and placed it in the voice of a young girl who is writing to her best friend about her visit to the South just before the Civil War. The stark black and white drawings set a powerful mood and the narrator asks childlike questions such as, "Why do they say they are 3/5 of a person? What are they missing?" After presenting the book I had a teacher say she would never use that book with her students. When I asked why, she said it was too depressing. However, in her attempt to shield her students from this reality she was doing them a deep disservice.

In this volume, Mariana Souto-Manning and Jessica Martell face diversity in early childhood classrooms head on. They write against notions of homogeneity as both normative and desirable. Instead, they point to the rich resources that come with diversity—for the students and their teachers. They talk back to the resurfacing discourses of deficit and the way code words such as *poor, at-risk, urban,* and *inner-city* are used to mean *without resources, less than,* and *deficient.* Even when students clearly have *more* resources, such as multiple languages, we have somehow contorted those resources to represent a form of deficiency.

Reading, Writing, and Talk is not a recipe or how-to book for early childhood educators. Instead it represents what I would term a set of *existence proofs.* In far too many classrooms I have heard educators declare that the children they serve are incapable of doing particular school tasks. They recite a litany of what the children (and by implication their parents, family, and community members) cannot do. They assume a lack of literacy skills in places where there are actually rich traditions of storytelling, such as *consejos, corridos,* talk-story, rap battles, signifyin', and playin' the dozens. They fail to understand that most of their students are submerged in language and that often the most revered members of the community are preachers and MCs (e.g., Martin Luther King Jr. and Jay-Z), and they have little or no way to leverage those literate traditions.

This volume provides powerful examples of what teachers who are willing to fully engage heterogeneity and difference can do with the multitude of diverse ways of being in a classroom. We read about teachers who engage students with a broad range of literature and word play. We read about teachers who understand the strength of bilingualism, multilingualism, and translingualism. Instead of bemoaning students' English language skills they recognize the added set of linguistic skills that their students bring to the classroom.

Reading, Writing, and Talk treats young learners with integrity and respect. It regards their questions about difference and diversity as valid points of inquiry rather than a place to shut off curiosity and wonder for the sake of polite fictions. It normalizes diversity and invites teachers to engage in the sometimes difficult work of trying to understand the contradiction between what we say we believe and how we actually treat others. For example, the initial discussion about how different members of a New York community experienced the events of September 11, 2001, is a powerful example of how young children can grapple with the multiple perspectives and differing viewpoints about similar events. Rather than focusing on one truth, the teachers in this volume help to underscore the way things can be true for one person while not true for someone else. This is not cultural relativism. This is life. When my older brother left home for the first time he was happy (and perhaps a little frightened), while I was extremely sad. Both feelings were true, yet we would tell this incident in very different ways.

My hope is that teachers of young children as well as teacher educators will use *Reading, Writing, and Talk* as a resource to encourage them to be bold enough to move beyond the narrow strictures of a standardized curriculum and tests and explore the expansive wonders of young minds. *Reading, Writing, and Talk* offers us a great opportunity to explore pedagogical strategies that are diverse and inclusive. It reminds us that a world of possibility exists in our young children and that we have a chance to embrace that possibility if we are willing to embrace them and their full humanity.

Gloria Ladson-Billings
University of Wisconsin-Madison
January 2016

Acknowledgments

As educators, it is our responsibility to recognize the potential and brilliance of racially, linguistically, and culturally diverse children and to teach literacy in culturally relevant ways. To do so, we must stop perceiving diverse children as being "at risk" and embrace their promise, bringing it to reality in our classrooms. We must make sure that diverse young children experience academic success, grow proud of who they are, develop cultural competence, and question inequities. After all, day in and day out, they are failed by schools and society.

In this book, we take the stance that literacy is reading words, but also reading worlds—and rewriting them transformatively, in just and inclusive ways. We believe that such an approach to literacy is greatly needed within a society where we must state that #BlackLivesMatter and where undocumented immigrants are routinely dehumanized. Education is political—and can be transformative!

This book is a collective effort—and a result of 3 years of work and collaboration. So, we first acknowledge each other's commitment to collaborating weekly and to learning from and with one another. We hope that the examples, concepts, and invitations included will serve to inspire and charge you.

There were key people and organizations that supported this work and the idea of this book from the very beginning. The National Council of Teachers of English (NCTE) funded our collaboration over the course of two years through its Professional Dyads for Culturally Relevant Teaching (PDCRT) Program. Robert O'Brien, principal of the school where Jessica taught for 17 years, supported our collaboration. Celia Genishi, Teachers College Press Language and Literacy Series Editor, read our very first draft of the proposal for writing this book, provided critical feedback, and encouraged us to move ahead. We extend our heartfelt gratitude!

As we wrote the book, multiple educators offered to read our manuscript and provided invaluable feedback. We are certain that the book has been much improved as a result. Others offered examples from their own classrooms, which enriched the text significantly. Thus, in addition to strategies and examples from Jessica Martell's classes, this book features the teaching of brilliant and caring teachers who refuse to give up on the children they teach—even in difficult times. These teachers are committed to unveiling the rich and sophisticated practices with which the children they teach enter their classrooms. They are (alphabetized by first name): Abigail Salas, Alicia Boardman, Ayesha Rabadi, Bessie Dernikos, Billy Fong, Carmen Llerena, Dana Frantz Bentley, Denise Villaseñor, Eileen Dougherty, Elizabeth Rollins, Gabriela Moscoso, Janice Baines, Jennifer Lopez, Julie Casper, Karina Malik, Lisa Wilson, María Inés Zanotti, Marisol Alicea, Megan Hanley, Meghann Snow, Patty Pión, Phillip Baumgarner, Sarah Zalcmann, Victoria Martínez-Martínez, Ting Yuan, and Zexi Ma. We are indebted to them. In a variety of contexts, these educators enact their beliefs in culturally relevant and inclusive literacy education in a variety of ways, yet they are each committed to enacting equitable education, learning from and with the children they teach, their families and communities. We met each of these amazing human beings and caring educators over the last 20 years, and knowing them has enriched our lives significantly. We thank them for their contributions to this book and to our professional growth. We also thank *all* of our friends and colleagues who continue to inspire us to engage in this work, including our PDCRT family.

The stories in the pages of this book are overwhelmingly the stories authored by the children who were members of Jessica's classes over the course of 3 years at a public school in New York City. While we do not name them, we acknowledge them and their families fondly and offer our deepest gratitude. If it weren't for them, their questions, their stories, and their learning, this book would not exist. In addition, a number of our current and former students have made important contributions to this book—here we acknowledge every one of them.

We are forever in awe of children's authors Jacqueline Woodson, Greg Foley, and Rafael Trujillo, who not only visited Jessica's class and talked about their craft, but graciously allowed us to write about their visits in this book. We also thank Tasha Tropp Laman, Lindsay Mann, Ebony Elizabeth Thomas, and Angie Zapata, who offered their expertise regarding children's literature, helping us identify resources for teaching diverse children in culturally relevant and inclusive ways. As we wrote this book, they reminded us to select books that would, in Rudine Sims Bishop's words serve as "mirrors, windows, and sliding glass doors." We are grateful!

We thank Carole Saltz, Teachers College Press Director, and Emily Spangler, Acquisitions Editor, for their encouragement, care, and patience. We also acknowledge Susan Liddicoat for her masterful edits, patience, and care. We thank Lori Tate for her support in the production of this book and Gail Buffalo for her careful and critical read of our manuscript.

We are truly honored that Gloria Ladson-Billings wrote the Foreword for our book. Her inspiring scholarship was foundational to our work and continues to shape not only our work but the field of education writ large in transformative and hopeful ways. In our collaboration, we sought to bring the tenets of culturally relevant teaching to life, challenging inequities in teaching and learning. Throughout our careers, Ladson-Billings's work has urged us to do right by our students. We acknowledge her paramount contributions to our careers as educators.

We are grateful to Anne Haas Dyson, Ernest Morrell, and Yetta and Ken Goodman for inspiring us to document the brilliance of diverse children and understand the sophistication of their literacy practices. We are thankful for their work and for their generous back-cover endorsements. We are humbled that they took time to review our work!

We thank Susi Long for her work in Jessica's classroom while she was a visiting professor at Teachers College; the *Name Story* and *Community ABC* books were first developed by her. We thank Georgia Heard for letting us adapt ideas from her book, *Awakening the Heart*.

Family is important to us; it is where our hearts live, where our memories come from, and where our roots are. We affectionately acknowledge our parents, siblings, aunts, uncles, nephews, and nieces. *Thank you! ¡Gracias! Obrigada!*

We extend our greatest gratitude and love to our spouses, Dwight and Boy. Without ever voicing a complaint, they supported and encouraged our work across time and space . . . even as we met weekly every Friday into the evening for a few years. We dedicate this book to them!

We thank our sons Lucas and Thomas Souto-Manning, and Nico and Lucas Martell for their energy, enthusiasm, and excitement—and for their love and admiration every day.

> Lucas, Thomas, Nico, and Lucas—we hope that this book will help teachers build on the brilliance and strengths of Boys of Color and of multilingual children like you! You inspire us each and every day. Through your actions and words, you urge us to fight for equity in education, for a more just tomorrow. Thank you! We love you!

A special thank you to Thomas, whose beautiful artwork is on the cover of this book.

Finally, we offer our gratitude to those who read this book. We sincerely hope that you find the strategies and examples included in this book inspiring and hopeful. We hope that you start engaging in or continue to develop culturally relevant and inclusive literacy teaching in your own setting, building on the brilliance, unique expertise, sophisticated experiences, and multiple strengths of diverse learners!

CHAPTER 1

Reading, Writing, and Talk with Diverse Children

On Sundays, CJ and his nana ride the bus across town to their stop on Market Street. But today, CJ's not happy about it . . . he's wondering out loud why they have to wait in the rain and why they don't have a car like his friend. (de la Peña, 2015, n.p.)

In the book *Last Stop on Market Street,* author Matt de la Peña wrote of the journey of a little boy, CJ, and his grandmother to Market Street. CJ wishes he had a car, like his friend: "Nana, how come we don't got a car?" Initially CJ sees himself as deprived, as lacking a car. CJ wishes he lived in a world where everyone had cars, just like his friend Colby. He yearns for a homogeneous world. But as he travels aboard Mr. Dennis's bus with his nana, he realizes the beauty of diversities and the richness of witnessing unique lives and diverse abilities. For example, when CJ asks "How come that man can't see?," he learns that the man who climbed on board the bus with a spotted dog can "watch the world with his ears," as his nana explains. By the end of the journey, CJ's nana has made clear the assets of this vibrant community, the unique benefits of their bus ride, and the value of relationships with diverse human beings.

ON THE BREATHTAKING DIVERSITY OF CHILDREN IN K–2 CLASSROOMS

The book *Last Stop on Market Street* serves as a metaphor for the need to understand and value diversities from positive perspectives, highlighting the possibilities and richness of a diverse world. As in CJ's journey, kindergarten, 1st-grade, and 2nd-grade classrooms in the United States (and throughout the world) are full of diversities. Yet these diversities are often seen as deficits—children who are emergent bilinguals may be seen as lacking language or having limited English, for example. This is similar to the way CJ initially saw his world, when he saw his family lacking a car and the man with the spotted dog as lacking sight. In this book, we invite you to see diverse

kindergarten–2nd-grade (K–2) classrooms as rich, colorful, and exciting—
from a strengths-based perspective, seeing diversities as integral and valuable to teaching and learning—and to position such richness as resources for
transforming teaching and learning.

As teachers, we do not have homogeneous classes. Our classes are composed of students who are diverse in terms of race, class, ethnicity, nationality,
language, gender identity, socioeconomic status, ability, faith, family composition, and sexual orientation. This diversity calls for culturally relevant teaching (Ladson-Billings, 1995a, 1995b)—especially when it comes to reading,
writing, and talk[1] (the practice of communicating through oral language;
to speak and to listen). It requires understanding that we are all unique and
worthy human beings with unique and worthy histories.

Yet, culturally relevant teaching is not in place in many classrooms. This
is not necessarily due to uncaring teachers (after all, it is too easy to blame
teachers), but to persistent deficit perceptions of diversities and to educational policies fixated on the standardization of curriculum and teaching, which
have shaped education over time. Both deficit perceptions of diversities and
the standardization of curriculum and teaching are grounded in the ideal of
a single story (and a singular set of resources and pedagogies) being enacted
in every classroom and applying to every child. This focus on standardization
ignores "the danger of a single story" in creating stereotypes, fostering exclusion, and promoting hostility and hate based on racial, linguistic, and cultural
identities (see our discussion of Adichie, 2009 in Chapter 3).

As Genishi and Dyson (2009) noted: "There is a very puzzling contrast—really an awesome disconnect—between the breathtaking diversity of
schoolchildren and the uniformity, homogenization, and regimentation of
classroom practices, from pre-kindergarten onward" (p. 4). While learning
standards continue to be mandated, meeting and exceeding such standards
do not necessitate the standardization of curriculum, teaching, or assessment
in ways that position monolingualism (or any dominant linguistic or cultural
practice) as the norm. Countering this puzzling disconnect, our book is built
on the proclamation "that difference and diversity are the new 'normal'"
(Genishi & Dyson, 2009, p. 10).

In this book you will find ways in which K–2 teachers honor diversities in reading, writing, and talk, fully valuing diverse children for who they
are. These teachers challenge this puzzling contrast between diverse children
and standardized curricula by teaching in diverse ways. They revise and re-
envision common practices such as read-alouds and writing conferences in
ways that challenge constrained and regimented curricular structures. In doing so, they purposefully move away from the current focus on fixing errors

---

1. We purposefully use "reading, writing, and talk" instead of "reading, writing, and
talking" as we seek to trouble standard notions of language use, resist and reject singular and
dominant language rules (Paris, 2009). This is especially important given the value given to
dominant language practices in language, literacy, and schooling.

and highlighting negatives—of the child, of their writing or reading, and ultimately of their worlds. Their practices focus on the strengths and possibilities of children from diverse backgrounds (many of which have been minoritized in society) and their unique experiences. These teachers expand the concept of texts in their classrooms. They listen to children and their families, learning from and with them. In doing so, they envision and inspire new possibilities, which are more culturally relevant and inclusive in their K–2 classrooms.

Most of the examples of culturally relevant literacy teaching and learning you will encounter in our book honor the histories of Children of Color (and their communities), engage children who speak languages other than English, and recognize the expertise of children whose families are socioeconomically disadvantaged. This is not an attempt to exclude higher-income English-speaking White students who have been exposed to schooling practices prior to attending school, but to counter deficit notions of diverse children's language and literacy practices, which position "the languages, literacies, and cultural ways of being of many students and communities of color as deficiencies to be overcome in learning the demanded and legitimized dominant language, literacy, and cultural ways of schooling" (Paris, 2012, p. 93). When authors and educators talk about children from diverse minoritized backgrounds, they often label these children as being "at risk," from a deficit perspective (positioning them as lacking something, as being inferior, as not having appropriate development). Yet such children represent a range of learners; they are brilliant, and their practices are unique and sophisticated.

In this book we provide you with tools, strategies, and approaches to open windows into the sophisticated learning practices of diverse children (from both dominant and minoritized backgrounds). And we invite you to take a stand to (re)position minoritized students as capable learners in classrooms, in schools, and in society. Throughout the chapters of this book, we explore ways of supporting children's reading, writing, and talk. In addition, we provide supplemental resources on the Teachers College Press website, tcpress.com (click on "Free Downloads" and scroll down to this title; each resource is cross-referenced in one or more of the forthcoming book chapters).

In the forthcoming pages of this book we invite you to learn with diverse children in K–2 classrooms, with hopes that this experience will inform your teaching. We encourage you to consider ways of teaching reading and writing that support and sustain children's cultural and linguistic practices, while simultaneously helping them develop academic excellence (Ladson-Billings, 1995a; Paris, 2012). The practices we share are many and do not illustrate one "best" practice because we don't believe in the homogeneity and exclusivity of one best practice. Rather we provide examples of approaches to teaching reading and writing and supporting the development of talk in kindergarten–2nd grade in fully inclusive and responsive ways, honoring the voices and stories of diverse children. But before we enter these classrooms and learn from these teachers and the unique students in their classroom communities, we challenge some assumptions that exist in society about diverse learners who are members of minoritized and historically disenfranchised communities—regardless of our individual stances and personal beliefs.

We start by inviting you to challenge language homogeneity as the norm and move toward accepting language variation, multilingualism ("the co-existence of multiple languages"), and translingualism (a hybrid and fluid language practice; operating "between and across languages"; merging language resources and negotiating new meanings), as the new norms (Canagarajah, 2013, p. 1) for language practices in classrooms. Then we invite you to take an expansive approach to languages and literacies—going beyond reading and writing—toward envisioning more inclusive and culturally relevant texts, varying communicative practices, and multiple ways of talking, reading, and writing. Finally, we conclude this chapter by inviting you to recognize how we are *all* language learners.

This first chapter, like this book, is full of invitations. We ask you to honestly and carefully consider each of them. Yet because we don't believe that one particular curriculum or way of teaching can ever be best for everyone, we expect that while you may accept some of our invitations, which may lead to transformed practices in your classroom, you may decline others. This is okay. We hope that in your classroom you take a similar approach and teach by invitation; after all, children are unique human beings with particular language practices, families, experiences, interests, and worlds.

HOMOGENEITY AS AN UNREAL NORM

Master teacher Vivian Paley (2000) wrote: "Homogeneity is fine in a bottle of milk, but in the classroom it diminishes the curiosity that ignites discovery" (p. 53). We invite you to stop and think about what your classroom would be like if the children you teach all looked the same, liked the same things, and spoke the same way. Would it lead to quality or excellence? We do not believe so.

Unfortunately, in early childhood education, this fixation with homogeneity being linked to quality is historical as well as contemporary. Throughout history, Children of Color have been positioned as genetically or biologically inferior, culturally deprived, or different from the norm (Goodwin, Cheruvu, & Genishi, 2008). These beliefs framed early childhood education, which was established "to work with the poor and unfortunate . . . in order to counteract children's inferior backgrounds and (lack of) upbringing" (p. 4). Historically, there were:

> pervasive conceptions of the poor as not just economically but also socially and culturally impoverished . . . .[And as] families were perceived to have the inability

or inadequacy to care for their young, the responsibility of this care shifted to the middle-class, typically white, community, which was presumed to know best what young children required in terms of moral and educational development. (p. 3)

Such beliefs and attitudes led to efforts to socialize Children of Color and children of low- and no-income families into a homogenized, standardized, and "White-ified" curriculum (Derman-Sparks & Ramsey, 2011).

Today, this deficit view of Families of Color and the overvaluing of homogeneity comes to life through the standardization of teaching. For example, early childhood researchers (New & Mallory, 1994) have critiqued the main early childhood education professional organization in the United States, the National Association for the Education of Young Children (NAEYC), for its "developmentally appropriate practice" (DAP); not because early childhood education should be developmentally inappropriate, but because there is no other word in the English dictionary as culturally loaded as "appropriate" (New & Mallory, 1994). Thus, it is important to take issue with commonplace definitions of learning and development and challenge the field's reliance on standardized measures as a "lens through which children's progress should be measured and assessed" (Goodwin et al., 2008, p. 7).

We believe that teachers who are committed to educating every child can benefit from more fully understanding the culturally grounded and informed nature of child development (Rogoff, 2003) and the "(mono)cultural specificity of the DAP guidelines" (Goodwin et al., 2008, p. 7). This is especially true at a time in which we are experiencing an expanded use of the specific and standardized to assess the diverse. For example, the *No Child Left Behind Act* (2001) and the more recent *Every Student Succeeds Act* (2015) are implemented through the use of (1) standardized teaching and curriculum and (2) narrow and homogenized forms of assessment—namely, the use of standardized tests with all enrolled students. Yet, in the midst of this fixation on homogeneity and standardization, economic and demographic changes point toward a school population that is ever more diverse (Cohen, Deterding, & Clewell, 2005; Genishi & Dyson, 2009; Maxwell, 2014; Stires & Genishi, 2008). As Genishi and Dyson (2009) wrote, "with a constricted focus on academic skills, those single-minded educators preoccupied with reading in English ignore the significant number of children in early education programs who are not English speakers" (p. 4).

It is important to acknowledge that in terms of language, monolingualism has not been the global norm. In fact, bilingualism and multilingualism are often associated with a global economic advantage. Throughout the world, there are many more bilingual and multilingual individuals than there are monolinguals (Baker, 2014; UNESCO, 2003; World Bank, 1995). In recent years, bilingualism has been associated with being smart—see, for example, the *New York Times* article that pointed out:

scientists have begun to show that the advantages of bilingualism are even more fundamental than being able to converse with a wider range of people. Being bilingual, it turns out, makes you smarter. It can have a profound effect on your brain, improving cognitive skills not related to language and even shielding against dementia in old age. (Bhattacharjee, 2012, para. 1)

The benefits of bilingualism are many. Yet, bilingualism and multilingualism are routinely discouraged in many settings because of the outdated understandings and beliefs of those who believe "a second language to be an interference, cognitively speaking, that hinders a child's academic and intellectual development" (Bhattacharjee, 2012, para. 1). Such understanding shapes the single story of language development in many settings, in particular those filled with children who speak multiple languages but possibly not English. Whereas bilingualism and multilingualism tend to be seen as assets for White English-speaking economically advantaged children, they are often positioned as liabilities for Children of Color from economically disadvantaged backgrounds.

In kindergarten–2nd-grade classrooms throughout the United States, monolingualism is not the norm. Monolingualism or fluency in the language of power, the so-called "standard English" (which we refer to as dominant American English), is positioned as a privileged practice, one often (and historically) associated with academic success. Yet, given the breathtaking diversity of children in K–2 classrooms today and predictions for even more diverse student populations in the future (Genishi & Dyson, 2009; Maxwell, 2014; Stires & Genishi, 2008), unless we are committed to failing students who differ from the norm (read: White, middle-class, speakers of dominant American English), we must change the way we teach.

MOVING AWAY FROM THE STANDARDIZATION OF TEACHING

Although many young children know how to communicate within and across two or more languages and dialects, books on teaching children how to read and write in kindergarten–2nd grade often assume that the "normal" child is monolingual, fluent in dominant American English, has been read to at bedtime since infancy, and is familiar with what Marie Clay (1979, 2000) titled *Concepts about Print* (to be discussed further in Chapter 2). This is a striking reality built on a fictional "norm," which continues to exclude the majority of young children in today's K–2 classrooms and ignores important research over the past 4 decades (for example, Genishi, 1976; Heath, 1982; 1983).

Today in order to be "ready" for kindergarten, the "normal" (or model) child must know letters and numbers in dominant American English, have the discipline and stamina to sit and write daily, and read books at higher and higher levels. These messages pervade current books on the teaching of reading and writing. The very reason why we decided to write this book is that as teachers, we could not find practitioner-friendly books on reading and writing methods that featured the voices and work of diverse children—of speakers of Spanish, Spanglish, and African American Language (AAL),[2] for example. We could not find books on teaching reading and writing in kindergarten–2nd grade that did not privilege White middle-class monolingual ways of communicating, interacting, and behaving as the (often unstated) norm. This silence reifies the maintenance of a norm linked to dominant American English and its conventions, contributing to the overprivileging of monolingualism in U.S. schools and society.

In this book we will introduce you to new ways of thinking about how young children have unique perspectives, valuable experiences, exciting interests, and multiple language practices. Each and every child is unique and beautiful. Thus, each child's voice must be valued in curriculum and teaching—along with her ways of making sense of and in the world. We, teachers and students alike, can learn from diverse language and literacy practices. We all can grow in the process. Every child has something to offer and strengths that need to be valued. Finding something to love in each and every child, caring for and about them, is essential so that we teachers can truly see their promise and potential.

Every child is a dream and their languages are part of who they are. We teachers have the responsibility of being *dreamkeepers* (Ladson-Billings, 1994), thus needing not only to understand or tolerate, but to truly value each child's language and literacy practices. Like dreams, children deserve to be nurtured and not deferred (Hughes, 1951). And to do so, we *must* listen to their voices, learn their stories, and, through our teaching, help them see themselves in our classrooms so that they can envision successful futures.

To illustrate this need to value many languages and multiple literacies, in the following section we invite you to enter a 2nd-grade dual-language classroom in a New York City public school and come to see the brilliance in the language and literacy practices of one boy, Juan[3] (Souto-Manning, 2013c). While this story takes place in New York City, we believe that it is truly a situated representation (Dyson & Genishi, 2005) of children who inhabit classrooms and schools throughout the country—maybe even yours! Read on.

---

2. Smitherman (1996) defined African American English (another name for AAL) as: "the result of the mixture of African language patterns with English words and patterns. Some linguists in fact refer to this as Ebonics—ebony for black and phonics for sound. It developed . . . from two different linguistic traditions . . . during enslavement" (p. 6).

3. We use pseudonyms, fictitious names, for most of the children portrayed in this book in order to protect their identities. Ms. Luna is also a pseudonym.

A STORY OF VALUING MANY LANGUAGES AND MULTIPLE LITERACIES

As the 10th anniversary of the September 11 attacks approached in New York City, television programs repeatedly showed scenes of the airplanes hitting the Twin Towers, the towers burning and then collapsing, and the rubble forming a thick cloud in the air as some individuals jumped out of windows and others ran for their lives. In early September 2011, subway and bus ads abounded, advertising free services for those whose health had been affected by the 9/11 events (City of New York, 2012). As the 9/11 Memorial in downtown Manhattan was inaugurated, family members were featured on broadcast interviews, often crying as they recounted the loss of loved ones. A fundraising campaign was launched and co-sponsored by a range of corporations (Elliott, 2011). There was little chance that any child attending public schools in New York City and regularly riding public transportation would be oblivious to the events that took place on September 11, 2001.

Officially and unofficially, young children in schools throughout New York City engaged in schooling activities that remembered the event. They read books and talked about what happened; yet young children in kindergarten–2nd grade had not yet been born by September 11, 2001. Their experiences were initially detached from the fear and pain felt by so many of their family and community members. However, as they looked at books exploring New York City (part of the official 2nd-grade curriculum at the time), 2nd graders recognized the Twin Towers and pinpointed their current absence in the city's skyline. Within and across New York public elementary schools, whether or not teachers decided to place 9/11 at the center of their curriculum and teaching, it was indeed a common topic of conversation in the fall of 2011 (Souto-Manning, 2013c).

Recognizing the children's interest in the 9/11 event and seeking to build on these interests in responsive and authentic ways, Juan's teacher, Ms. Luna, extended her students' learning by taking her class on a field trip. Then, she introduced a variety of texts to the class (e.g., ads, newspaper and magazine articles, photos, children's books), which added a number of perspectives and facilitated a class discussion that identified gaps in their knowledge (silenced and disprivileged voices). This led her students to learn from family members, considering additional points of view and grappling with multiple perspectives and differing points of view regarding the same event. We briefly recount each of these below.

Together, Ms. Luna and her 2nd graders went on a field trip to the *Faces of Ground Zero—10 Years Later* exhibit, which was on display in the Time Warner Center a few miles away from the school. They discussed those who were directly and indirectly affected by the 9/11 events. The exhibit featured life-size pictures of firefighters and other uniformed rescuers, survivors, caregivers, politicians, and students at nearby schools. In reading the exhibit as a text and considering its silences, the 2nd graders realized that some affected by the 9/11 events, like firefighters and healthcare professionals, were featured in the exhibit, but others were not, including family members of those who lost their lives.

Seeking to build on her students' observations and offer the perspective of a person who had lost a loved one on this tragic day, Ms. Luna read aloud *The Day the Towers Fell* (Santora, 2011), a book written by a New York City teacher and mother of a firefighter whose life had been claimed in one of the Twin Towers. After reading the book, Ms. Luna invited students to engage in a conversation and think about whose perspectives had not yet been considered. Citing conversations they'd previously had with family and community members, students acknowledged that many people who were not there, or didn't even know anyone who was there, were indeed affected by the 9/11 events. So Ms. Luna invited her students to interview a family member who had been in New York City on September 11, 2001.

As the children engaged in dialogue, they were at first confused since they had been socialized into the fiction/nonfiction binary (sometimes referred to as narrative and informational texts) often present in the K–2 English Language Arts curriculum and standards. If there were so many available "true" accounts of 9/11, why would they ask family members about it? However, one student put forth the idea that everyone experienced 9/11 differently and that all who experienced 9/11 had different stories to tell about their lived experiences. Juan affirmed that family members truly knew about 9/11 "*quizás hasta más que los que escribieron los libros porque no todos ellos estaban aquí en Nueva York*" [perhaps even more than those who wrote the books because not all of them were here in New York].

In class the students brainstormed possible questions they would like to ask family members who had directly experienced 9/11, rejecting "certain types of questions [that] assert the priority meanings in the written text over reality" (Heath, 1982, p. 71). The questions they settled on were:

- Where were you when the Twin Towers came down?
- How did you first hear about the Twin Towers coming down?
- What image from that day do you remember the most?
- What are your strongest memories from the day and the days right after 9/11?
- How did you feel when you heard the Twin Towers fell or saw them falling? and
- What lesson did you learn from 9/11?

Because English and/or Spanish were spoken by the families who made up the classroom community, after agreeing on interview questions for family members, the students in the dual-language class translated the questions from English to Spanish. Together, students decided that each family member could choose their language for responding. To offer a true option to those being interviewed, interview questions were printed on a single sheet of paper—one side in Spanish and the other in English. Students were to take the questions home, interview a family member, and write their answers down, bringing the written assignment back to school the following morning.

Through such a seemingly simple act, Ms. Luna was combining the official and unofficial curriculum and bringing together official and personal accounts, traditional and nontraditional texts, effectively positioning multiple authorings of September 11, 2001 as complementary. She was not allowing standard (or standardized) curricula to be positioned as more important than the lives, interests, and families of the children she taught. She was honoring Spanish and English as equally valid languages for the interview and utilizing family voices and resources as a way to enrich the curriculum. She was including multiple languages and literacies in her teaching. She was enacting a curriculum based on children's (and their families') funds of knowledge, "the historically accumulated and culturally developed bodies of knowledge and skills essential for household or individual functioning and well-being" (Moll, Amanti, Neff, & Gonzalez, 1992, p. 133). In doing so, Ms. Luna was making learning more authentic, engaging, culturally relevant, inclusive, and accessible.

Listening to Juan

According to the school's assessments, Juan was reading at the lowest level in his class and was not at "grade level." Yet the way that he orally responded to Ms. Luna's assignment (interview a family and record his answers in writing), although not written down, was very powerful (Juan's response is forthcoming). Nevertheless, because schools tend to overprivilege written language, in most classes Juan's oral homework response would likely not have been accepted or validated.

Here we pause and invite you to carefully read Juan's transcribed narrative at least twice, once for meaning and again to identify his expansive knowledge and sophisticated use of languages. We know that it is lengthy and the *italicized* translations may tempt you to scan through or skip ahead, but in doing so, you would miss the ways in which Juan displays great syntactic, semantic, and pragmatic knowledge within and across dominant American English, African American Language, and Spanish. From a deficit perspective, Juan's language shifts may be conceived as errors. But we ask you to reject such a deficit perspective as you read Juan's narrative. Here are his words, as transcribed from an audiorecording with *italicized* translations [in brackets], which seek to enhance your access to Juan's knowledgeable language practices:

I was at the table. My food was there but I wasn't eating. I was reading my Pokémon when mi papi [*my daddy*] had got home from work. You know, he work all night every night. I was 'posed to be eating breakfast. Me dijo: ¿qué estás leyendo? [*He said to me: What are you reading?*] I jumped. Papi asked: ¿Hiciste tu tarea? Bueno . . . . [*Did you do your homework? Well . . . .*]

I looked down to the floor. I don't like no school book. I like Pokémon. My friend like Pokémon. Pokémon is fun, not reading homework. All this was inside my head, you know. I didn't say nothin'. No quería molestar mi papi. Y no quería una paliza ni un castigo. [*I did not want to upset my daddy. And I did not want a beating or a punishment.*] He always be sayin' he work so hard. So yo tenía que trabajar duro también en my tarea y en la escuela. [*I had to work hard also on my homework and in school.*]

Pero, los libros de la escuela eran so boring y mis amigos like Pokémon. Cuando yo leyo los libros de la escuela estoy solo, you know? Y nosotros jugamos Pokémon, jugamos juntos [*But the schoolbooks were so boring and my friends like Pokémon. When I read books from school I'm alone, you know? And we play Pokémon, we play together*] like everyday, you know? And I take my Pokémon and read it every day. I read it under my school book my teacher give me.

Then, I was thinking all of this and I felt the floor moviendo violentamente [*moving violently (shaking)*]. I thought I will always do what mi papi want. Always. Mi papi me dijo que no sabe lo que está pasando . . . y me abrazó. [*My dad told me he did not know what's going on . . . and hugged me.*] I was so scared. We went outside. The building was falling, like collapsing. Hundreds of feet tall. Like falling, you know. Someone say "the plane hit the building." Papi said "no creo" [*"I can't believe it"*]. And people crying and screaming. And people saying they be good from now on, you know.

Papi took me inside. We turn the tele [*TV*] on. It was happening. All before I come to school. And you know I didn't have no time to write all the words mi papi told me. He didn't write no word down. He just told me. Like I tellin' you.

In closely reading the transcription from Juan's oral narrative, you may have seen how he knowledgeably employed three languages aptly and in concert, making shifts that did not compromise syntax, semantics, or pragmatics. That is, those familiar with these three languages will find that his story sounds right (syntax), makes sense (semantics), and is appropriate for the specific task or context (pragmatics).

Through this oral account, Juan had responded to the book read aloud by Ms. Luna and displayed mastery of many of the language and speech objectives of the Common Core State Standards for 2nd grade, 3rd grade, and beyond. Yet, he was "below grade level" according to the formal assessment system in place (Souto-Manning, 2013c). In this book, we challenge this deficit view of racially, culturally, and linguistically minoritized students like Juan. Instead, we value such sophisticated practices and share inclusive teaching strategies that build on the brilliance, strength, and sophistication of diverse learners' "ways with words" (Heath, 1983).

Literacies—Privileged and Dismissed

Juan's story displays some of the literacies privileged as relevant in school learning and some of the literacies that are often invisibilized or dismissed. We highlight them below.

First, Juan knowledgeably navigated within and across *dominant American English, Spanish, and African American Language* (Souto-Manning, 2013c) as he remixed languages in a sophisticated and purposeful way (Ladson-Billings, 2014). He illustrated that we cannot assume homogeneity, in terms of language and literacy practices, in a child—much less in a classroom, school, city, state, or nation. In Chapter 2 we will develop a better understanding of the diversity of children's language and literacy practices through observing and documenting their ways of reading, writing, and talking—taking into consideration the role of sociocultural knowledge and experiences.

Second, Juan's narrative highlights the *social nature of learning* (Souto-Manning, 2013c). Juan stated that when he read schoolbooks, he was alone. So official reading practices and materials in Juan's narrative were related to individual learning processes and did not have an authentic function in his social life. Juan positioned himself individually when talking about "los libros de la escuela" [schoolbooks]. Yet when referring to Pokémon, he took on a collective stance, positioning himself as part of a group of Pokémon experts or at least of friends with a common interest. This social aspect motivated Juan to take his Pokémon book to school and read it every day. He understood what he was reading—even though his Pokémon book was much beyond his official school-sanctioned "reading level." Juan invites us to (re)conceptualize literacy teaching and learning in more inclusive and relevant ways. In Chapter 3 we will consider ways to build and support literate communities that honor diversities.

Third, in his story Juan clearly articulated how in school *doing home-work and producing written evidence were associated with academic success, with being a good student* (Souto-Manning, 2013c). Yet Juan challenged the separation of oral and written authorial practices as he explained that he did complete his homework. He interviewed his father and orally shared his narrative. His lack of written documentation did not hinder his authoring process. His oral narrative was complex and sophisticated, having an orga-nized and clear structure, consisting of setting, catalyst, crisis, evaluation, resolution, and coda (Gee, 2005). Juan invites us to see how oral and written narratives (his original assignment was to write down answers to the inter-view questions) can serve similar functions, troubling "current dichotomies between oral and literate traditions" (Heath, 1982, p. 49), which position written language as a privileged way of communicating. Here we question this dominant practice and propose that it is important to listen to what Juan said, because by not opening up possibilities for students to display the many ways in which they make sense of their worlds, teachers may be missing invaluable insights and excluding students from learning. Even worse, they might be viewing students like Juan from a deficit perspective. Positioning written language as one of many "types of literacy events" (Heath, 1982, p. 74) while focusing on oral language traditions, Chapter 4 will explore the power and possibilities of talk in K–2nd-grade classrooms.

Fourth, Juan's story distinguished between *official reading* (leveled books) and *clandestine reading* (Souto-Manning, 2013c; Sterponi, 2007), which in Juan's case was Pokémon and served as a way for him to engage in pleasure reading that facilitated play and friendships (Paley, 2007). According to Ms. Luna, Juan was not interested in official reading—that is, the leveled books he was deemed able to read. Official reading may be defined as school sanctioned and teacher initiated. Unofficial readings are often directed by friendships and peer cultures (Dyson, 2003) and include an array of texts. The books Juan read for pleasure, unofficially, were much more advanced in terms of text complexity than his official leveled books. Juan displayed great competence as he engaged in them. This is often the case when children read for pleasure.

From listening to Juan, we can learn that so-called unofficial texts can be brought to the classroom to better educate all children. Interest, authen-ticity, and peer cultures matter in reading—for children—much more than mandated reading levels. If teachers can recognize the sophistication of such practices, they can engage children like Juan in reading in their classrooms, reorganizing teaching and learning by bringing official and unofficial reading practices together. In Chapter 5 we will explore ways in which teachers can negotiate these inclusive literacy spaces and consider diverse possibilities, per-spectives, and points of view in K–2 classrooms.

Finally, *Juan brought together nonfiction and fiction, crossing time and space boundaries and creating a compelling narrative* (Souto-Manning, 2013c), which could easily be dismissed by the impossibility of him personally experiencing the collapse of the Twin Towers given his age. Juan engaged in fantasy play in his narrative—a prominent characteristic of early childhood (Paley, 1986). Yet he intertextually employed accurate detail in his narrative from the book Ms. Luna had read to the class, *The Day the Towers Fell* (Santora, 2011). Juan situated the time of day as when many people "were bringing their children to school" (p. 30). Here, present and past were brought together as Juan brought his schooling experiences together with his father's responses to the interview homework. His narrative displayed comprehension of the text read in class and the use of that text and other nontraditional texts (such as the Internet, television, advertisements, and the interview with his father) as mentor texts (defined on p. 138), creating a multimodal text set. For example, Juan employed the word *collapsing*, which came from Santora (2011). He displayed knowledge about the height of the Twin Towers in "hundreds of feet tall" from the Internet. He brought knowledge from television footage when he narrated that "Someone say 'the plane hit the building.'" Then his father's voice (in response to one of the interview questions) was woven in. Temporally, the real timeline of 9/11 was blurred in Juan's personal timeline of all the narrated events that occurred before school started that day. Juan illustrates the varied ways that children can come to author texts, engaging in individualized authoring processes. In Chapter 6 we will explore ways of writing a curriculum that honors the brilliance of diverse children as they author diverse worlds employing diverse ways with words.

Moving Beyond Scripted Practices

Juan's story invites us to consider the need for moving beyond traditional definitions of what counts as educational success, language, and literacy practices. Given the raced, classed, cultured, and linguistically biased ways in which these definitions have been established, they are likely to exclude children who navigate within and across multiple languages and literacy practices (Derman-Sparks & Ramsey, 2011; Goodwin et al., 2008; Nieto, 2000; Valdés, 1996). This book seeks to move away from standardized and scripted conceptualizations of worthy language and literacy practices.

In his oral narrative, Juan, a young multilingual Student of Color, complicated simplistic notions of inclusion, exclusion, time and space as he positioned academic and social realms linked, respectively, to official and clandestine reading practices. His narrative exemplifies a complex (albeit often unrecognized and undervalued) authoring process. Juan invites us to consider such texts within the contexts in which they are located. His narrative offers powerful insights and invites us to challenge the universality of "best" or "traditional" language and literacy practices.

Juan's narrative reveals the urgent need to negotiate multiple and changing communicative competencies, literacies, and texts (very broadly conceived and including curriculum and materials as well as social/interactional contexts) in today's schools if we are to honor the expertise of children who have been historically marginalized and excluded. His narrative points toward the need to pay close attention to the ways in which multicultural and multilingual Children of Color navigate educational experiences, moving away from seeking to compare and understand them against White middle-class monolingual experiences (Derman-Sparks & Ramsey, 2011).

By listening to Juan, we are invited to recognize (to *name* in the Freirean sense—Freire, 1970) and challenge such normative language and literacy practices pervasive in today's classrooms. We are urged to embrace "a pedagogy that empowers students intellectually, socially, emotionally, and politically by using cultural referents to impart knowledge, skills, and attitudes" (Ladson-Billings, 1992a, p. 382).

TEACHING "ENGLISH LANGUAGE LEARNERS"— AND WE ARE ALL LANGUAGE LEARNERS

In today's classrooms, many languages and cultural practices interact with one another. In this book, we argue that recognizing and building on the strengths of multiple language and literacy practices can be productive for both students and teachers. In doing so, we invite you to learn from teachers who are engaging and valuing a multitude of languages and literacies in their own classrooms. We invite you to learn from the children in their classrooms—children like Juan, who navigate within and across languages and who may not have been introduced to schooling, books, and reading prior to entering kindergarten (Heath, 1982).

While you may be questioning the benefits of this approach with children who were introduced to schooling practices prior to entering kindergarten and are fluent in the language privileged within schools (dominant American English, the so-called Standard English), we have observed that they too benefit, becoming more aware of language form and function in authentic ways. They come to understand and articulate grammatical rules (phonological, semantic, syntactic, and pragmatic) in ways that will not need formal and/or direct instruction (Genishi & Dyson, 1984). They understand how language is used across social contexts—and within a context across interlocutors. They develop the awareness that they are *all* language learners and begin to see English language learning from more positive and promising perspectives. By acknowledging multiple languages in the classroom and valuing them in authentic ways, you will be teaching every child to respect each other in ways that will forge an inclusive and culturally relevant learning community—while maintaining high expectations and addressing their academic needs (Ladson-Billings, 1995a).

Yet a firm commitment to fully include multilingual and multicultural learners requires a nuanced understanding of the communicative practices that language learners (read *all*) negotiate. To come to this nuanced understanding, we teachers may benefit from positioning ourselves as learners and creating spaces for students to be positioned as experts, making learning processes visible. Teachers (who are also learners) and students (who are also teachers) then learn from one another about the diversity of communicative practices that take place in their classroom and in their worlds (Freire, 1970). In this way, we are all positioned as language learners.

Through listening to children and learning about the ways in which they navigate within and across texts (official, clandestine, fiction, nonfiction), curricula (reading, writing, speaking, listening), and broader contexts (home, school, community), teachers can develop ways of teaching that build on diverse children's strengths, leading to stronger understandings of learning processes (and of how they are culturally and linguistically shaped). Building curricula that honor these multiple texts and contexts centrally in K–2 classrooms can serve to value the diversities students (re)present. Further, teaching in culturally relevant ways has the potential to disrupt the doctrine of pathology linked to traditional and deficit-oriented approaches to remediation (Gutiérrez, Morales, & Martínez, 2009).

As teachers, we need to conceptualize language and literacy in more diverse, multiculturally sustaining (Souto-Manning & Cheruvu, 2015), and expansive ways. After all, language and literacy practices are "not abstract systems of normative forms but rather a concrete heteroglot conception of the world" (Bakhtin, 1981, p. 293). From this perspective, and as exemplified by 2nd-grader Juan, language and literacy practices are not matters of merely acquiring specific skills, but of becoming more humane. That is, language and literacy learning are predicated upon becoming more aware of other human beings, respectful of multiple cultural practices, and committed to including (or at least understanding) various positionalities, points of view, and ways of making sense in and of the world.

We suggest that we can all start by genuinely seeking to understand the language and literacy practices of children who constantly navigate within and across languages and cultures as we reflect on our own. And instead of emphasizing so-called basic skills (Dyson, 2013), which are framed as problems of the individual, we must engage in a serious reorganization of curriculum and teaching if we are to educate children equitably (Gutiérrez, Morales, & Martínez, 2009). In the coming chapters, we invite you to learn with and from K–2 teachers and children who have brought such reorganization to life in their own classrooms. Aware of the brilliance of multiple language and literacy practices (such as Juan's), in the next chapter we delve into ways of more fully understanding the diversities of children's language and literacy practices.

CHAPTER 2

Understanding the Diversity of Children's Language and Literacy Practices

In the early 21st century we seem to be stuck in a time warp in which children who embody certain kinds of diversity have become the problem, and standardization has become the "fix." (Genishi & Dyson, 2009, p. 10)

In this chapter we invite you to explore the diversity of children's language and literacy practices. In doing so, we address the importance of observing and documenting children's languages and literacies to identify each child's unique ways with words. In observing children's ways of knowing and documenting how their many languages and varied literacies develop, we do not assume a lockstep, linear, and hierarchical trajectory. After all, we know that instead of "building one language concept at a time, children simultaneously build knowledge about myriad aspects of language" (Owocki & Goodman, 2002, p. 5).

We affirm that all children have diverse and sophisticated language and literacy repertoires. They bring rich notions of language and literacy to the classroom—notions that may be new to us teachers, but are well known to the children we teach. Instead of measuring children's language and literacy practices against ours or against what is expected in school, further advantaging normative practices, in this chapter we make visible how young children's rich language and literacy repertoires are developed through a variety of social, historical, and cultural tools and activities. In doing so, we explain how children construct unique meanings within unique sociocultural worlds (Gutiérrez, 2008). We emphasize that the value, function, and meaning of each literacy experience or event must be determined by the child who is having the experience (Owocki & Goodman, 2002), rather than by adults (even teachers)—because the very concept of *literacy* is socially, historically, and culturally defined. Thus, experiences more meaningful to young children will likely result in deeper and more meaningful learning.

Given the time, space, and opportunity, children will share their language and literacy repertoires with us, demonstrating the ways in which they are capable and knowledgeable. We can also learn about children's language and literacy practices by reaching out to their families, learning from them, expanding our understanding of what counts as rich literacy engagements, which may ultimately lead us to rethink our very definitions of literacy. We teachers can then use this information to foster and cultivate a classroom community that more broadly welcomes and values diversities.

We authors invite you to blur the roles of teacher and learner, so that teachers are also learners and learners are also teachers (Freire, 1998). We invite you to see language and literacy as sociocultural practices and family *funds of knowledge* as essential parts of language and literacy practices that are fully and truly inclusive. As children explore their histories, their emerging interests and questions will initiate many and varied learning journeys in powerful ways. This necessitates an understanding that "knowledge is obtained rather than imposed by adults" (Moll & Greenberg, 1990, p. 326). Children must be engaged in learning—making connections that are meaningful to them. In bringing such concepts to life, we share examples of diverse K–2 classrooms.

We make visible the importance of valuing oral language and making room for storytelling and talk in K–2 classrooms (Fassler, 2003; Heath, 1982). We also explore Concepts About Print (Clay, 1993) while pinpointing some of the ways in which current understandings of print concepts and assessments (even informal and low-stakes) are full of problematic cultural assumptions—for example, that English rules apply to all languages and that left-to-right, top-to-bottom directionality in reading is universal. Further, we disentangle the concepts of authoring and writing.

OBSERVING AND DOCUMENTING CHILDREN'S LANGUAGE AND LITERACY PRACTICES

Every day, children enter our classrooms with rich language and literacy practices. They may already know how to navigate across languages and contexts, having sophisticated pragmatic understandings of social language and how language works. They may be very familiar with the rules of social language (pragmatics) in one context but not in another. For example, students may speak Spanish, Spanglish, or African American Language at home, but may be expected to speak only dominant American English (the so-called Standard English) in school. Not doing so may result in them being seen as incapable due to the misalignment between their home language(s) and the language of schooling. After all, the closer a child's home language and communicative practices are to the practices valued in schools, the more likely it is that the child will be perceived as communicatively competent and academically successful (Souto-Manning, 2013a).

When home and school communicative practices are misaligned, children are often perceived as having trouble communicating, needing help, or even, as some educators say, as "not having language." The truth is that they do have language, but their language use and rules for social interactions are not aligned with those expected in school. This can be frustrating and lead children to doubt themselves, feel incompetent, and even question their own intellect (Hilliard, 2014). Their peers may also assign deficit identities to them, which may result in their exclusion from peer groups and segregation within classrooms.

As teachers of diverse children, we need to understand the communicative experiences of each child along with their functions, formats, meanings, rules, and features—learning from them and not judging them against what is (over)valued in classrooms, schools, and society. Doing so requires documenting how young children from diverse minoritized backgrounds:

- Use language for different purposes (greeting, informing, requesting);
- Change language according to the needs of a listener, situation, or context (talking differently to a teacher than to a peer, giving contextual information to an unfamiliar listener, speaking differently in a classroom than on a playground); and
- Follow rules for conversations and storytelling (taking turns, rephrasing when misunderstood, attending to facial expressions, eye contact, and distance to stand from someone when talking).

We also need to find ways to document how *all* learners do this, within and across languages. Further, we must include ourselves, as our language and literacy practices influence *how* and *what* we teach. "The more we learn about the diverse experiences . . . of our students, the better prepared we will be to question existing practices" (Faltis, 1997, p. 28). This requires recognizing our own linguistic identities, rules, experiences, and practices as situated and not as the rule against which all students' communicative practices should be judged. Only then will we create inclusive classrooms that honor, cultivate, and build on the diversities of the children we teach and their cultural and linguistic practices.

Because indicators of pragmatic language problems at times match cultural misalignment between homes and schools, we must be careful not to equate differences with deficits or dis/abilities. As the American Speech-Language-Hearing Association (ASHA, 2015) states on its website:

An individual with pragmatic [language] problems may:
- say inappropriate or unrelated things during conversations
- tell stories in a disorganized way
- have little variety in language use.

Although, in addition to being indicators of speech and language disorders, these are all real possibilities for children whose communicative practices and languages are not aligned with the language and communicative practices employed in schools. Shirley Brice Heath wrote about this more than 30 years ago in *Ways with Words* (1983). She documented "children learning to use language at home and at school in two communities a few miles apart," making visible "the deep cultural differences between these two communities, whose ways with words differed strikingly." She raised "fundamental questions about the nature of language development, the effects of literacy on oral language habits, and the sources of communication problems in schools and workplaces" (Heath, 1983, n.p.). Unfortunately these cultural misalignments often result in misunderstandings regarding communicative practices, having roots in deficit perceptions of differences (Goodwin et al., 2008; Valdés, 1996).

In reality, it is not unusual for children to experience issues with pragmatics—communicating appropriately in a variety of situations (Genishi, 1998)—in a few situations teachers observe. After all, *appropriateness* is culturally grounded. Even as adults we experience similar issues when we enter unfamiliar settings and negotiate various communicative rules. So, building a fuller understanding of children's communicative practices requires creating space for a variety of structured and unstructured communicative spaces in the classroom and beyond—that is, spaces for child-initiated and teacher-initiated interactions, for one-on-one exchanges, for small-group conversations, and for whole-class discussions (Owocki & Goodman, 2002). These spaces allow teachers to observe, document, and learn about their students' wide range of communicative practices.

More fully accessing students' communicative repertoires requires expanding teaching and learning beyond the walls of the classroom. For example, we teachers can engage in visiting with families (in their homes or at a location where they would feel comfortable) to better understand the children we teach within their home context and identify funds of knowledge in the extended classroom community. It is important to know that some families might not be comfortable having teachers in their homes (at least until a more solid relationship is formed). Instead of questioning or judging, in such cases we suggest engaging in community visiting or meeting at a mutually agreed place—of the family's choosing. After all, home and community visiting has been shown to be an effective tool for learning from young children and their families. Here, we propose it can also be a tool for fostering more culturally relevant and inclusive teaching.

There are many ways of learning more about children's communicative and linguistic practices. Designing learning opportunities that build on their home and community literacies is one of them. Children may not be interested in reading about Ancient Greece or Early Civilizations (which are Core Knowledge units for 2nd grade) or Kings and Queens (Domain

7 of Core Knowledge for kindergarten, featuring all White kings). At the same time, young children in New York City may know how to read subway maps and how to navigate the great distance from Staten Island to upper Manhattan, even though there is no subway line connecting these boroughs. And they may know their own histories. They may not know how to write a procedural text, but they may be masters at looming rainbow bracelets or weaving complex narratives or dances. They may not be experts in the teacher-selected topic for the "All About" books they are expected to work on in kindergarten—for example, one teacher-selected topic in a New York City kindergarten was *All About Pigs*, a topic unlikely to be relevant to many children living in a big city. Yet, they may know how to play Pokémon, be experts in Angry Birds, or know how to get from home to school in a crowded, bustling city. As teachers, it is essential that we develop a commitment to discovering, uncovering, and learning who our students are as well as what they know, care about, and can do. Believing that every child has strengths is necessary, but not enough. We must seek to understand their unique ways of communicating, constructing, and expressing what they know. We must listen to our students' stories and voices. Only then can we connect with them—and connect what they already know with what they are learning in our classrooms.

To do so, we must not judge, but learn, respect, and appreciate the languages and cultures of their homes and communities, not only supporting these in our classrooms but also positioning them centrally in teaching and learning. After all, there are multiple pathways to literacies, and as teachers we need to learn about children's multiple paths and varied literacies so that we can support them. Some of these pathways and literacies will be more conventional and more widely accepted (Gregory, Long, & Volk, 2004). Others will be less conventional and more contested, such as using African American Language to teach and learn. Nevertheless, we must be committed to justice (racial, cultural, linguistic, and social) and to understanding the sociocultural nature of literacy (Au, 2014; Gutiérrez, 2008).

We must see children as capable, and learn from them about teaching, language, literacy, and learning. We must position diverse children's experiences and expertise at the center of our teaching, making visible the interconnectedness of their own experiences and lives with the knowledges (over) valued in school. To do so in an authentic and foundational way, we must engage in observing and documenting their literacy practices, focusing on what they can do, the ways in which they participate in many communities within our classroom and beyond, *making sure that our teaching builds on their strengths*. Teaching is about learning to see what children are capable of, what they can already do, focusing on their strengths. It is also about valuing who they are, their practices, experiences, and identities. Ultimately, we can use these as ways to access the standards mandated by school districts and state and federal departments of education and enable children to achieve academic excellence (Ladson-Billings, 1994, 1995a). In doing so, we enact the understanding that having high standards does not necessitate the standardizing of teaching and learning. By learning about children's ways of knowing, we can better (re)organize our classrooms and curricula to support learning (Gutiérrez et al., 2009).

RECOGNIZING SOCIOCULTURAL KNOWLEDGE AND EXPERIENCES

Literacy and learning are sociocultural processes (Gutiérrez, 2008; Rogoff, 2003). Young children are active members of multiple cultural and linguistic groups; membership in a group is not a fixed or linear process. As Gregory, Long, and Volk (2004) explained: "Children do not remain in separate worlds but acquire membership of different groups simultaneously, i.e. they live in 'simultaneous worlds'" (p. 5).

A sociocultural approach assumes that social interactions and culture are central to learning. Socially, as Vygotsky (1981) proposed: "Any function in the child's cultural development appears twice, or on two planes . . . on the social plane and then on the psychological plane" (p. 163). Considering culture and biology in human development, Rogoff (2003) explained that "development is biologically cultural" (p. 34). That is, while "all cultural communities address issues that are common to human development worldwide, due to our specieswide cultural and biological heritage, different communities may apply similar means to different goals and different means to similar goals" (Rogoff, 2003, p. 34). For example, while acknowledging diversities within communities in India, Rogoff makes visible how distinguishing between left and right hands tends to occur earlier in specific communities in India than in the United States, where such distinction does not have great cultural importance in toddlerhood. She explained:

> Children everywhere learn skills in the context of their use and with the aid of those around them. This is how toddlers in India learn at an early age to distinguish the use of their right and left hands (a difficult distinction for many older children in other communities). The right hand is the "clean" hand used for eating and the left one is the "dirty" hand used for cleaning oneself after defecation. (pp. 69–70)

Rogoff, Matusov, and White (1996) defined learning as "a community process of *transformation of participation* in sociocultural activities" (p. 388). So, within this Indian context, a U.S. child would be considered to be developmentally delayed or "behind" when not distinguishing between right and left hands by 3 years of age. This distinction would define a whole culture in terms of deficits instead of recognizing that "development is biologically cultural" (Rogoff, 2003, p. 34).

Culture is central to learning, and its role must be acknowledged in teaching. This may be done by purposefully and intentionally connecting school, home, and community practices and contexts. After all, it is important to connect children's home knowledges, languages, and literacies to what is happening in the classroom. As García and García (2012) proposed, there should be fewer schooling practices entering homes and more home practices entering schooling.

Funds of Knowledge

Moll and colleagues (1992) proposed the key importance of drawing on family *funds of knowledge* when teaching and learning with diverse children (see Chapter 1 for definition). Funds of knowledge extend more traditional sociocultural understandings of what Vygotsky (1978) called the "zone of proximal development" and thus serve as "extended zones of proximal development" (Moll & Greenberg, 1990, p. 344). Countering deficit perceptions of young children as inferior or deprived (Goodwin et al., 2008; Valdés, 1996), the concept of funds of knowledge allows teachers to see young children and their families as skillful and resourceful. Inherent in the notion of funds of knowledge is that all families have worthy language and literacy practices. (See Supplemental Resource 2.1 at www.tcpress.com for a list of children's books that may depict selected funds of knowledge.)

Some family funds of knowledge and cultural practices are not seen as valuable in schools and have historically been neglected and considered to be taboo—such as celebrating the dead, an important cultural practice for many Mexican and Mexican American families. For example, lighting candles for the dead may not be considered "normal" or "appropriate" for young children. As a result, children may not share their rich experiences because their cultural practices do not match what is seen as normal or appropriate according to dominant cultural norms. Thus, students may keep quiet and shut down or choose not to share their rich funds of knowledge.

From a sociocultural perspective, literacy is dialogic and social; that is, literacy is co-constructed with others. Many times, our students feel and say that they have nothing to share or write about. This may be an unfortunate result of their cultural practices not being valued. And while most teachers do not want to ostracize children by positioning such cultural practices at the center of teaching and learning forcefully, we have the responsibility to expand what counts as normal, what is valued in classrooms, pedagogically making diversity the new norm.

Examples of Home and Community Connections

An example of reframing traditionally marginalized ideas and discourses in powerful ways comes from a dual-language 1st grade in which the construction of altars for loved ones positioned *Día de los Muertos* (Day of the Dead) altars as *mentor texts* (refer to page 138 for definition).

After interviewing a parent and visiting a *Día de los Muertos* altar, 1st graders created their own altars in shoeboxes, putting together objects representing those whom they missed—either because they had passed away or because they were on the other side of a geographical border. Acknowledging the separation of families due to international geographical boundaries and limiting social policies allowed for a pedagogical practice that built connections between family funds of knowledge and academic standards. From the construction of altars to the oral description of the artifacts and how they represented the person the child was missing, to writing about the altar and its components, the 1st graders were engaged in meeting several learning standards regarding the writing of informational texts (for 1st, 2nd, and 3rd grades), in culturally relevant and authentic ways.

Another example from an inclusive kindergarten classroom involves creating an ABC book of community images entitled *On Our Way to School* (coauthored by the class), through which teachers clearly scaffolded and connected what children knew (symbols in their communities) to what they should know (such as letter-sound correspondence, and producing a word's primary sound) according to the CCSS for *Reading: Foundational Skills* for kindergarten (Common Core State Standards Initiative, 2016). The children were able to talk about their community, to capture it through digital photography, to write about it, and to become fluent readers of their alphabet book. For instance, because most of the children rode the subway to school, they were familiar with the MTA MetroCard. Thus, MetroCard became the word they saw on their way to school starting with the primary sound /*m*/ and the letter *M* (see Figure 2.1). As they read this book multiple times, they reflected on the many words they saw every day on their way to school. They became more purposeful readers of environmental print (Clay, 1993). They talked about how many words there were in their neighborhoods. They read these words and used them in their own writing. They also recognized these words in reading books and signs in their classroom and school. They talked and learned about how to use their worlds to read words.

Finally, an example comes from a 1st-grade after-school program in a New York City public school. Noticing that many of the 1st graders had an incarcerated family member and aware of negative stigmas often associated with having incarcerated family members, teachers Bessie Dernikos and Gabriela Moscoso decided to read the book *Visiting Day* by Jacqueline Woodson. They wanted to invite children to have the space to talk about an often-silenced issue. Reading *Visiting Day* aloud created the space for the children to make meaningful and knowledgeable connections to the text, drawing on their lived experiences, and allowed Dernikos and Moscoso to teach sophisticated comprehension strategies. While they were careful not to victimize, objectify, or single out children who had incarcerated family members, they

Figure 2.1. Page from *On Our Way to School,* an ABC Book of Community Images

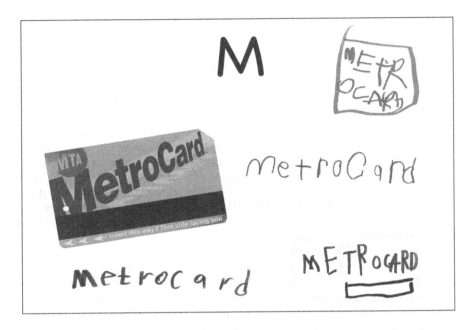

recognized this to be an important generative theme[4] for teaching and learning. As they read the book, children who did and children who did not have incarcerated family members made connections, asked questions, and represented the story. The teachers then engaged in a close reading of the text, focusing on what the author wrote, her purpose, the meaning of particular words, and the text structure (CCSS, 2011). They used a culturally relevant text to engage students in meeting learning standards with which many of them had previously experienced difficulty.

Incarceration is a complex issue, with People of Color disproportionately incarcerated (Alexander, 2010). It cannot be addressed simply by reading one book, which might perpetuate stereotypes of People of Color. Recognizing such complexities, Moscoso and Dernikos were able to create a safe space for critical dialogue. Children were able to voice uncaring comments they had heard about their family members or someone they knew being in jail or prison. The children were also able to make analogies to detention practices in their school (including racial disproportionality), to question "being good" and "being bad," and to talk about the racialization of incarceration—even as represented in the book, which portrays the incarcerated man and his family as African American and the guard as a White man.

---

4. Generative themes emanate from the tensions and concerns in the lives of members of that learning community (Souto-Manning, 2010a).

TALK

In their early years, children are celebrated for their talk as they attempt to communicate. Their approximations are valued—for example, when they say "ma-ma-ma" for *mami, mamá, mamãe,* mommy, or mom. Their language attempts are rarely deemed wrong and unworthy; they are seldom corrected. Imagine how ridiculous it would sound if a mother turned to her 9-month-old child and said, "Until you say 'mommy,' I am not responding to your calls." As children enter schools, and especially in K–2nd grade, there is a dramatic shift. Talk is no longer valued—in fact talk is discouraged in classrooms. We hear again and again, "No talking until your work is done" and "Stop talking so that you can get to work." Yet talking is a way of making meaning, of making thoughts concrete, of conveying and testing ideas and hypotheses. As a result of such common (albeit constricting) messages, children may learn that it is better not to talk. Their communicative development is compromised—in terms of functions and interactive competencies. They are encouraged to disengage.

Oral language is inherently important in K–2nd grade. For most children, it is key to how they make sense of the world. Yet there is less and less space for oral language to develop in authentic, meaningful, and deep ways in today's K–2 classrooms. Even though the Common Core State Standards outline learning standards in speaking and listening, these are typically underprivileged in classrooms and schools. This may be due to a lack of understanding of the centrality of what Vivian Paley (1986, 2007) called the three Fs of childhood—fantasy, friendships, and fairness—to learning, growing, and being a young child or to a lack of understanding of young children's oral language development (Genishi, 1998). Nevertheless, underprivileging talk marginalizes linguistic diversity. If teachers do not take the time to learn about children's linguistic practices, they cannot help but impose situated understandings and personal experiences onto the child. This is very problematic, as it casts deficits onto children simply because their ways of speaking are different from those of their teachers.

As you seek to document and support children's language development, specifically oral language, here are some questions, informed by the work of Owocki and Goodman (2002), that may be helpful:

1. How comfortable is the child when talking in different settings (self-talk, one-on-one, small group, whole group, and play)? What language(s) is the child favoring in each of these settings? Is the child dominant in one language? What does this tell you?
2. Is the child using talk as a tool for learning? In what language(s)? As a tool for thinking? How? Does this change across contexts? How?
3. What language(s) is/are most beneficial to the child according to your observations? What does this tell you about language use in your classroom? What actions can you take to promote language equity?

These questions can help you not only document children's oral language use across purposes, number of participants, medium, interaction, and cultural differences (Cazden, 2001), but plan for culturally relevant teaching as well. For example, if a child uses Spanish in play and home settings and is often very talkative, while being very quiet in class when English is the dominant language, you can plan so that both languages are present and valued in the classroom. This shift is likely to result in the child's academic and linguistic growth.

When linguistic diversities are not understood and valued in K–2 classrooms, children are effectively excluded from learning. For example, in kindergarten, George had been sent to detention often during the school year simply because his style of communication differed from his teacher's (Souto-Manning, 2009). While his teacher meant a command when using the question "Would you like to sit down?," George understood this as a real question, and after considering whether or not he really wanted to sit down, he often responded "No." His teacher assumed such a response to be an act of defiance. This perceived defiance resulted in George spending most of his kindergarten days in detention. Because George spoke African American Language at home and thus had been socialized into a much more direct way of talking than what characterizes the so-called Standard English (with its pervasive use of indirectness to signal politeness), his teacher's limited understanding of language variation and communicative diversities put George in jeopardy. Had she taken the time to learn how he talked and created meaning through words, she may have realized that he was simply operating in a different pragmatic realm; that is, he had a different point of reference for how to communicate with adults. Yet she imposed her own communicative referents and excluded George from learning.

Here, we invite you to foster classrooms filled with talk, taking a stand against the erroneous conflation of talk as distraction and detraction, and recognize the inextricably linked nature of reading, writing, and talk (Lindfors, 2008). These three work hand-in-hand as children develop multiple aspects of language and thinking. Talk helps children focus their thinking, make their understandings known, and learn from others. And unless their voices are heard, the classroom cannot be reflective of their cultures. "In a classroom in which children have agency to talk and collaborate, they not only develop language, they develop their ability to use it as a tool for learning" (Owocki & Goodman, 2002, p. 60).

PRINT

From a very young age, children are socialized into reading their worlds, making meaning of symbols such as environmental print. In New York City, it is unlikely that children in K–2nd grade would not know how to "read" subway stations. Yet, these may be foreign texts for adults visiting from other locales. In many places throughout the United States, young children read McDonald's when they see the "golden arches," or Target when they see a white plastic bag with a red target (even though there are no words). They are readers from a very young age. Even in infancy, children read the world—caregivers' faces, for example. When adults stick their tongues out while looking at infants, infants will read that image and author their own tongue-sticking-out gesture (Anisfeld, 1991). "Around age 5 or 6, children become capable of using notation systems, such as alphabet letters," to represent spoken words, which "often first appear in artwork" (Dyson, 1990, p. 53). So, we propose that the concept of print must be expanded beyond letters, words, and sentences—beyond books. This is an imperative if we are committed to valuing diverse children's rich language and literacy practices.

Children have multiple experiences with print prior to entering kindergarten. Nevertheless, these experiences can be traditional (as expected by schools, reading books and being read to at bedtime) or not so traditional or school-related (but no less valuable, such as navigating subway rides, cashing checks, identifying particular products in grocery stores, paying bills, and reading texts such as the Bible—Compton-Lilly, 2003; Heath, 1983). As teachers, we need to access the kinds of literacy experiences children have had instead of focusing on the experiences they should have had according to our own personal upbringings. Children's literacy practices are sophisticated; we teachers have the responsibility not only to identify them but to build on them, recognizing them as strengths.

Over the last four decades, we in the teaching field have learned that the communicative practices and literacy experiences of different communities (even when geographically close) are each unique and worthy (Heath, 1983). Yet in schools and classrooms we still see the prevalence of one-size-fits-all understandings of children's language and literacy experiences (Genishi & Dyson, 2009). These assumptions must be examined and questioned if we are to foster truly inclusive and equitable educational experiences.

Books, Book Handling, and Concepts About Print

"What have children learned about the way we print language?" (Clay, 2000). This is the question guiding what Marie Clay called *Concepts About Print*, "the rules of the road" that must be taught "so that all children become knowledgeable about these essential concepts so they open doors to literacy" (pp. 24–25). Concepts About Print indicate children's understandings of "how print encodes information" (Clay, 1993, p. 1) and include "the front of the book, that print (not picture) tells the story, that there are letters, and clusters of letters called words, that there are first letters and last letters in words, that you can choose upper or lower case letters, that spaces are there for a reason, and that different punctuation marks have meanings" (p. 47).

In some homes, children become familiar with these concepts in very central ways, through bedtime stories and read-alouds. In other homes, the exposure is more peripheral (Heath, 1982; Heath, 1983; Owocki & Goodman, 2002). Yet, as teachers, we must remember that children's Concepts About Print develop not only from book reading, handling, and sharing, but also from many other day-to-day experiences with print in their homes and communities.

Clay (2000) explained that teachers who have an understanding of what aspects of print their students are attending to can introduce students to print conventions through authentic and meaningful experiences in both reading and writing. Some of these concepts regarding book knowledge can be informally observed. They include (adapted from Owocki & Goodwman, 2002):

- *Book handling* (holds book upright, turns pages from right to left);
- *Print knowledge* (knows what letters and words are, is familiar with orientation and layout of text, tries to match voice and print); and
- *Interpretive knowledge* (is eager to select a book to read independently or with someone else, makes personal connections to books). (p. 104)

These can be documented informally in the classroom, observationally. There are a variety of checklists that can aid teachers in documenting Concepts About Print. While some are more standardized and require the purchase of special books (for example, Clay, 2000), others are more generic and can be employed with any book (for example, Owocki & Goodman, 2002).

It is important to note that assessments of Concepts About Print are most accurate when books are in the home language of the child, feature directionality familiar to children's experiences in languages of their homes and communities, and have direct relevance to children's interests, experiences, and background knowledges. Some of the measures are very cultural and contextual, such as the front of the book and directionality. For example, East Asian languages can be written either horizontally or vertically, as they consist mainly of disconnected syllabic units, each occupying a square block of space. Languages such as Kapampangan, Mongolian, and Manchu are written vertically. For children familiar with print in any one of those languages, the Concepts About Print put forth by Clay (2000) would be irrelevant and misleading. Simple requests such as "show me the book cover" can be problematic for many Japanese children as Japanese book front covers are what we in the United States (and much of the Western world) would consider to be the back cover.

On Authoring and Writing

As adults, we tend to equate authoring with writing. Yet we may know of authors of books who have hired ghostwriters. Young children do not need ghostwriters, but it is important to see the authoring and writing processes as separate, so as not to impose a glass ceiling over children's authorial practices. Children's fine motor skills or graphophonic awareness may not be (and are likely not) as developed as their imaginations and creative capacity for authoring. Children can author in more informal or formal ways. Children's storylines are often developed through play. As Vivian Paley (1990) documented, they story act, demonstrating sophisticated pragmatic, semantic, and syntactic understandings. Young children workshop their stories through multiple renderings and performances. They refine character traits. They engage in authoring their own stories performatively. They offer feedback to their peers. As teachers, if we are to harness children's diverse potentials we must create spaces for story acting to take place in our classrooms.

READING

"During the early years children become fluent and inventive users of symbols, including gestures, pictures, spoken words, and written ones" (Dyson, 1990, p. 51). Young children enter kindergarten reading multiple symbols. They "interpret objects and actions in their world as signs and thus create meanings" (Siegel, 1984, p. 1). According to Anne Haas Dyson (1990), around five or six, young children start making meaning of notation systems, using one symbol (for example, written letters) to represent another (for example, spoken words or objects). They start making meaning of squiggles on a page, a process heavily influenced by prior social and cultural experiences.

Many educators mistakenly assume that if children cannot read print by the time they enter kindergarten or 1st grade, it means that they are unable to read. Perhaps, though, it merely signals that the child did not engage in book reading before entering school. After all, young children enter kindergarten as competent and knowledgeable readers of multiple symbols. It is often in K–2nd grade that they develop their ability to read notation systems, such as words comprised of the letters of the alphabet, more systematically (Dyson, 1990). Much of young children's reading development should happen in play and authentic interactions, on timelines that are as unique as they are.

In today's K–2 classrooms, one of the most prominent approaches employed by teachers to support this development is based on the balanced literacy framework, which combines phonics and whole language approaches to teaching reading. The balanced literacy approach is designed to foster the gradual and progressive release of responsibility from teachers to children, moving from demonstration (e.g., through read-alouds) to shared practice (e.g., through shared reading) to scaffolded support (e.g., through guided reading or partner reading) to independent reading (Routman, 2003). This approach seeks to support and scaffold children's reading practices and processes, going from greatest support (read-aloud) to least support (independent reading).

Introducing the practice of reading books through demonstration (such as read-alouds) can be helpful. Nevertheless, in seeking to bring home and school practices together (thereby creating bridges of access), it is important to document the everyday practices in which young children and their families engage. Such practices can be represented by books selected for read-alouds, making stories more contextually accessible for children who are already familiar with or can relate to the story being read.

As we have noted earlier, drawing on children's prior experiences and interests can lead to deeper understandings. So, for a child who celebrates *Día de los Muertos,* books such as *The Dead Family Diaz* by P. J. Bracegirdle and *Funny Bones: Posada and his Day of the Dead Calaveras* by Duncan Tonatiuh may be helpful and culturally appropriate. And while those unfamiliar with *Día de los Muertos* are not likely to have such a great understanding of the context of the stories told in these books, we also see value in having books as windows into other cultures, practices, and ideas (especially when they can learn about such disprivileged contexts from their peers, families, and communities).

Books portraying the diversities of children should be employed not only for read-alouds but for independent and partner reading as well. We affirm the importance of young children reading books that portray the experiences and practices of people from diverse minoritized backgrounds. We have noted that when we had children read books that represent their interests, expertise, and realities, we were more likely to obtain a more accurate measure and fuller understanding of their reading (Bishop, 1990). For example, in Jessica Martell's 2nd-grade classroom in New York City, this came to life as her students read books from the Fountas and Pinnell (2011) benchmark set (selected by the school). In reading the book *Trucks* by Maryann Dobek (level H), Jessica's students, who live in an urban setting, displayed higher accuracy on the page portraying an ice cream truck than on the page with a rural mail truck—a less familiar kind of truck in New York City. This illustrates how prior experiences influence children's ability to make sense of a text and supports our suggestion for books that serve as mirrors (Bishop, 1990). Books about and by diverse minoritized people are beneficial for *all* children and are an imperative for *all* children as they develop as readers.

LISTENING TO AND VALUING THE STORIES CHILDREN TELL

As we have emphasized throughout this chapter, it is essential to listen to the stories children tell and to genuinely value them in our teaching. But—how? One of the first meaningful stories about a child is the story of his name. According to Lucy Calkins (1991), in reading, writing, and talk it is important to start with meaningful concepts. It is hard to think of a more meaningful concept for a child than his name.

Figure 2.2. Children's Names: A Pattern Book

Lucas, Lucas, who do you see?

I see Thomas looking at me.

Children's Names

A child's name signifies her identity (Souto-Manning, 2007). It is likely the first word the child hears repeatedly. It often elicits positive affective connections. But—how can we teachers position children's names in teaching beyond having children learn how to write them? We know that there are important and unique stories behind children's names.

In terms of writing, kindergarten teachers may start with coauthored books. For example, using the book *Brown Bear, Brown Bear, What Do You See?* by Bill Martin, Jr. and Eric Carle as a mentor text, children can author their own pattern books (see Figure 2.2). This allows children to learn about mentor texts, use patterns in the English language to read, learn sight words in meaningful ways, and ultimately see themselves as readers and writers.

But *Name Storybooks* can be much more complex and culturally relevant than shown in Figure 2.2. For example, students may interview their families regarding the history of their names, which can serve to develop oral language and involve families in meaningful ways. A name storybook may include high-frequency words and contain not only narratives but also rhymes, repetition, and patterns in multiple languages, being a multilingual text that represents and honors the languages spoken in the classroom and community (Figure 2.3). Note that the pages in the name book shown in Figure

Figure 2.3. The History of Our Names: A Class Book

Amairany Machuca Elvira

Amairany is my name,
No Amairany is the same.
Read along to find out
What my name is all about.
Amairany es mi nombre,
Otra Amairany como yo no habrá.
Lee sobre mi nombre,
Y verás lo que aprenderás.

My name is Amairany Machuca Elvira. I was born in
the United States but my parents are from the
historic municipality of Cuaulta Morelos in México. I
was born on Mother's Day (in the United States)! My
maternal grandmother decided to call me Amairany.
I share my name with an older cousin who lives in
México. My uncle Rodolfo calls me "ojos de capulín"
which means "eyes like black cherries". I have many
nicknames and I have written a song about it:

"My name is Amairany,
But my family calls me Nani.
My name was picked by my granny,
My friend Danny calls me Ami.
Machuca comes from my father,
Elvira comes from my mother,
Yamilette and Mixdale are my sisters,
And I am the youngest daughter."

My name story
Has come to an end
Turn the page
And meet my friend!
La historia de mi nombre
Ha llegado a su final.
Pasa la página
¡Y a mi amiga conocerás!

2.3 contain English and Spanish as they came from Jessica's classroom,[5] a
dual-language Spanish-English 2nd grade. To make the book more fully bilingual, we asked students to write the entire story in their preferred language
(English or Spanish). Thus, while Figure 2.3 portrays a story written in English, other pages of this same book portrayed name stories written in Spanish.

In Eileen's and Carmen's inclusive kindergarten (1/3 of the class was
comprised of children with autism spectrum disorders or ASD), the name
book includes English and additional languages spoken in a child's home,
such as Spanish, Mandarin, Hebrew, and Patois. Family members and other individuals fluent in each language helped with the writing and with the
translations of the English pattern text into multiple languages. The class
titled their book, *No Name is the Same: Name Stories from Ms. Carmen's and
Ms. Eileen's Kindergartners.* The children also included common parts of a
book, such as a dedication and a copyright page. This allowed the teachers
to address learning standards for kindergarten in authentic and meaningful

5. Examples from Jessica's classroom span 3 academic years. The pattern for this book
was developed by Susi Long and translated into Spanish by Victoria Martínez-Martínez.

ways and led the children to always ask: "What is the title of this book? How did the author decide on it?" along with "How old is this book?" and "For whom did the author write this book?"

In Supplemental Resource 2.2 (available at www.tcpress.com), we offer suggestions of books for reading, writing, and oral language activities that position children's names at the center of teaching and learning. Most of the books listed are by and about People of Color and address issues such as gender-name associations (e.g., *I am René, The Boy* by René Colato Laínez), linguistic and cultural privileging (e.g., *My Name is Jorge: On Both Sides of the River* by Jane Medina), the translation of names (e.g., *My Name is Yoon* by Helen Recorvits), names that mix languages (e.g., *Marisol McDonald Doesn't Match* by Monica Brown), and the teasing and exclusion related to having a name that is deemed to be "different" (e.g., *The Name Jar* by Yangsook Choi). There are many other books about names, and we encourage you to use our list merely as a resource as you teach and learn from the names of the children in your class—and from the history of your own name.

We have found that by positioning children's names centrally in our teaching, they not only feel honored, but learn the histories of their own names. This often results in children developing pride in their names and growing more confident of their identities. Through interviewing their parents and other members of their families, children see that their families (and the families of their classmates) are knowledgeable and worthy. Even if they may not have had the opportunity to experience formal schooling or learn dominant American English—the language of power in U.S. schools and society—parents and family members are the experts on their children's name stories.

As you engage in teaching from children's names and identities, consider the following questions:

- What strategies have you used to welcome all children's names in your classroom?
- How could these be extended to support multilingual children?
- How can you use children's books to consider multiple representations, points of access, and engagements? and,
- Are you as a teacher ready to embrace your vulnerabilities and share your own name story?

We hope so!

Children's Histories

In addition to their names, another important topic that matters for young children is where they are from. We are all historical beings. The book *Momma, Where Are You From?* by Marie Bradby offers possibilities for an activity

Figure 2.4. "I Am From" Activity (adapted from Cahnmann, 2006)

My name is . . .	*My name is* _____
1. I am from [familiar places]	1. I am from _____
2. I am from [familiar foods you eat with your family]	2. I am from _____
3. I am from	
[familiar sayings or expressions you hear at home]	3. I am from _____
4. I am from [people you love]	4. I am from _____

in which children can develop a better understanding of their everyday histories—what they eat, those they love, the expressions they hear. In Bradby's book, a little girl asks her Momma "Where are you from?" Momma poetically evokes memories of her own childhood: "I'm from Monday mornings, washing loads of clothes in the wringer washer." However, Momma's memories also include inequities she witnessed in her childhood, including her siblings not attending "the school right up the street," but being bussed to a school across town "where all the children were brown—some light, some dark, some in-between" and living just past where the sidewalk ended.

Following a read-aloud of Bradby's book and a discussion, we invite you to engage children in documenting their own everyday histories through poetry, using the template shown in Figure 2.4 (Cahnmann, 2006, p. 343). This is a time in which teachers and students learn together as they "write four stanzas" (p. 343). This can start through a simple yet representative and relatable poem. *Show Way* and *This is the Rope* by Jacqueline Woodson, *Let's Talk About Race* by Julius Lester, and *Tar Beach* by Faith Ringgold are other books that could help extend this learning opportunity.

Children's Racial Identities

Exploring children's racial identities in the classroom is very important. Many times in the early years, Children of Color draw themselves White in portraits and illustrations. To honor children's racial identities, we teachers need to engage children in reading their worlds racially, developing *racial literacy* (Twine, 2004).

Although many educators may think that children are not ready to start discussing issues of race, research has shown that as early as 6 months of age, young children start attributing emotions to race. In fact, children as young as 6 months of age displayed positive emotions when seeing White faces and negative emotions when seeing Black faces (Bronson & Merryman, 2009). There are many other studies of young children that put forth similar findings, including line drawing experiments (Clark & Clark, 1939) and the well-known White doll–Black doll experiment (Clark & Clark, 1947), which found that young Black children displayed preference for and attributed positive characteristics to the White doll. As Clark and Clark (1950) underscored: "The discrepancy between identifying one's color and indicating one's color preference is too great to be ignored" (p. 350). So, while children may or may not be talking about race, their feelings regarding race are already developing when they are in kindergarten, 1st, and 2nd grades. Thus it is important to teach in ways that young Children of Color see the beauty in their racial identities and in ways that White children recognize the beauty in the racial identities of People of Color.

Here are some ideas. We suggest engaging in a study of what children look like. You may find it helpful to start with mirrors, inviting children to look at themselves and describe what they see (what they look like) in a Think-Pair-Share.

> The Think-Pair-Share strategy is designed to differentiate instruction by providing students time and structure for thinking on a given topic, enabling them to formulate individual ideas and share these ideas with a peer. This learning strategy promotes classroom participation. . . . Additionally, this strategy provides an opportunity for all students to share their thinking with at least one other student, which, in turn, increases their sense of involvement in classroom learning (Simon, 2015, para. 2).

Students can ask each other questions, offer additional descriptions, and make connections. You may invite them to use metaphors (a figure of speech that identifies something as similar to an unrelated thing—e.g., my eyes are fireflies) and similes (a figure of speech comparing one thing to another thing of a different kind, used to make a description more emphatic or vivid—e.g., my hair is dark as the night sky). Then children can draw and describe themselves. They may even create elaborate portraits! Here are some helpful books for read-alouds:

- *Chocolate Me!* by Taye Diggs
- *Looking Like Me* by Walter Dean Myers
- *My People* by Langston Hughes
- *Viva Frida* by Yuyi Morales
- *Let's Talk About Race* by Julius Lester
- *Black is Brown is Tan* by Arnold Adoff

Chocolate Me! features a 5-year-old boy who is unhappy with his name, his nose, his hair, and his skin color. After all, young children learn to associate having brown skin with negative feelings early on. For example, a 4-year-old child in a New York City pre-K classroom asked the center director, "Is your skin dirty? Why is it brown?" In *Chocolate Me!* Taye Diggs captures a similar comment: "Look where your skin begins! It's brown like dirt. Does it hurt to wash off?" (n.p.). He even captures the emotional rawness of receiving such comments. This book can serve as a conversation starter for issues of fairness and racism. It can serve as a tool to teach *all* young children how to restate, challenge, and reframe hateful, prejudiced, and racist language.

If you teach younger children, you can read books such as Bobbi Kates's *We're Different, We're the Same, and We're All Wonderful!* or Todd Parr's *It's Okay to Be Different*. After doing so, you may find it helpful to have children explore how they are different and how they are the same—making a list, talking, developing peer Venn diagrams. This allows the children to compare different versions of a text—of humanity!

Then, it may be helpful to follow up with *The Best Part of Me* by Wendy Ewald as an example or mentor text. In the book, a group of children wrote descriptions of their favorite body parts in response to the question: "What is the best part of you?" Their answers are written in their own handwriting (including a few misspellings), making it all the more real as a mentor text for young children. This book can be used to discuss body image, to enhance self-esteem, and to explore diversities with children. The children you teach can take photographs of their body parts and write about them—engaging in informational writing (emphasized by the Common Core State Standards) in authentic and culturally relevant ways, making their very own "The Best Part of Me" book. (See also Supplemental Resource 2.3 at www.tcpress.com.)

Children's Voices and Rhythms

As we have emphasized throughout this book, it is important not to judge the stories and voices of young children but to value them. Janice Baines, 1st-grade teacher in Columbia, SC, shows us that by suspending judgment teachers can build meaningful bridges between children's home literacies and expectations for school (Long, Volk, Baines, & Tisdale, 2013; Souto-Manning, 2013b). One year, Baines noticed that the children in her class were singing Soulja Boy's "Pretty Boy Swag" on the playground, in the cafeteria, and around their homes (as observed during home and community visits). Instead of doing what many teachers would do—declaring the lyrics of the song inappropriate for young children and perhaps even banning it from her classroom—Baines spent her energy building meaningful connections between the song and school knowledge. She authored "I Can Read Swag" to the tune of "Pretty Boy Swag." Her lyrics were full of sight words mandated by her school district to be mastered by the end of 1st grade. Instead of judging, she built a bridge, using a familiar structure so that the children she taught could more easily access sight words. Never were the children so excited to practice their sight words as when singing "I Can Read Swag" individually, in classroom shared readings, and when reading a class-made book with the lyrics to their "I Can Read Swag" song. As they got started, they sang and read:

This right here is my book
Watch me turn the pages, look!
Every-body pay attention
This, right here is my —
I can read swag—read!
(Long et al., 2013, p. 427)

As Baines underscored, it is important to "get to know the worlds of your students," to "think about cultural relevance as learning," and to "consider this work foundational, not an add-on" (Long et al., 2013, pp. 434–435). Let's pay attention to children's practices and create bridges to school expectations, fostering academic success in culturally relevant ways.

REFLECTING ON DIVERSE LITERACIES AND LOOKING AHEAD . . .

In this chapter we explored ways of understanding diversities in children's language and literacy practices. We reviewed ways of using children's diversities to scaffold access to academic standards. In the following chapter, we will address ways of building learning communities that honor diversities. In doing so, we invite you to consider the stories your classroom and materials tell, (re)writing them in more inclusive ways, in ways that support multiple languages, literacies, and cultures.

CHAPTER 3

Building a Learning Community That Honors Diversities

To build learning communities that honor diversities through culturally relevant teaching, it is essential that teachers find something to love in each and every child they teach—to truly love. We don't propose that this is easy or quick; yet it is essential and foundational. So, if you don't immediately find something to love in each and every child you teach, learn about the student outside of the classroom environment, during recess or other school times. Go on a home or community visit. Learn from families and community members. Conduct assets inventories, intentionally and systematically documenting all that each child can do well.

To ensure that all students succeed in our classrooms and schools, we need to value them as worthy and capable individuals, and provide learning conditions that convey our faith in each student as a successful learner. It is the responsibility of every teacher to love each child they teach, as love and care are essential for fostering positive identities as learners (Heath, 2012), understanding that love is "an act of freedom, it must not serve . . . for manipulation. It must generate other acts of freedom; otherwise it is not love" (Freire, 2000, p. 90). Our actions and interactions matter—and they must position children's interests, identities, and experiences centrally.

In this chapter we introduce ways of engaging in culturally relevant teaching practices by building a learning community that honors diversities. We invite you to start where you are, to look around and carefully document the stories your classroom and its community members tell. We also share ways for rewriting stories and pedagogical practices, creating more inclusive teaching and learning opportunities. We offer ideas for how you can set up a classroom that supports multiple languages and literacies while making authentic connections and developing caring relationships with students and their families. After all, the strongest predictor of reading achievement is the quality of student–teacher relationships (Routman, 2003). We encourage you to make your own language and literacy practices visible in the classroom, positioning them as culturally situated (not as the norm against which children's practices are to be judged or assessed), and to further connect and strengthen your relationships with your students in the process.

In addition, we highlight the power and possibility of—and really, the need for—listening to and valuing students' stories (moving away from defining literacy solely as reading books and writing texts). We focus on ways to authentically develop meaningful family partnerships that support students' learning journeys (Allen, 2010), highlighting the importance of valuing reading, writing, and talk within and across the diverse communities of which children are members (Long, 2011).

Finally, since we regard each child as a unique human being, we discuss the importance of authenticity, interest, and play (Lindfors, 2008; Paley, 1986). We conclude with an invitation to engage in literacy teaching that builds on the strengths of children and honors diversities.

LOOKING AROUND: WHAT STORY YOUR CLASSROOM TELLS AND HOW YOU CAN REWRITE IT

When we think of stories, we often think of books. Here we invite you to read your world (Freire, 1985) and, more specifically, read the stories you, your students, and your classroom tell. Look around your classroom. What do you see? What do the walls, the children you teach, the materials, the interactions reveal? Who is visible? Who is made invisible? These are important questions to consider as you start reading your classroom. (See also Supplemental Resource 3.1 at www.tcpress.com for additional questions to consider.)

If you already have a classroom, take an inventory (Earick, 2009). If you are getting started, consider planning a classroom that is inclusive and honors diversities. But what exactly does this mean? It means that when children enter your classroom they see inclusiveness and diversities portrayed in the materials and arrangements, in the schedule and tasks.

The inventory must start with yourself and with your own practices. While it can be helpful to employ reading inventories, such as the Burke Reading Interview (Goodman, Watson, & Burke, 1987; see Chapter 5), it is even more important to know what contextual, linguistic, and cultural knowledge children bring to the classroom. After all, as we pointed out earlier, teaching is not culture-free. Nor are curricula. Teaching practices should be (re)centered to both honor children's cultures, languages, and identities and to foster academic success. This involves getting to know children and positioning their interests, identities, and experiences at the center of the curriculum and teaching.

Classroom Environment

Many teachers perceive their physical classrooms to be much more diverse than they actually are, especially in terms of materials and opportunities for interactions (Earick, 2009). Because of this misalignment between the reality of the classroom and teachers' impressions, we posit that there is a need for us teachers to *document the walls and materials of our classrooms.* After all, it is important to identify an issue in order to problematize and address it (Souto-Manning, 2010a). If classroom materials are perceived as already being diverse, there is less incentive to actively seek to diversify them. But before assessing materials, we have found it helpful to consider questions that can help make differences and inequities visible, such as: Is the diversity of my classroom characteristic of the composition of the school (or larger community) as a whole with regard to race, gender, and language? Then, we can engage in taking an inventory to assess the adequacy of our classroom's physical environment (materials, texts, resources, room arrangement) for facilitating the learning of diverse students—especially those who have historically been minoritized and excluded.

Earick (2009) suggested that we teachers rate items documenting how diverse the landscape of our classroom is using numbers: 1 for meeting expectations, 2 for in progress, and 3 for beginning, learning. For example, ask: do the texts in my classroom balance racial, linguistic, cultural, and gender images with the ever-present privileged positions? Then, after rating items, Earick (2009) invited us to quantify the percentage of resources (photos, artwork, and books) of each racial, language, cultural, and gender group. This can reveal whether your perceptions of the classroom environment match its reality. It will also avoid the perpetuation of a "single story" (Adichie, 2009) about any one cultural group, which too often leads to stereotypes.

Classroom Library. It is important for us to have classroom and school libraries that reflect multiple diversities (languages, cultures, identities) in the world, to have books in multiple languages, even if we teachers do not understand those languages. We must remember that the classroom belongs to its community of learners and not to us alone. A well-organized and representative classroom library can positively impact independent reading in powerful ways (Routman, 2003). Children read more when they have easy access to books. As teachers, our first goal for our classroom library should be to foster easy access to books. Ultimately, the availability of reading materials can significantly impact a child's literacy development. (See Supplemental Resource 3.2 at www.tcpress.com for more specific guidance in setting up your classroom library.)

According to Rudine Sims Bishop (1990), "books are sometimes windows, offering views of worlds that may be real or imaginary, familiar or strange. . . . Literature transforms human experience and reflects it back to us" (p. ix). So, regardless of how diverse our students are, it is essential to have books that allow children to see themselves in their narratives and to learn from different experiences in the stories we read and tell. This allows them to walk into and participate in multiple story worlds.

Too many children from nondominant backgrounds and identities have been deprived of seeing their images in the mirrors of stories, and as Junot Diaz (2009) stated, "if you want to make a human being into a monster, deny them, at the cultural level, any reflection of themselves. And growing up, I felt like a monster in some ways. I didn't see myself reflected at all." Bishop (1990) explained that when our images are mirrored in books, "in that reflection we can see our own lives and experiences as part of the larger human experience. Reading, then, becomes a means of self-affirmation, and readers often seek their mirrors in books" (p. ix). It is also important for children across racial identities to see themselves in the authors of the books displayed in the classroom and the books that make up the classroom library—providing mirrors into the authoring process. After all, books and their stories serve as a way of knowing (Short, 1997). Keep in mind that in addition to books that serve as mirrors, students need books that serve as windows, so that they can learn from and about other cultures.

Room Arrangement. A key aspect of setting up a classroom is to keep in mind the need to set up an environment in which children can have choice and control. Our role as teachers is to facilitate the learning and plan the environment in which our students will spend most of their day. We have found the following question to be of help in reading and reflecting on our classroom arrangement: Does the set-up of my classroom allow students opportunities to work in mixed-gender, mixed-race, and mixed-language groups during both academic and social events? The setup of desks or tables should be strategic and functional decisions. This means that setting up areas for whole-group community meetings, small-group work, pair work, and independent work is essential—not all at once, but throughout the day.

In K–2 classrooms, there should be room for movement and choice. For example, read-aloud may be done in the meeting area (an area large enough to fit the whole class), then students can move to their tables where they are grouped to work. Every student should see her name on a desk, table, or cubbie but even those should be flexible. So if students work in math groups at a certain table, they may work at a different table for writing. Groups should always be flexible.

Keep in mind that students learn best when they feel comfortable and at being comfortable is different for every student and for different activ s and times of day. A student might love to read while sitting on a rug does his best writing while standing up or lying on the floor. And that is The focus should not be on taming students but on creating classrooms they can learn and grow, classrooms that respect their needs and pref s as human beings.

recommend that the whole-group area accommodate a circle where nts can sit facing others to allow for more productive and equita rsations to happen. We have found it helpful to contain the area shelves (at least two or three sides of it) and to set up crates with pillows so that students can sit on their bottoms or sit on the crates (which can store books inside). This area often has a dual purpose. It can become the meeting area and the classroom library. When not being used for whole-class activities, it can be used for small-group work or as a reading area. Some classrooms also have lofts, which can be helpful and add more work areas in a classroom. The key is to have a variety of possibilities for students so that they can engage in the learning task at hand as opposed to learning how to contain their bodies in a limited or constraining area.

We have found tables where three or four students sit and work together to be conducive for learning. It is important to reorganize the groups at least once a month so that students have the opportunity to work (and develop friendships) with everyone who is a member of the classroom community. The seating arrangements should be strategic, but also flexible. We suggest keeping in mind language use, personality, friendships, and previous seating arrangements when arranging and rearranging seats—or asking students to keep these in mind if they select their own seats and workgroups. While it is not necessary to separate students from their friends, we suggest creating opportunities for students to expand their friendship circles by working with every member of the classroom community. For individual work, clipboards and breakfast lap trays are helpful so that students can spread out throughout the classroom. These should always be available so that students can select the most conducive setting for reading, writing, and learning.

Curriculum

Examine your curriculum to ascertain where gaps may occur and to expand, supplement, revise, and envision it in more inclusive ways as it is enacted in your classroom. When we ask students to connect to the curriculum, connections are much easier for children who see themselves and their experiences represented. Drawing on the work of Peggy McIntosh (1990) and her categorization of how curriculum can racialize academic success and on the work of Mary Earick (2009) and her call for moving beyond Whiteness by engaging in racially equitable teaching, we invite you to rate your curriculum in terms of whether or not it portrays:

- Exclusively or mostly history of people who are White;
- Popular individuals who are often positioned to represent their entire racial and cultural groups (such as Rosa Parks and Martin Luther King, Jr.);
- Minority groups as problems—in terms of anomalies, absences, and as victims;
- The lives and cultures of People of Color everywhere as general history (as opposed to singular representations that equate February with Black history month, for instance); and

- History redefined and reconstructed to include each and every one of us—all cultural groups, especially those historically marginalized.

As teachers committed to supporting all students, we need to move from histories of people who are all-White and male to seeing women and People of Color as inherent and central parts of the curriculum. For instance, the Core Knowledge Foundation's (2013) approach to Kings and Queens exclusively features White kings (kindergarten unit in *Tell it Again! Read-Aloud*). This results in normative and privileged racial, cultural, gender, and linguistic identities being foregrounded in the curriculum, as the unit privileges people who are White, economically wealthy, and male. While the supplemental guide regards ELL accommodations, they are seen as add-ons and do not lead to making the curriculum and teaching more inclusive. While Core Knowledge is mentioned here by name, we encourage you to look at any curriculum guide for equity and representation. Core Knowledge is merely a situated representation of boxed and ready curricula, illustrating our point that ready curricula are ready for no one. They simply continue to reify inequities as they overprivilege the culture and language of power or the culture and language of those who have power (Delpit, 1988). In reading and writing, this has to do with who is present or absent in the books read as well as which languages and communicative practices are honored in our classrooms and schools.

Teaching Strategies

What kinds of teaching strategies foster the participation and engagement of students across racial, gender, and linguistic identities? Some of the teaching strategies in reading and writing include teacher-directed read-alouds, minilessons, interactive writing, shared reading, guided reading, independent reading, and writing workshop (further explored in Chapters 4, 5, and 6). It is important to ensure that an array of strategies is employed throughout the day, providing multiple opportunities for engagement—ranging from more teacher-directed to more student-directed. At the same time, it is essential to identify which curricular and instructional structures appeal to students. We cannot assume that all strategies will engage students in similar ways. They will not. Largely, the way that a student engages in learning as a result of particular teaching strategies depends on the strategies' alignment or misalignment with home and community literacy practices. Thus our teaching will be more effective if we pay attention to and document which strategies are most effective for which students, and if we note patterns around racial, linguistic, and gender groups.

As we seek to foster more equitable learning environments and communities, we must take a close look at the messages we communicate to our students, directly and indirectly. We can ask the following questions, which seek to unveil messages we communicate during each of these teaching contexts: whole class, large group, small group, and individual conferences.

- To which students do I give the most positive messages?
- To which students do I give the most negative messages?
- To which students do I not give any messages?

Then, we assess whether or not our answers communicate equity. We can do so by taking a close look at racial patterns, for example. If our answers do not communicate equity and inclusion, we have the responsibility to ask: Why not? And then, seek to change our teaching and interactional practices to foster a more inclusive and equitable classroom.

A helpful strategy for beginning teachers, in particular, may be to audio- or video-record yourself for a period of time each day (varying the time of day and setting). Listening to or watching the recording can assist you in learning to identify your messages and planning to teach more inclusively and responsively. Partnering with a colleague and asking her or him to observe you and offer insights and feedback might also be effective here.

In addition, we make *Today's Schedule* visible in the classroom, outlining our plan for the day. This is important for students so they know what to expect. Yet we ensure that our students know that changes may occur along the way; that the daily schedule is akin to a forecast, which may change according to a variety of conditions—including but not limited to students' engagement and investment in an activity. While it is essential to plan, we must remember to be flexible—to observe and honor the rhythms of children. Students will in turn be flexible.

In seeking to create inclusive teaching and learning environments with an expansive curriculum, it is important to always ask ourselves whose knowledge is privileged—the students' or the teacher's? And consider, as a result of what we learn from taking inventory of our own classroom environment and teaching practices, what inclusive teaching strategies and learning opportunities we will enact to ensure racial, cultural, and linguistic justice in our own classrooms. We teachers have the power to enact education that fosters the practice of freedom, "as opposed to education as the practice of domination" (Freire, 1970, p. 81). This enactment starts within the text and context of our classrooms.

VALUING CHILDREN'S LITERATE LIVES

We know that prior to entering our classroom, many students already have had experiences that did not convey respect for them and their families and did not acknowledge their brilliance. Pre-kindergarten teacher Dana Frantz Bentley (Cambridge, MA) explained that 4-year-olds entering her class see themselves as not knowing much. In turn they expect that she knows everything. This banking approach to education (defined by Paulo Freire, 1970), which posits that teachers deposit knowledge in students' brains as people deposit money in banks, is detrimental to many of our children. It creates obstacles and leads them to see themselves as not being capable or knowledgeable. It is no surprise that many of them claim: "I can't read!"

In Columbia, SC, when met with an avalanche of "I can't read" comments, kindergarten teacher Donna Bell put together a book entitled *We Can Read*, which featured wrappers and images of common foods and brands known to children (Bell & Jarvis, 2002). Upon introducing her big book to rising kindergartners, she invited the children to engage in a picture walk (reading the book's illustrations). To their surprise, they were able to read every single page of the book. Donna had put images of Kraft Macaroni & Cheese, McDonald's, Doritos, and other images of items the children's families had sent in. Donna's action allowed students to feel capable and is an action that teachers anywhere can take.

Extending Donna's idea may result in a word wall (an alphabetized collection of words displayed in large letters on a wall, bulletin board, or other display surface in a classroom) with not only words used frequently in the language(s) of classroom members and texts, but also images of common household items that are part of the children's lives. Eventually the pictures can be replaced by words, perhaps going from the actual wrapper to a black and white Xerox copy of the wrapper, to the word only, then to the word written in a more uniform font. This represents the process whereby children engage in making sense of a word—from a meaningful object to its written representation.

Also in Columbia, SC, 1st-grade teacher Janice Baines had students read the instructions for using Blue Magic, a coconut-based hair conditioner used by many of the children in her class. Then she invited her students to compare the written version to the practice enacted by the family members who got their "hair did" (Souto-Manning, 2013b). Valuing students' lived experiences in her teaching, not only did Baines cultivate relationships with the families of the children she taught, but she regarded them as experts. She also made sure that she was leveraging the knowledge and practices in which children engaged to ultimately acquire school knowledge, which would allow them to succeed academically. In so doing, Baines was able to address multiple learning standards in culturally and contextually relevant ways, showing students that their lives and practices outside of school mattered, thereby positioning them as knowledgeable and competent. While Blue Magic was a product relevant to the lives of Baines's 1st-graders one particular year, we invite you to identify what is important in the lives of your students, enabling them to study procedural texts in knowledgeable and culturally relevant ways—in ways that matter to the young children you teach.

The examples above, while specific to Donna Bell, Janice Baines, and their respective students, shed light on the many possibilities that lie ahead for us teachers to put our commitment and love into action in culturally relevant and academically demanding ways. We hope that you can draw inspiration from their practices and recreate their ideas in your own setting, valuing your students' resources and positioning them capably.

INVITING FAMILIES INTO THE CLASSROOM TO SHARE EXPERTISE

One way to build communities that honor diversities is to bring families to the classroom in ways that expand and deepen the curriculum, broaden teaching, and honor family funds of knowledge. Jessica, who has been teaching in New York City public schools for about 20 years, regularly invites families as teachers to her classroom, sometimes to read aloud, sometimes to be interviewed as experts on the day their child was born, and other times to bring a unique expertise that deepens the curriculum and addresses children's interests and inquiries.

Jessica teaches Spanish-English dual-language 2nd grade in a high-needs New York City public school. Each year she has around 25 students in her class, about half who are Spanish dominant and come from immigrant families (mostly of Dominican and Mexican origin). Thirty to forty percent of her students either have identified dis/abilities or are in the process of being referred and tested. The families of the children she teaches vary in terms of income (close to 70% of the children receive free or reduced meals and many live in single room occupancy (SRO) housing or in homeless shelters). They vary also in family composition, ethnicity, and race (most identify as Latina/o, Afro-Latina/o, or African American). The school's dual-language program follows a rollercoaster model of bilingual education, with language alternating by school day (one day English, one day Spanish). Bilingual teachers remain in the classroom and teach in both languages.

In her classroom, Jessica invites families to share their expertise and engage as members of the extended classroom community in ways that feel comfortable to them. In doing so, she expands traditional notions of family involvement. Although Jessica honors the interests and literacies of the students in her class, she acknowledges that she is not an expert in all their areas of interest and that students' families and communities have much to contribute to their education. It is within this context that we share two examples of how she effectively positioned family members' technical knowledge and cultural practices to enhance curriculum, teaching, and learning in culturally relevant ways.

Technical Knowledge

One day, one of Jessica's 2nd-graders brought to class an issue of *AM New York* (a free newspaper distributed at New York City subway stations) and shared an article about two window washers getting stuck high up on the Freedom Tower (New York City's tallest building, which replaced the World Trade Center Twin Towers). Observing the engagement of the class with this article, Jessica invited her students to engage in a close reading of the text and to write down questions they still had. Some of their questions had to do with the fact that the window washers remained nameless. "They are people. They have names!" one of her students said. So, they did research (consulting Internet resources, watching the news, and reading periodicals) and learned more about the two Latino men, both named Juan, who had gotten stuck washing windows high up.

Yet some of their questions were technical and required architectural knowledge. Knowing the human resources of her class families, Jessica invited one student's mother, a Boricua (Puerto Rican) architect, to come to the class to explain the structure of the building's windows, the safety procedures related to window washing, etc. After answering the children's questions, this architect noted: "They have really good questions. They are asking the same questions my coworkers have been asking all day in the office." Through knowing the families that make up her classroom community, Jessica was able to expand the curriculum in ways that not only addressed learning standards for grades beyond 2nd, but that met the interests and answered the questions of the children in her class.

Cultural Knowledge

Another example from Jessica's 2nd grade developed in response to guided reading, small-group reading instruction designed to provide differentiated teaching that supports students in developing reading strategies. Having observed that her student Martín was not confident in his guided reading group, Jessica consulted with Mariana, coauthor of this book and early childhood teacher educator. They decided to select a book for guided reading that showcased one of Martín's funds of knowledge. Jessica explains her observations about Martín and her strategy to engage him in small-group discussions:

> Martín is an engaged and intelligent boy. He is fluent in Spanish and English. He loves soccer and rugby. He is charismatic, loving (regularly displaying affection for peers and teachers alike), and clearly cares for his classmates. He is an avid reader. Yet he often excluded himself from small-group book discussions and from whole-class conversations, as he thought of his own home experiences, practices, and culture as irrelevant and unworthy.

Despite markers that would position him as being "at-risk" (such as his family's income and his English language learner label), I saw Martín as clearly being "at promise" (Swadener & Lubeck, 1995). Based on classroom interactions and discussions as well as more formal measures, including assessments such as the Benchmark Assessment System (Fountas & Pinnell, 2011), Martín is ahead of what is socially expected of a second grader; that is, he is above the social construct of his grade level per New York City measures of progress in reading and mathematics.

Seeking to draw on Martín's strengths, value his voice, and more fully include him in small-group book discussions, we selected one of the few books available in the school's book room featuring a Mexican American extended family (like Martín's) to be read in guided reading: Gary Soto's *Too Many Tamales.* I knew that Martín lived with his extended family and that his mother made tamales. Although one of many children from Mexican immigrant families in my class, Martín was the only Mexican American child in that guided reading group. Both connections would allow him to shine during the small-group book discussion that followed guided reading.

After introducing and reading the book, the students and I engaged in a discussion, which sought to deepen our understanding of the story, make connections, and foster Martín's participation. Martín spoke much more than he had in previous discussions. He was knowledgeable and could explain to the children what "cornhusk" and "masa" were, for example. Yet our efforts to select a book that had connections to Martín's life and experiences initially served to reify stereotypes. The other students in the group initially assumed that Martín ate tamales. To everyone's surprise, while Martín was knowledgeable about tamales, he stated: "I don't like tamales." Many of the children seemed confused. They had developed essentialized definitions of Latinos and had come to believe that if you are Latina/o, and especially if you are Mexican American, you must like tamales.

Martín shook his head and smiled. He looked at his peers and knowledgeably invited them to rethink their assumptions, firmly saying: "When my mother makes tamales, she makes tortas for me. I really like my mother's tortas." This stood in contrast to Martín's often tentative and soft-spoken comments. This is what we were hoping for in selecting a book that had visible connections to Martín's experiences and life.

Omar, an English-dominant White boy, looked at Martín and asked what tortas were and tried to compare them to tamales. But before Martín could answer Omar's question, an English-dominant White girl stated, confidently, "Tortas are what we call sandwiches."[6] Looking down at the book, Martín softly and reluctantly stated that tortas de queso (cheese tortas) are not like sandwiches. "It's like flour and cheese. My mother, she fries it," he said, raising his eyes from the book to look at his classmates. Even

---

6. *Tortas* may be either sandwiches or fried patties (a kind of *fritura*) across various Latin American countries.

Figure 3.1. Reading _Too Many Tamales_ by Gary Soto

though Martín had the answer, it was as if he recognized that the voices of his White, English-dominant peers resounded louder.

A week later, when Mariana reconvened the group, she asked what they thought of the book, if they had read the book during that week, and if they had talked with anyone about the story (see Figure 3.1). Kya, a child who spoke Hindi as her home language, and was learning Spanish as a third language, immediately shared that she had read the book so many times that she dreamt she was eating a tamale, and that tamales tasted like hot-dogs, with bread and a hot dog.

Martín frowned but did not say anything. The children were not sure about the tortas Martín had talked about. They were puzzled. Omar stated: "I don't know what tortas are really." They were curious and asked Mariana questions like: What are tortas? What do they taste like? Where can you get them? They assumed that Mariana would know more than Martín. Yet Mariana was also unfamiliar with the tortas to which Martín referred.

While it would have been easy for Mariana to push through to the next task or text, she deliberately created the space for Martín to share his expertise. She invited the children in this guided reading group to listen to and learn from Martín. Martín tried to explain to the group what tortas de queso were. He said: "Tamales are cooked. Tortas are fried. Tamales have meat. A lot of times they have meat. Tortas have eggs and flour and cheese. That's it. And you fry it. They don't have corn husk." "Do they have masa?" Fisher, a White, English-dominant boy asked. Martín shook his head. "Where can you get tortas, Martín?" Omar asked. "My mom makes them for me," Martín said, shrugging his shoulders.

After the meeting, Mariana approached me and said that the children were interested in learning more about tortas and that maybe their interest could be connected to the informational writing Common Core State Standards (the learning standards in place). I thought: Yes, we can invite his mother and they can interview her. I immediately thought that they could write a procedural piece; procedural writing would come to life. Additionally, this would serve as an opportunity to show not only Martín, but the whole class, how capable Martín's mother was.

I asked Martín, "¿Crees que tu mamá puede venir y enseñarnos cómo hacer tortas?" [Do you believe your mother can come and teach us how to make tortas?] Martín did not respond immediately. Finally, he looked down, raised his shoulders, and tilted his head to the right as he softly muttered "Creo que sí" [I believe so] and hesitantly agreed to my request. He said he was nervous, that it was the first time his mother would ever come to his classroom; she had never done so before. He said: "Esta es la primera vez que mi mamá viene a mi salon. No vino en el jardín [de infancia]. No vino en el primer año. ¿Por qué ahora?" [This is the first time my mother comes to my classroom. She didn't come in kindergarten. She didn't come in 1st grade. Why now?]

The weeks that followed were not exciting ones for Martín. As much as we played up the idea of his mother coming to share her knowledge with us, Martín did not seem to be looking forward to the day. In fact, it seemed as if he wished the day would never come. No one knew for certain exactly what Martín was thinking or what he was feeling, until he asked Mariana: "Why did you tell Mrs. Martell that my mom can make tortas?" Then we knew Martín was feeling uncomfortable. As uncomfortable as he felt, we knew (and hoped) having his mother come into the classroom would allow for a life-changing experience. Maybe not life changing, but certainly a new experience for everyone involved, which would invite them to cast a new light on individuals who are Spanish speakers as capable and worthy. My hope was that her visit would challenge the idea that Spanish is an obstacle and illustrate how Spanish-speaking individuals are knowledgeable and competent.

As we prepared for the day, we explained how Martín's mother was the only person who knew how to make cheese tortas (tortas de queso). In preparation, the children wrote questions in Spanish. They knew that they would be using their Spanish language knowledge to access this very valuable information. I made clear connections between what we were learning in 2nd grade and what they would be learning from Martín's mother—specifically related to the listening and speaking, language, reading, and writing strands of the Common Core State Standards. I wanted to communicate that this was important, that it was academic, and that it was valuable for their learning. I purposefully wanted to move away from their thinking of this as simply extra or nice. Thus, I communicated the curricular connections in clear and deliberate ways, letting them know that they would need the knowledge they learned in the subsequent week as we worked on informational writing.

The day finally arrived. For Martín's mother, Alba, it was the first time she had been asked to be the teacher in a classroom. According to Martín, "it was the first time she came to my classroom since kindergarten and first grade." He later explained that she had never been personally invited into a classroom for anything other than a parent–teacher meeting or a publishing party (which had taken place within the first 8 weeks of school, prior to this visit). She also hesitantly agreed to come, share her recipe for tortas, and demonstrate how they were made. For Martín, this was the first time his mother would be the most knowledgeable person in his classroom. It would be the first time his mother, teachers, and peers would interact with one another. His mother and her knowledge would be at the center of our learning.

For Martín's classmates, it would be the first time they would experience a cooking demonstration in the classroom. Although most of the students had been in a dual-language setting for at least 2 years, since kindergarten, many of the English-speaking students had never experienced having to speak in their second language, Spanish. While they spoke English on English days and Spanish on Spanish days, they all knew that the classroom teachers were bilingual and would understand either of the languages. For many of the English-dominant children, it would be the first time they would have to communicate completely in Spanish, in an authentic rather than didactic manner, in order to have their questions answered. If they wanted to communicate with Martín's mother, it would have to be in Spanish. It would be the first time the balance of power would be shifted.

For that hour, Martín's mother, Alba, held all of the knowledge. She spoke Spanish and answered the questions the children had for her. One student asked, "Cuántos años tenías cuando aprendiste a cocinar?" [How old were you when you learned to cook?] She smiled and nodded, almost as if the question had evoked a sweet memory. "Ah, cuando muy niña. A los 6 años en México. Mi mamá me enseñó." [Ah, when I was very young. At the age of six, in Mexico. My mother taught me.] Another student asked, "¿Por qué no hay tortas para venta en las calles de Nueva York como tamales?" [Why aren't there tortas for sale on the streets of New York, like tamales?] She responded with a large smile: "Por qué las tortas de queso son especiales. Son de mi familia. Tamales todos lo hacen. Pero las tortas no. A Martín le encanta mi torta de queso. Las preparo con mucho amor." [Because tortas de queso are special. They are from my family. Everyone makes tamales. But not the tortas. Martín loves my tortas de queso. I prepare them with much love.]

Figure 3.2. Writing About Our Family Funds of Knowledge

While she was hesitant at first, soon she grew confident, as she knew all of the answers. She stayed longer than the time she had initially agreed on. As she prepared and cooked the tortas, she also answered questions. She was often the only adult in the room able to answer the questions the children posed. We did not know many of the answers. Alba was the expert. The assigned texts, mandated curriculum, and reading assessments were not guiding our learning. Martín's mother was.

Martín and his mother did a lot of smiling and hugging when all was said and done. The children were very excited about all they had learned from Martín's mother. They saw value in their Spanish language skills—they needed Spanish to access information only she had. Martín was extremely happy. As he said, "It was great; it was fantastic, really." He hugged us many times throughout the day. Some of the children told him in both English and Spanish that they would be teaching their parents what they learned from his mother. He responded, "Really?" and smiled. For once, he experienced (instead of being told) that his mother was knowledgeable—that she was worthy.

Other students also changed their perception of Spanish-speaking parents during the visit and in their writing. For example, Aurora said: "I didn't know his mother knew sooo much." Other students asked for the recipe for tortas de queso, remarking how lucky Martín was to have a mother who would make these tortas for him. Still others wrote in Spanish and/or English about their own experiences with a family member who cooked with them (see Figure 3.2).

For example, children who had been reluctant to write, such as Orlando, wrote about traditions like the ones Martín's mother talked about.

Orlando read aloud his very first draft: "Yo como arroz con pavo y es delicioso. Mi mami y mi papi hacen bueno arroz con pavo. Es mi favorito porque sale bueno. Es arroz con pavo. El pavo tiene carne adentro." [I eat rice with turkey and it is delicious. My mommy and my daddy make good rice with turkey. It's my favorite because it comes out good. It is rice with turkey. The turkey has meat inside.]

We recognize that this is a first step, and many more were taken throughout that year. After Martín's mother came to visit, was interviewed by the children, and demonstrated her process of making tortas, bringing a procedural text to life, we invited many other family members to come. They talked about many topics, including Palestine, Greensboro sit-ins, Brazilian music and culture, Tanzania within the context of Africa, and the sociocultural histories of the children who made up our classroom community.

Family members communicated in English, Spanish, Portuguese, and American Sign Language (ASL). While most of the students did not speak Portuguese and ASL, they were able to depend on their classmates to give them access to what was being said. For example, when a family spoke Portuguese, students were able to draw connections to Spanish, to draw on the expertise of a Brazilian student who spoke Spanish and Portuguese, and to call on Mariana, whose first language is Portuguese. They relied on a student's family members to understand messages communicated in ASL.

Family members answered many questions the children asked, such as: "Why isn't Palestine a country?" and "Why is there a civil war in Syria?" They helped children do away with misconceptions, such as the ones illustrated by these comments: "I thought Africa was a country" and "I didn't know there were big beautiful houses in Tanzania." The students did not know the answers to the questions they asked (and many times neither did we), but they were confidently seeking to expand what they knew, adding new perspectives to their bodies of knowledge.

While there are many possibilities for inviting families, here we underscore the power of having families in the classroom, expanding the very curriculum in central and meaningful ways.

FOCUSING ON AUTHENTICITY AND INTEREST IN READING, WRITING, AND TALK

Children seem born not just to speak, but also to interact socially. Even before they use words, they use cries and gestures to convey meaning; they often understand the meanings that others convey. The point of learning language and interacting socially, then, is not to master rules, but to make connections with other people and to make sense of experiences. (Genishi, 1998, p. 2)

Young children make use of reading, writing, and talk to make meaning and communicate within and across contexts. That is, reading, writing, and talk serve specific purposes and have social and interpersonal meanings. In our classrooms, it is important for us to foreground authenticity and interest in reading, writing, and talk. "We need to look for, listen for, and feel the heartbeats in our students. That's where the energy is, for us and for them" (Graves, 2004, p. 90).

In Jessica's classroom, reading, writing, and talk are linked to specific purposes, visible to the children with whom she teaches and learns. This happens day in and day out. The children in her class don't write a letter because it is part of the curriculum, but because they want to communicate with someone who is outside their immediate context. And so it was in the winter of 2014–2015, when Jessica introduced one of her favorite children's authors to her class, Jacqueline Woodson. Jessica shared, "I am reading a wonderful book that won many prizes. It is called *Brown Girl Dreaming*. It is written by one of my favorite authors, Jacqueline Woodson." Then, she went on to say, "A very special thing about this author is that she writes books for adults and for children. I have two of her children's books that I'd like to share with you." Jessica then introduced and read both *Show Way* and *The Other Side*.

The children were so enthralled and had so many questions that Jessica suggested they write to the author. She didn't yet know how the letters were going to get to Jacqueline Woodson, but she was determined to make it happen. After all, the children's letters were not meant to decorate a bulletin board, but to communicate meaning. Figure 3.3 features an example of how empowering the process of reading and writing authentically can be, captured by a child's letter.

Upon hearing Jessica say that she wanted to do this in a way that would allow any other teacher to achieve similar results, instead of contacting friends or personal connections, Mariana reached out to Jacqueline Woodson via her fan-mail e-address (publicly listed), asking if she would consider responding to the children's letters. She replied positively and immediately, but after reading the letters she decided to respond in a more personal way, by visiting Jessica's class. When Jessica let the children know that Jacqueline Woodson liked their letters and questions so much that she was coming to visit, the children literally and enthusiastically jumped up and down. They decided that they should read all of her books written for children. Jessica then read *This is the Rope, Each Kindness, Visiting Day*, and *We Had a Picnic This Sunday Past*. They read and discussed her books, her writing style, and the themes she wrote about. They composed questions to ask her during her visit. They visited her website. They did research. With contributions from an Internet crowd-sourced campaign, PTA, and families, Mariana and Jessica

Figure 3.3. Letter to Jacqueline Woodson

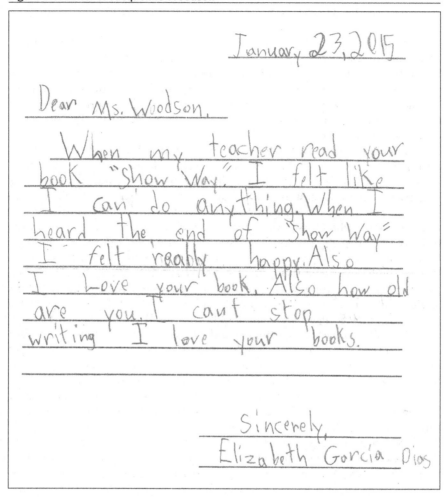

January 23, 2015

Dear Ms. Woodson,

When my teacher read your book "Show Way," I felt like I can do anything. When I heard the end of "Show Way" I felt really happy. Also I Love your book. Also how old are you. I can't stop writing I love your books.

Sincerely,
Elizabeth Garcia Dias

purchased 25 copies of *The Other Side* so that the children would each have their very own book for Woodson to sign. We knew that their signed copy of *The Other Side* would not merely mean one more book, but would become the example, the mentor text for authorship, a mirror and a window for future possibilities for many of them.

When the day came, all children were present; in fact, they had all arrived early. They were excited. One of them said she leapt out of bed at 4:30 A.M., jumping and singing, and waking her entire family up for the special occasion. Some of them were dressed in their best clothes, and a couple had even convinced their family members to go to bookstores to purchase other books authored by Woodson.

When Jacqueline Woodson came, she answered questions about her life and about writing. The Children of Color in particular sat a bit taller as they listened to Jacqueline Woodson; they had a special "light in their eyes" (Nieto, 2010). As one child recalled, "She said you have stories inside of you, and you need to get them out." Another one said, "It doesn't matter if you don't write the words right, or if you forget your periods. What matters is that you get to tell your stories." Finally, one of them said, "I have so many stories to tell that I want to be an author like Jacqueline Woodson when I grow up." And another noted, "And do you know how many times you have to write a story to get it just right? Like 31!" referring to the fact that Jacqueline Woodson had revised the multi–award winning *Brown Girl Dreaming* more than 31 times (she had said that she stopped counting at her 31st revision).

They had seen their images in Woodson—and understood the authoring process firsthand—and the many possibilities for their futures. They had read, written, and talked—in real and authentic ways, in ways that will remain in their memories for years to come. They had seen the powerful effect of writing. As second-grader Elián voiced: "You know, Jacqueline Woodson came to visit us because we read her work and wrote her letters. So, you never know what will happen when you write. Things like this just might happen, you know?"

PLAY, LANGUAGE, AND LITERACY

One of the prime times we teachers can see children's language and literacy practices is when they are playing. Yet there is rarely time for play in today's K–2nd grade. Play is often misunderstood—and positioned by many apart from learning. We propose that a daily time for play is a time not only to provide authentic scaffolding, but also to explore the multiple worlds of children. To establish such a time, it is important for teachers to educate families, colleagues, and administrators about the power and possibility of play in the early years, so that they can support play in our classrooms. After all, as kindergarten-2nd-grade students move in and out of play, they expand their knowledge of the world (Owocki, 1999).

"Play is like a gold mine in its potential for facilitating literacy" (Owocki, 1999, p. 3), as play brings literacy concepts to life in the social realm. It provides lots of clues for sorting out aspects of written language, for example. Because children's play involves what is familiar to them or what they are interested in, it is a meaningful context for children to build new knowledge and for teachers to marvel at children's brilliance and competence and to document and facilitate this construction. Play allows children to "build on their current understandings at individualized paces" (p. 4).

Recognizing the importance of play, Jessica has a playtime called *Nuestro Tiempo* (our time). It is not academic in nature. It does not overprivilege traditional definitions of literacy. It is not comprised of closed-ended literacy centers. It is a time for children to engage with each other in meaningful and authentic ways. In observing during this time, Jessica noticed how this setting was ideal for children to take risks and learn in the process. And children have to take risks to learn, which makes play very important for building new knowledge (Harste, Burke, & Woodward, 1981; Owocki, 1999). Jessica also realized that as they engaged in the complex tasks they selected—whether looming rainbow bracelets, playing chess, or building a ramp that tested hypotheses about car speeds related to incline and surface texture (see Chapter 4)—the children were engaged in problem-solving together. They were using language. They were developing relationships. They were growing as learners and developing as human beings.

REFLECTING ON BUILDING LEARNING COMMUNITIES AND LOOKING AHEAD . . .

We conclude this chapter by inviting you to consider options—in intentional ways, each and every day. We realize that competing demands and dwindling resources can make it hard to honor each and every child's diversities, but we encourage you not only to see the beauty in diversities but to represent these diversities through the materials in your classroom and through your teaching practices. We hope this chapter serves as a valuable resource.

In Chapter 4 we focus on oral language because it is so important yet it is often ignored and misunderstood in language and literacy education and in K–2 classrooms. Through a variety of examples, we illustrate the power and multiple possibilities for learning authentically from and with children . . . and of creating spaces for oral language to be seen as an imperative in the K–2 classroom.

On Oral Language

Considering Meaningful Possibilities and Learning Authentically from Diverse Children in K-2 Classrooms

"Shhhh!! It is time to learn, not to talk." In classrooms throughout the country, talk is often seen as a distraction that gets in the way of learning. Yet it is through talk that many children learn—they observe ("Look at that!"), report ("I saw Yesenia . . . "), question ("Did you see that? Why did she do that?"), make predictions ("I think . . . "), make connections ("Guess what?"), and inquire ("What if? Why?"). In this chapter, we invite you to reclaim oral language's important role in learning.

Talk is important in the classroom and beyond—not via Daily Oral Language (DOL) exercises and sentence diagrams, but through communicating and talking. Rather than presenting formulas, we offer vignettes of classrooms to help you see possibilities for engaging in teaching and learning with diverse children in your own setting. These narratives are organized around storytelling, play, and culturally relevant oral-language engagements, encouraging you to (re)consider the role, importance, and definition of each of these in your classroom. We build on the work of Vivian Paley (1986, 2007) as we talk about oral language in terms of friendships, fairness, and fantasy—the building blocks of early childhood. Most of all, we explain the prominence of communicative functions and explicate the importance of consistently including time and space for oral language, not for the sake of reading comprehension or to scaffold writing, but for its own value.

This chapter highlights the promise of oral language to culturally relevant teaching through bringing in stories, traditions, and bodies of knowledge (texts in a general sense) that are traditionally absent from the official (and often prescribed) curriculum. Overall the chapter briefly explains the components of oral language, illustrates the importance of children engaging in storytelling and negotiating friendships, fairness, and fantasy through storying worlds. It also illustrates how to fully engage in recognizing and valuing the varied linguistic repertoires of the extended classroom community, including families and communities (Ladson-Billings, 1994). It concludes by making visible possible ways for connecting oral and written language meaningfully in K–2 classrooms.

ORAL LANGUAGE

Oral language is a "complex system that relates sounds to meanings" (Genishi, 1998, p. 2). It includes "the rules for combining sounds" (phonology), the knowledge that "the smallest units of meaning that may be combined with each other to make up words (for example, paper + s are the two morphemes that make up papers), and sentences" (semantics), "the rules that enable us to combine morphemes into sentences" (syntax), and the "ability to speak appropriately in different situations, for example, in a conversational way at home and in a more formal way at a job interview" (pragmatics) (pp. 2–3). Oral language is thus comprised of phonology, semantics, syntax, and pragmatics (Genishi, 1998). Young children orchestrate and further develop these components of oral language as they talk.

Although these components (phonology, semantics, syntax, and pragmatics) exist across languages and cultures, they are culturally grounded. That is, with regard to phonology, while the sound –ng can start words in languages such as Tagalog (as in teeth, *ngipin*), Thai (as in easy, *ngāy*), and Cantonese (as in the family name *Ng*), children who speak "English, for example, know that an English word can end, but not begin, with an -ng sound" (Genishi, 1998, p. 2). Thus, phonology is culturally shaped and situated. With regard to pragmatics, in Brazil, for example, it is appropriate to kiss someone on the cheek upon meeting them, even in a business setting. In the United States, this would be inappropriate. With regard to talk, in Northeastern Brazil, it is appropriate to use the term *minha filha* (my daughter) in addressing women who may not be related to the speaker at all—including adults, many times older than the speaker. The same action would be framed as inappropriate in the United States.

Young children who are socialized into pragmatic rules that differ from what counts as appropriate in U.S. schools and schooling are often disadvantaged by teachers' expectations that young children would understand how indirectness may signify politeness, how questions may mean commands, and how some questions are not meant to be answered (Souto-Manning, 2009; 2013a). As Genishi (1998) underscored: "Learning pragmatic rules is as important as learning the rules of the other components of language, since people are perceived and judged based on both what they say and when they say it" (p. 3).

By the time they enter kindergarten, most children are able to communicate orally and their talk features complex sentences (Genishi, 1998). Although their oral language continues to develop in K–2 classrooms even as they develop written language. Young children's oral language develops through authentic interactions with teachers, peers, families, and community members. Thus, it is essential to make room for talk in our classrooms—not only for the sake of oral language development, but for the sake of learning; after all, learning is mediated by and enhanced through talk. Doing so can socialize children into multiple culturally situated pragmatics, varying phonological and semantic rules, and myriad syntactic structures.

STORYING IN THE EARLIEST YEARS

Oral storytelling traditions are well known and very important in a variety of cultures—Native American/American Indian, West African, African American, and Japanese, for example. However, oral storytelling is not adequately valued in classrooms that overprivilege print. The practice of overprivileging print is exclusionary and communicates to many children and their families that their traditions, although rich, are not valuable in classrooms and schools because those stories are not recorded in a book (Heath, 1982). Such practices are seen from a subtractive perspective (Valenzuela, 1999) and their richness for developing phonological, semantic, syntactic, and pragmatic knowledge and understandings is ignored.

To move away from Eurocentric stories as well as Eurocentric conceptions of what counts as literacy (Souto-Manning, 2010c), we teachers need to listen to children's voices and stories (Ladson-Billings, 1992a). By moving beyond often-privileged Eurocentric stories through oral storytelling and the acting out of stories in the classroom (originals and adaptations of stories that have historically portrayed characters who are White), we trouble the prototypical image of American families as White represented in almost 90% of children's books published today (Cooperative Children's Book Center, 2015). For example, noticing that Goldilocks was blond and not African American like them, the children (all African American) in Janice Baines's 1st grade in Columbia, SC, coauthored the story *Starbraid and the Three Bears*, which was orally recorded and featured an African American main character (Souto-Manning, 2013b). This was done as children sought to author themselves into fairy tales, which, despite many published versions, featured only White human characters.

Questions, Questions, Questions!

Parents usually get extremely excited when our young children utter their first comprehensible words. As those words continue and develop exponentially, usually around the time children enter school, we often ask them to be quiet and stop asking questions. Why? Many times their questions don't make sense to us, or we don't have an answer (Why is the sky blue? Why are there so many stars in the sky?). At other times we read into their questions and see them as challenges to our directions (Why do I have to clean up?). We usually judge their questions based on our own cultural expectations of what is appropriate, as adults, employing our own culturally situated pragmatic rules. Here, we invite you to consider the many affordances of asking questions—to learning and to oral language development. If we want young children to develop their communicative practices and repertoires, we need to understand that this development happens in authentic social interactions.

In asking questions, children are constantly trying to construct meaning. They are trying to understand their worlds and author their stories. Every child has stories to tell. And each story has a beginning, a middle, and is often "to be continued. . . ." Allocating the time and space for our students to express themselves orally—by promoting self-talk, one-on-one talk, small- and large-group talk—is invaluable in a variety of settings. "We have to plan more deliberately for the many purposes of talk in our classrooms, and create the best environments—physical and interpersonal—for them" which requires giving up "ways of speaking that have seemed so normal in our own past" (Cazden, 2001, p. 77). Thus, we also have to make ourselves vulnerable, recognizing that we will not have all of the answers or be familiar with multiple ways of talking. That is perfectly fine! We must allow students to see us as inquirers, learners, and problem-solvers as well.

Children need to be heard and need to hear each other. We teachers can learn from the kinds of questions the young children we teach ask in their homes and communities, and use them for teaching. In many homes, *what* questions are less frequently used, as questions have the purpose of eliciting stories with particular morals (Heath, 1982). By recognizing the purpose of such questions and leveraging them in our teaching, we can engage families and communities in storying in our classrooms. Through storying, children learn from their family and community members how to be expressive, include details, use transitional words, and show emotion. Does this sound familiar? Yes, it's literacy. It's all literacy!

When they are not reduced to "guess what I'm thinking" formulaic "known-answer questions" or questions used simply for recall (Cazden, 2001; Heath, 1982), in the K–2 classroom, questions can leverage powerful, inclusive, and culturally relevant learning. They can serve to construct narratives and establish meaning. They can be used to learn from and with others. In the following section, we share how Jessica Martell's 2nd graders used questions to learn from their families, orally co-constructing their own histories.

The History of Us, An Oral History Project

When asked "What is the most important aspect of your life as a cultural being?" many adults' answers have to do with family. Many children feel the same, even though they may not express it. Families are the vital thread that

Figure 4.1. Learning from Families

connects any child to the world. The connection begins long before a child walks into your classroom. Each has a history, at least 5 years long, depending on the grade you teach (K–2). That history is important. Not just to the child, but to everyone who meets that child, teachers especially. How do you learn that history? Listen. Listen to your students. Listen to them talk about their likes, their dislikes, their adventures. Listen to their families. Family perspectives are invaluable and can afford teachers a fuller picture of the child, including his experiences, strengths, and histories. Teachers cannot consider themselves to be the sole experts on the children they teach. The teacher may have information on how a particular child negotiates meaning and grows within a classroom setting, but will always learn from the child's family and community members in order to unveil her potential.

In Jessica Martell's dual-language 2nd-grade classroom in New York City, she invites families to come in and talk about what happened on the day their child was born. She uses birthday celebrations to connect history and storying. Family members come in and are interviewed on or around their child's birthday (see Figure 4.1).

This is a yearlong project. Families offer unique insights and contribute to the oral history project entitled *The History of Us*, which is based on the idea that we all have unique and worthy stories to tell. It acknowledges that our stories are well known to our family members. It also acknowledges that we are historical beings; that we are stories that started even before the day on which we were born (Freire, 1970).

The project starts when Jessica reads the book *On the Day You Were Born*, by Debra Frasier. She explains to the children how on the day they were born the world stopped and only their family members know and can share what happened. Family members are initially apprehensive about speaking in class, but are soon overtaken by the children's excitement and many questions. While the children ask questions such as "What was his favorite food as a baby?" and "Did she have hair?" other questions are very profound, and substantially extend children's reading of their worlds.

Because a class is a community of learners, it is vital for everyone in that community to understand each student's value. It is imperative for the children to see the importance of their own story and to understand their own history as a central part of the classroom and of its history. In order to foster this while recognizing that there are learning standards to be met, Jessica engages her class in an oral history project. She anchors this yearlong oral history project on the Common Core State Standards for Speaking and Listening (2011)—meeting and going beyond the grade 2 standards and addressing more advanced standards for grades 3, 4, and 5. Jessica explains:

> Each year, *The History of Us* begins on the day the first family asks if it would be okay to celebrate his or her child's birthday in class. I respond with an excited, "Yes! Of course! I will need something very simple from you." Usually the family member is confused as I elaborate: "I need you to share that story." "What story?" I then explain that the reason for the celebration is to celebrate the day his or her child became part of the Earth. Through this oral history project, students come to understand the importance of each other and what a treat it is to learn from and with families as they expand their own understandings of history.
>
> Students in my class prepare for this first celebration by composing interview questions. Most students are familiar with interviews by 2nd grade. Students are asked to think about what they want to know about their classmate. We select questions by focusing on what their classmate could not answer without the help of the experts—in this case, family members. This allows students to see all families as experts, after all, only families can tell the history of a child's birth. Usually questions are as simple as: "Did _____ cry when he was born?" or "Who held _____ first when she was born?" As we celebrate more birthdays and hear more stories, the questions become more complex; not because I want them to become more complex, but because students are able to evaluate what kinds of information their questions elicited and revise accordingly. They then learn how to write different kinds of questions, addressing learning standards for grades beyond 2nd grade. For example:

- How did you decide on a name for _____? Who was part of that decision?
- Did you have an alternative name? Why?/Why not?
- What made you realize that _____ was ready to come out?
- What were your thoughts when you learned you were going to be a mom/dad/parent?

On the day of the visit, students are ready. Family members come in, begin the story, and show photos. Families who don't have printed photos send photos via email to be projected onto the SMART Board. The children know that this is a unique opportunity. The information relayed is not part of textbooks and cannot be acquired later. They are focused—eyes on the speakers, our experts. The guest speaker(s) use their preferred language—English or Spanish or both. You can hear a pin drop. After listening to the speaker(s) and taking notes, the students ask their questions. We end the celebration by singing "Las Mañanitas" and finally "Happy Birthday." If there is an edible treat (not always the case), we enjoy the treat. While students are eating the treat, they will often continue to ask questions.

There are many accommodations and adaptations made. Three of the most common have to do with when parents cannot come during the school day, when students' birthdays are not during the school year, and when parents are separated by borders. I address the three of them briefly here. While it is important to know that adaptations will need to be made, the important thing is to keep in mind the inclusive nature of this learning event.

When parents can't come during the school day, anyone in the student's family life is welcome to share this birth story. Some celebrations have involved one family member (typically a mom or a dad) while others have involved many—mom(s), dad(s), grandma(s), grandpa(s), and younger siblings. In the cases where an adult family member cannot come to the school, older siblings might come and share the story from their point of view. There have been several times when a babysitter or nanny will share the stories. A foster child may choose to invite a sibling or a caseworker.

The students who have summer birthdays are invited to celebrate during the last month of school. By then, they take proactive roles in planning for and scheduling their special event. They know that this is a special time. They want to make it happen.

One student's parent lived in a different state, but wanted to share her daughter's story, so we Skyped with her, using technology to make our classroom more inclusive. The mom shared the story. The students asked her questions, and we sang to the celebrant. The fact that the person cannot be physically present should not preclude that person from participating—even if virtually. The children often problem-solve, negotiate, plan, and facilitate these special learning opportunities with great ease and with genuine interest and curiosity. They know their questions matter.

For example, on Henry's birthday, his two mommies came to class. The children were intrigued about the idea of two mommies. One child asked: "So—who is your real mommy?" While the teachers froze, Henry responded confidently: "Well, they both are. Mary carried me in her belly for many months and Pat was the first one to pick me up." The children smiled, nodded, and understood that Henry's two mommies were real and loved by him. It was clear to them that the definition of parents and families was broader than traditionally portrayed. They immediately learned to associate parents with love, rather than thinking only biological parents are "real" parents. While there are books that portray LGBTQ families, such as *And Tango Makes Three* (Richardson & Parnell, 2005) and *The Family Book* (Parr, 2003), it is important for children to see diversities as the new normal in their immediate setting (Genishi & Dyson, 2009). So these opportunities are important not only to address standards in authentic and culturally relevant ways but also to expand children's worldviews.

On Umi's birthday, her adoptive mother came. Umi is an African child adopted from Tanzania and her immediate family is comprised of herself and her adoptive mother (an African American woman). Umi's mother explained: "Some mommies carry their babies in their tummies and then they give birth. I carried Umi in my heart." Once again the children were expanding their knowledge of what a family is and how families come to be.

Many times, during the interviews with family members, children were challenged to communicate completely in Spanish to access the information being shared by family members. They were very interested, and thus invested a significant amount of time and attention to the task at hand. They genuinely relished the opportunity to learn about the histories of their peers. As Emilia said: "You know, your birthday is not about goody bags. That is not what is really special. What is really special is that it was the day you were born. That is why it is special." And it is special because everyone has a unique and worthy story to tell.

Through this oral history project, children learned not only about the importance of oral language and of families, but also about who they are—and who their classmates are—as historical, social, and cultural beings. As Owocki and Goodman (2002) explained:

> Families contribute another layer of influence to children's literacy . . . [B]ecause different families and different cultural groups stress different kinds of activities, knowledge, uses of language, values, work, social interactions, and social organization, children develop knowledge differently. Individual, familial, social, and cultural forces make each child's literacy history unique. (p. 5)

While valuing family funds of knowledge and the histories of the children who made up the classroom community, Jessica made sure that she was addressing the mandated learning standards, as noted earlier. Our approach is not in conflict with the CCSS (2011) or other learning standards, but centers on children's lived experiences, identities, and worlds. While doing so, it also meets standards for the grade level and beyond—in culturally relevant ways (Ladson-Billings, 1995a, 1995b, 2014). (For a sample of the CCSS Jessica addressed in Speaking and Listening, see Supplemental Resource 4.1, at www.tcpress.com.)

In *The History of Us* project Jessica also addressed other standards related to reading and social studies. In authentic and meaningful ways, Jessica's teaching demonstrates that meeting (and surpassing) academic learning standards does not necessitate the standardization of curriculum or teaching. And culturally relevant teaching is not antithetical to high academic achievement. In fact, as Gloria Ladson-Billings (1995a) explained, high academic expectations are an inherent part of culturally relevant teaching. After all, "culturally relevant teaching rests on three criteria or propositions: (a) Students must experience academic success; (b) students must develop and maintain cultural competence; and (c) students must develop a critical consciousness through which they challenge the status quo" (p. 160). Keeping the focus on fostering literacy success for all children, especially those who have been historically disempowered and minoritized in schools and society, necessitates embracing these three principles.

ROLE OF PLAY IN LITERACY DEVELOPMENT

Through play, children use their imagination, and engage "with the three F's—fantasy, friendship, and fairness" (Paley, 1988, p. 107), developing oral (and at times written) language. Through fantasy play, they develop skills that will help their literacy development across content areas and grades (Owocki, 1999). After all, language and literacy development are inextricably linked (Dyson, 1983; Lindfors, 2008). Daily play is not just useful in developing language practices and literacies but also necessary in developing friendships and social skills, for learning to get along. "In play a child always behaves beyond his [or her] average age, above his [or her] daily behavior; in play it is as though he [or she] were a head taller than himself [or herself]" (Vygotsky, 1978, p. 102).

Even with the push for more academics in K–2, social skills are just as important as academic skills in "successful" students. Play is children's work. The false separation of work and play is an adult invention that should not be imposed on children. Young children in kindergarten through 2nd grade learn through play. But—how? According to Vygotsky (1978), "play creates a zone of proximal development of the child" (p. 102), which is

the distance between the actual developmental level as determined by independent problem solving and the level of potential development as determined through problem solving under adult guidance, or in collaboration with more . . . peers. (p. 86)

Children need to engage in

> playing, experimenting, acting on objects, and exploring, instead of listening to a teacher talk, watching her demonstrations, and filling out dittos and worksheets. Hands-on action and exploration are children's natural tools for discovering the world. (Owocki, 2001, p. 45)

Indoor and outdoor play provide different contexts for children to develop oral language. Outdoor play could include negotiating which part of the playground or yard should be played in. Students will often initiate group games such as freeze tag. They come up with a plan to get started and negotiate rules for playing, revising them when they don't work. Where are the bases? What happens if someone doesn't freeze when tagged? When is it time to switch out? Who is "it"? Will we play this game again tomorrow? These are just a few of the questions students may come up with. They may also engage in playing pretend and change the meaning of things—a shirt becomes a cape, a twig becomes a wand. In play they attribute different meanings to objects. How young children negotiate space, time, and the rules of play is evidence of oral language development, of speaking and listening, to use CCSS language.

Why Create Space and Time for Play?

In the classroom, teachers can plan for a time in which children are engaging in talking, thinking, and hands-on learning through play. Teachers may call this choice time, work time, or use another name. This is a time when students are given the space within the classroom to select where and how and with whom they would like to work. In Jessica's classroom, as explained in Chapter 3, it is called *Nuestro Tiempo* [Our Time]. This is the time Jessica would allocate for students to work and play together. While she initially identifies and sets up some options for play (what some teachers call "stations"), such as Legos, art, and board games, her community of learners always develops additional ones.

For example, three boys, Nestor, Devin, and TJ, were pretending to be race-car drivers. While they'd done so on the floor on previous occasions, one day they asked Jessica if they could use two shelves to create a ramp (see Figure 4.2). They set one end of the shelf against a chair, creating a ramp diagonal to the floor and anchored it with another shelf. They designed and created a parking lot, measured speed, and tested a variety of surfaces for the shelf (paper, plastic, cloth, water, sand) to see which surface would allow the cars to reach the greatest speeds. They also adjusted and recorded the speed of cars at different inclines. In doing so, they were not only developing oral language in an authentic context, but were engaging in sophisticated mathematics and science learning, thus developing academic language as

Figure 4.2. Learning Through Play

well. Extending that play engagement, another boy, Caleb, brought his *Hot Wheels* car with the original packaging, which had a QR code for access to a race-car virtual world. Borrowing Jessica's iPad, they engaged in (re)creating their ramp and employed their learnings through their interactions in this virtual world, thus developing technologically.

Another group of children proposed that they loom rainbow bracelets. While Jessica was initially not thrilled with the idea, she asked the children to make an argument for what they would learn through looming rainbow bracelets. Upon close observation (and realization about the sophistication of the activity), Jessica asked the children to teach her how to loom a bracelet (see Figure 4.3). While she was being taught, she said: "This is hard! You are using great memory skills, problem-solving, math. You are making amazing patterns. You are collaborating. Wow!"

In order for this work/play time to provide students with freedom, yet include all students, it is important for the teacher to develop a plan with the children, so that everyone can play. Jessica developed a "You can't say you can't play" rule inspired by Vivian Paley's (1992) strategy, so that no one could be excluded from play or rejected by their peers. Groups were fluid and there were no caps or maximum number of participants. Yet children understood that they were responsible for the materials and that Jessica expected them to work as a community. During the time the children played, Jessica observed, documented, extended, and facilitated. She recognized that "as in the focus of a magnifying glass, play contains all developmental tendencies

Figure 4.3. Teachers Also Learn Through Play

in a condensed form and is itself a major source of development" (Vygotsky, 1978, p. 102). This was not a time for teacher planning or for a break. It was time for teacher learning. Jessica learned much from her students as she facilitated *Nuestro Tiempo*.

Play as a Motivator for Learning

Here we want to share a specific episode to illustrate some of the affordances of play to oral language development—and to bilingualism and multilingualism! In Jessica's dual-language 2nd grade everyone is encouraged to communicate—in English, in Spanish, and in any other language in which they are fluent (even if Jessica is not fluent in the language). Cali was a new student who entered Jessica's 2nd grade halfway through the year as a monolingual speaker of English. She was resistant to using Spanish until the need presented itself during *Nuestro Tiempo*. Carolina, who spoke Portuguese and had a beginning understanding of both Spanish and English, arrived in Jessica's class after Cali. Carolina wanted to learn to loom rainbow bracelets, a skill Cali had already learned and wanted to share with Carolina. Cali resorted to Google Translate (https://translate.google.com/) and to experimentation, and even asked her mother for a tutor so that she could develop her Spanish as a tool for teaching and learning (due to the great lexical overlap of Portuguese and Spanish, both of which are Romance languages). As Cali stated: "I wanted Carolina to feel good about herself, so I learned Spanish so that I could teach her how to loom bracelets." An authentic need for communication presented itself, and Cali's desire to connect with Carolina motivated her to use Spanish as the link, in intentional and purposeful ways. Here she clearly illustrated Halliday's (1993) theory that children learn to speak, they learn a language, because it serves a purpose. A parallel can be drawn to reading and writing.

As teachers, we must think about the purpose of reading, writing, and talk in our classrooms, ensuring that they are authentic for each child. It is also important that we acknowledge the centrality of language to learning itself, and come to see language learning as a lifelong process, thus creating "room for talk" in K–2 and beyond (Fassler, 2003).

Whether written or spoken, language should not be seen as a distraction from learning, but as foundational to learning. Halliday (1993) explained that "when children learn language, they are not simply engaging in one kind of learning among many; rather, they are learning the foundation of learning itself" (p. 93). Thus, talk should be encouraged in K–2 classrooms and beyond. Yet it is important to also rely on other means of communication. "Many teachers, when confronted with linguistic diversity in the classroom, find themselves for the first time in a situation where they cannot take for granted what they can accomplish through oral language" (Fassler, 2003, p. 4).

Even as children learn to communicate by reading and writing, in more conventional ways, it is important to recognize the sophisticated ways in which they learn how to communicate—and the very reasons that lead them to do so. As Vygotsky (1978) proposed, learning happens first in the social realm. Through talk, children facilitate their own thinking and learning, constructing meaning with others, including peers, teachers, family, and community members. After all, language is the "primary symbol system through which children learn about the world" (Owocki & Goodman, 2002, p. 49). Learning is likely to happen first through talk. Here is an example of how this may happen: After communicating orally in Spanish with a new student during *Nuestro Tiempo* as she sought to teach Carolina how to loom rainbow bracelets, Cali went on to use oral and written Spanish in a variety of settings. She wrote a letter in Spanish to an independent Latino bookstore in New York City's *El Barrio* (East Harlem), *La Casa Azul*. After all, "children's writing ability [can be developed] by building upon their proficiency in oral language" (Dyson, 1983, p. 1). Cali also started selecting more Spanish language books, but it all started with talk in a social situation.

While meaningful and child-centered, Cali's learning experiences required planning from the teacher. Jessica designed opportunities that allowed Cali to experience support and take risks in Spanish, both through *Nuestro Tiempo* as well as through planning a visit to a Spanish-language bookstore where the children learned about Frida Kahlo and Diego Rivera. After the visit, noticing how excited the children were about *La Casa Azul*, Jessica suggested that they write to the bookstore personnel, letting them know how much they enjoyed their visit. Of course, this being a Spanish-language bookstore, she suggested that the children write in Spanish. These spaces were created in intentional ways to support children's language development—going from talk to reading and writing. The children did not want to let their voices and messages go without being heard. Therefore they made every effort to use all of the resources available, including their knowledge of Spanish, Spanish books, and the Internet, to write letters to the bookstore personnel. They knew they had an audience who would read these letters; they had made that connection at the bookstore. After delivering the letters, Jessica noticed that some of the letters were posted on La Casa Azul's Facebook page. The next day, Jessica showed the class the letters, which were not just posted on Facebook but were being commented on and even "liked" by many. The students were ecstatic to have such a broad audience for their writing.

To fully understand children's capabilities, it is important to document their talk across settings, as such a practice "reveals their knowledge of language functions and forms, their interactional competencies, and what they know about the world around them" (Owocki & Goodman, 2002, p. 49). Whereas Cali was quiet during teacher-led small-group and whole-class discussions in Spanish, in self-selected peer groups during *Nuestro Tiempo* she began to take risks. Not only was that setting more comfortable—as there were fewer risks and greater support from peers who were Spanish dominant—but it was a setting that fostered relationships. The importance and value of a literacy task is determined by students and is often related to social relationships. In this case, Cali benefitted from the play setting, but also from her relationship with Carolina and the need to speak Spanish for communicating with Carolina.

EXAMINING CLASSROOM TALK

Looking closely and listening carefully to many kinds of talk that serve a variety of functions can offer us windows into children's thought processes. Here are some of the kinds of talk in which children engage: self-talk, one-on-one (with adult or with peers), and within peer-group (self-selected or teacher-selected), small-group, whole-group, and play settings. It is also very valuable to observe children's talk in their home and community settings. What are some of the other kinds of talk you have observed children engaging in? Now is the time to pause and consider, as our list (above) is incomplete at best. Take a few minutes and write down the kinds of talk in which children in your classroom engage.

As you seek to encourage talk in your own classroom, it is important to evaluate the learning environment you have fostered. We have found the following questions to be helpful.

1. Which settings promote exploratory talk? (For teachers working with emergent bilingual and multilingual students, which settings promote exploratory talk in each language?) How can I recreate these settings in my own classroom?
2. Am I doing most of the talking in my classroom? What language(s) am I using? How can I flatten the linguistic hierarchy I am demonstrating? How can I foster times in which children are doing most of the talking so that they actively engage in making sense of their worlds? How can I foster times in which children are doing most of the talking in dominant American English and in other languages, so that they actively engage in making sense of their worlds? And, do I have evidence that children who are not talking are indeed learning? What is this evidence? Does it fully capture the child's learning processes?
3. How does talk relate to reading and writing for particular children?
4. What do I learn about the children I teach through documenting and analyzing their talk across time and space?
5. Are my classroom environment and schedule set up so that there is space and time for exploring multiple functions of talk and a variety of topics through talk in multiple languages?

Beyond fostering environments where oral language is valued, it is essential that we engage in self-evaluation. At times we are so focused on what we want children to do, achieve, and learn that we are not prone to value the resources and assets children bring to the classroom. Consider asking yourself the following questions:

1. How do I use talk to negotiate concepts and understandings *with* the children I teach?
2. What language(s) do I use when asking questions? What language(s) do I use when responding to them and offering feedback?
3. What functions of talk do I value?
4. Which languages are students encouraged or allowed to use in response to questions (in small-group, one-on-one, and whole-class settings)?
5. Are attempts at using multiple languages valued? Is translanguaging appreciated?
6. What interactional competencies do I deem important?
7. What topics do I value?
8. What languages do I cherish? Do I appreciate language that is not talk? Do I respect languages I may not understand? In what ways?
9. How do I support the children in developing multiple language functions and interactional competencies? How does my talk support this development?

All in all, it is necessary to understand that children use language for a variety of purposes. For example, children express points of view (even through the socially undesirable *Eeewww!*), take leadership (*You do it!*), and ask questions (*Do I have to? Why?*). At certain times they share stories, retell events, report information, or explain how to do or make something. At other times they may use language to express what they know about language, literacy, and other content areas. Nevertheless, there are very important kinds of talk that are often ignored or undervalued in schools. These can include using talk to create imaginative worlds (and friends); to take social action (e.g., refusing to exclude peers from specific roles in play based on gender, or telling a peer it is not fair that she took the last milk carton); and to plan events. These different purposes of talk may or may not exist in our adult world. There are so many functions of talk, and they vary across time and space.

Many times, what we teachers consider to be interruptions are important to the development of talk and learning. It is important to listen to children, documenting the functions of their language use. As Owocki and Goodman (2002) proposed: "with every function comes a set of language forms, or structures that take their shape depending on the purpose and meaning of the language" (p. 56). It is essential that children explore language functions orally so that they have the foundational knowledge to develop reading and writing. "For example, children who learn to report information or explain how to do something have important knowledge for writing nonfiction text.

Children who can tell a cohesive, logically sequenced story have important understandings for structuring a story in writing" (p. 57).

Over time and across settings, children expand and develop their language functions and forms through use. Documenting these uses through observations or conversations with family members can help us identify and better understand the language(s) children employ, which allows us to create bridges between what children know and the academic language of schools and schooling. Even when we don't understand what children are saying, we can document their interactional competencies observationally. We can document if and how a child participates in group activities, for example. It may be a good idea to develop a tool to capture these observations over time.

With talk, distinct from writing, we need to capture the moment and develop a way to document and understand each child's practices and growth. We cannot do so relying only on our memories. Checklists and forms may be helpful. However, we do not provide these here as we believe that you best know your own setting, personal preference, and available time, so you have the essential information that will allow you to develop a relevant tool. In Supplemental Resource 4.2 (www.tcpress.com), we provide some suggestions regarding the kinds of tools you can develop.

ORAL LANGUAGE AND FRIENDSHIPS, FAIRNESS, AND FANTASY

As noted earlier, oral language supports the development of friendships, fairness, and fantasy (Paley, 2007). For example, earlier you read about Cali and Carolina developing a friendship and their bilingual communicative practices. You read about young children who pretended to be race-car drivers and zoomed down the ramp they'd constructed in the classroom. In addition, young children pretended to be Minecraft characters, soccer players, and animals. Through oral language, they developed friendships and engaged in fantasy play.

Because they were in a very child-centered environment filled with play, Jessica's 2nd graders did not shy away from issues of fairness. One poignant example of the children's quest for fairness took place in 2014 upon the exoneration of the White police officer who killed Eric Garner, a Black man. Many of the children had previously taken part in Black Lives Matter marches (http://blacklivesmatter.com/) and were well aware of the murder of Trayvon Martin in 2012. Yet when Eric Garner was murdered a few miles from their school, in another of the New York City boroughs, the children became very interested in fairness, in racial justice. While conversations about race and racism had taken place, especially after read-alouds and critical discussions of books such as *The Other Side* by Jacqueline Woodson (2001) and *Freedom on the Menu: The Greensboro Sit-Ins* by Carole Boston Weatherford (2005), the children had never been so enraged as they were that morning.

TJ walked in with a copy of the newspaper *AM New York*, displaying the headline "Grand Jury on Garner Death: No Charges." He looked at Jessica and said loudly: "No charges. Can you believe it?" Soon Amber said: "I saw a newspaper that said it was not a crime," referring to the *New York Post* front cover. Rashod, an African American boy, muttered: "Yeah. I guess Black lives don't matter." Ana, a Puerto Rican girl with light skin, said: "All lives matter. Not just Black lives."

At this point Jessica stopped the regular morning routine in which children read and talked over in-class breakfast and called the class for a meeting. She wrote "No charges," "Not a crime," "Black lives matter," and "All lives matter" on the easel to capture the children's words as she invited them to problematize what they had said critically. She asked Ana to explain her statement. Ana based her explanation on some of Jessica's prior statements that all human beings are unique, and thus she deduced that all lives mattered. Then Jessica asked Rashod to explain his rationale. He looked at Ana and said: "I'm afraid I'm gonna get shot and die. They killin' people like me, not people like you." Ana looked at him silently. Rashod continued: "They killing Black people. Black men and Black boys. Like me." Ladson-Billings (2011) shed light on this phenomenon—on how young Black boys are not seen as children, but rather as men; how they are constantly marginalized within the context of classrooms, schools, and society. After the silence, which seemed to have lasted an eternity in a classroom where children are never at a loss for words, Ana responded: "I guess you are right. You know, I hadn't thought of that." Without missing a beat, Rashod said: "You don't have to." The discussion progressed to an understanding of segregation, racism, unjust laws, racialization, and the immediate need for reparations.

The children were very respectful of each other but pushed each other's understandings in significant ways. For more than an hour, the children developed not only their oral language, exposing arguments, basing their statements on documentation, and demonstrating many of the learning standards for 2nd grade and beyond, but they also engaged in a much-needed examination of why Black Lives Matter cannot become All Lives Matter. As one of the children said: "It is not fair that people think that you are bad because you are Black." Another added: "Yeah. And some police are really violent with Black people. I don't think they would be with a White person." Their comments displayed an understanding of the situation lacking in many adult circles. For example, one of them explained:

> It is not fair because since slavery Black people are not treated as humans. What if President Obama treated White people the way Black people have been treated in the history of the United States? Like slaves?

They understood the need to have an honest and critical conversation about the marginalization of Blackness within schools and society, where a deep education debt exists (Ladson-Billings, 2006). They understood the need for reparations. They understood that Black lives matter. It was just fair!

ORAL LANGUAGE AND CULTURALLY RELEVANT TEACHING

Oral language can be an important avenue for developing culturally relevant teaching (Ladson-Billings, 1995a, 1995b). It can serve for children to learn about their family funds of knowledge and honor language variation as the norm.

Jessica found that she could not truly bring language diversity as the norm to her classroom until she understood and challenged the hierarchy of Spanishes as a way of oppressing or controlling, coming to understand that her own Boricua Spanish from Puerto Rico was not worse than Spanish from Spain. Instead of omitting or substituting words used in Puerto Rican talk (such as *quenepa* and *guagua*) as she had previously done, she started explaining to her students what these words meant. She also encouraged students to share words used in their own Spanishes and Englishes, explaining their meaning and use. In doing so, she was honoring language variation while honestly discussing issues of linguistic hierarchies. Such experiences created spaces for the children to discuss how they may have previously seen language diversities as deviations or deficits. Sharing one's learning journey as a reader of worlds and words is thus essential to transforming learning and to creating more inclusive learning environments. Students need teachers who recognize and value many languages and multiple ways of speaking, reading, and writing.

The following descriptions of events show how Jessica sought to sustain students' languages and cultures by involving the extended classroom community—family members!

Learning about Authoring Bilingual Books

Rafael Trujillo is a children's book author. He is also a parent of a child in Jessica's classroom. One special thing about Rafael's books is that they are written either entirely in Spanish or in Spanish and English (bilingually). After engaging in an author study, reading the books Rafael Trujillo had authored, Jessica's 2nd-grade class invited Rafael Trujillo for a visit. They wanted to learn about the craft of writing books. They had prepared many questions. As they asked their questions, the children listened carefully to Rafael's answers.

During his visit, Rafael Trujillo honored language variation as the norm, being interviewed and responding in English, Spanish, and Spanglish. He talked about his authoring process and then signed copies of his book *La última ola de Marianela* (Trujillo, 2009) for the children. This was a powerful example of culturally relevant learning in action as the children learned about

Figure 4.4. Learning from Author Rafael Trujillo

authoring and, since most of them had not met a children's author before, had their first encounter with an author who was a Spanish-speaking Man of Color. This served to disrupt the dominant story that authors are White and English-speaking. It also fostered high expectations for the children to author in English and in Spanish, to revise their writing multiple times, and to hone their craft so that they too could become published authors.

While Rafael's visit (Figure 4.4) did not involve writing a book or a story (at least not during the time he was there), the children had prepared questions and learned lessons they later applied to their own writing. One of these had to do with unstated character traits. While this is a learning standard for 4th grade, the children in Jessica's class had authentically learned it in 2nd grade.

Learning about Palestine and the War in Syria

Hibah, one of the students in Jessica's class, is Palestinian American. As she was about to visit Palestine with her mother, she suggested that her 2nd-grade peers write letters to students in a Palestinian school to learn more about where she comes from. So Jessica asked if Hibah's mother would be interested in coming and talking about Palestine. She answered questions from the 2nd graders such as: Why isn't Palestine a country? Why is there a civil war in Syria? Why are schools being bombed?

Sophisticated questions gave students access to advanced knowledge while they learned about part of Hibah's identity. To employ Bishop's concept of windows and mirrors (1990) on the macro level, the story of Hibah's mother's childhood provided a mirror for Hibah while providing windows into another culture for Hibah's peers. At the micro level, the children made connections between the food they eat and the foods Hibah's mother ate in Palestine as a child, such as fish and hummus, while recognizing that not everyone in Palestine eats these foods. In this way, Jessica's students were exposed to multiple stories and did not fall prey to the danger of a single story, which often creates stereotypes and promotes hate (Adichie, 2009). Additionally, putting a face on Palestine helped children understand multiple perspectives and add to some of their understandings, which had been shaped by Israeli communities in New York City. At the end of her mother's visit, Hibah said: "I am so happy my friends know about Palestine, because Palestine is part of who I am."

"Africa is Not a Country": Learning about Tanzania

Aware that many of her students conceptualized Africa as a poor (under-resourced) country—instead of a rich continent—Jessica used *The History of Us* oral history project (discussed earlier in this chapter) to start educating her entire class about Africa. When the mother of Umi, a child from Tanzania, was interviewed, the 2nd graders were able to problematize their prior assumptions and limited perspectives of Africa. As one of Jessica's students, Nico, said: "I thought all people in Africa were poor. . . . I don't know why, but I did. . . . Now I know that there is great rich[ness] in the countries of Africa. You know, because Africa is not a country."

REFLECTING ON ORAL LANGUAGE AND LOOKING AHEAD . . .

All in all, it is essential that we teachers create spaces for children to develop oral language and engage in storytelling in our classrooms and schools, so that they can negotiate friendships, fairness, and fantasy and learn through storying worlds. To do so we teachers can start by creating authentic and respectful relationships with families, inviting them into our classrooms *as teachers* from whom the classroom community has much to learn. It is also essential that teaching and learning centrally value the linguistic features employed by the extended classroom community—including students, families, and community members—so that children come to see the diverse world in which they live in terms of strengths.

Oral language, in addition to being important on its own (as explored in this chapter), can scaffold written language development (Dyson, 1983). For example, children are often ready to tell and enact their stories much sooner than they are ready to write them. They are still engaging in authoring, but the cumbersome nature of forming letters and words is removed. Later, once the child has the fine motor skills to write letters and has mastered (or is developing) the process of writing words and sentences (recognizing the patterns in language), they already have the knowledge of how stories work, pragmatically and semantically. They also know how sentences work, how they are structured in their language(s). Thus, children can compose stories without ever touching a pencil (or crayon) to a paper.

In Jessica's class she made direct connections between oral language and written language by: (a) having the students discuss the newspaper articles brought to class about Eric Garner's case; (b) writing a book entitled *The History of Us* emanating from the oral history project; and (c) writing a manual for looming bracelets and a book about toy car speed, ramps, and inclines. In an inclusive kindergarten classroom in New York City, teachers Carmen Llerena and Eileen Blanco made a practice of writing down on chart paper songs, chants, and rhymes from children's play, inviting them to see the connection between oral and written language and positioning the children in capable ways. While it is perfectly fine not to make such connections with every activity (Carmen and Eileen did not write down everything they heard), there are many possibilities for connecting oral and written languages in meaningful ways.

Chapter 5 focuses on reading words and worlds, continuing to expand on the definition of what counts as a text. In doing so, it considers diverse possibilities, perspectives, and points of view in K–2 classrooms.

On Reading Words and Worlds

Considering Diverse Possibilities, Perspectives, and Points of View in K–2 Classrooms

"Reading is not walking on the words; it's grasping the soul of them." (Freire, 1985, p. 19)

Reading is about making meaning, making sense. Yet reading too often gets diminished to the simple act of decoding, of calling out words. While we recognize that reading involves decoding words, simply calling them out is far from reading.

In this chapter we expand the notion of reading beyond accuracy, comprehension, and fluency to include critically problematizing one's world. We see literacy as a tool to address political and social issues, to question inequities, re-envision and revise realities (Freire, 1970; Souto-Manning, 2010a). To do so, we consider diverse possibilities, perspectives, and points of view in the K–2 classroom.

We explore strategies that have been typically associated with labels such as *emergent reading* (such as directionality and one-to-one correspondence), *early reading* (semantic, syntactic, and graphophonic cues), *early fluent reading* (such as rereading the text and self-correcting), and *fluent reading* (such as self-monitoring) (Cappellini, 2005). Although, because children in K–2 classrooms are diverse and because reading does not develop in a linear and lockstep fashion, we focus on who children are as readers and explain authentic, meaningful, and culturally relevant ways in which we teachers can support their learning.

Thus, we invite you to get to truly know the young children you teach, learning about their identities and documenting their cultural and linguistic practices. In doing so, we teachers can unveil the multiple ways in which young children read words and worlds within and across contexts, even if they have not mastered the letters of the alphabet or the required sight word list. Learning from and with the young children in our classrooms allows us teachers to document their assets, to better understand the multiple contexts they inhabit, and to assess what they already do and know, instead of simplistically reducing them to labels such as "emergent readers" or "early readers," which reify a single story about all children (Adichie, 2009). After all, any "experience is always what it is because of a transaction taking place between an individual and what, at the time, constitutes his [or her] environment" (Dewey, 1938, p. 43).

READING

Reading is a transactional act. It is a way of constructing meaning. That is, the reader and the text interact with one another and make meaning together. Reading is a "two-way transaction" (Rosenblatt, 1978, p. 170) where "the reader always approaches the text with a set of culturally acquired assumptions, values and ideas" (p. 170) and "any text embodies semantic, literary, and cultural elements or 'codes' . . . being susceptible to multiple readings" (p. 171). The reader writes a new meaning to the text as she reads it. At times this process involves reading words; at other times it involves reading other symbols (such as facial expressions, pictures, or spoken words).

Regardless of symbol system, each "reading act is . . . a transaction involving a particular reader and a particular configuration of marks on a page, and occurring at a particular time in a particular context. . . . The "meaning" [of a text] does not reside ready-made in the text or in the reader, but happens during the transaction process" (Rosenblatt, 1988, p. 4). As we emphasize throughout this book, reading, writing, and talk are social and cultural practices. That is, the meaning (or meanings) a child makes of a text is influenced by her identity, culture, experiences, and communities. Reading is influenced by who the child is. Thus, in teaching reading, we teachers need to learn about the children we teach.

Focusing on the Child as a Reader and a Learner

To cultivate and foster reading growth and development, we teachers first need to get to know the young children who inhabit our classrooms— regarding them as capable literate beings, developing relationships, noting interests, learning about community experiences and family funds of knowledge. We need to actively reject the notion that children are empty banks into which we deposit reading knowledge. Reading is not achieved through banking education; nor are knowledge and skills simply transferred from one person's brain to another's (Freire, 1970).

Young children are social, historical, and cultural beings. To teach them in culturally relevant ways, we need to learn where they are from—their families, communities, and histories. We need to learn about who they are! While this certainly can take place informally, to better understand reading from the perspective of the children, we have benefitted from interviewing them (for sample questions and guidance in developing the interviews, see

Supplemental Resource 5.1 at www.tcpress.com). After interviewing and learning from them, we can make connections to the curriculum and learning standards, fostering educational success in culturally relevant and sustaining ways (Ladson-Billings, 1995a, 1995b, 2014; Paris, 2012).

Inclusive teachers are engineers. They envision, plan, and build bridges between students' interests, expertise, experiences and individualities, and curricular goals. They are intellectuals. They identify strengths and interests in children, unveiling what motivates them. Then they make connections between the children and curricular goals and standards. In this way they avoid the standardization of teaching and learning by placing children front and center in curriculum and teaching. They recognize that "although children bring unique literacy histories from their specific communities, they all come to school with the same intellectual *potential* for literacy" (Whitmore, Martens, Goodman, & Owocki, 2005, p. 305).

Empowering Young Children as Readers

After learning about children's worlds, it is important to empower them by showing them that they are already readers—even before they enter kindergarten. This will mean that even though children may tell us that they cannot read, we can find ways to show them otherwise. This is not to prove the child wrong, but to problematize the message that they have received again and again throughout their earliest years—that they aren't able or ready, that they don't know, that they can't read. In Chapter 3 we described how Donna Bell used the labels from empty packages of common household products to show the children that they *could* read (Bell & Jarvis, 2002). Once children realize that they can read, we teachers can add the words they can read (along with children's names) to the word wall (a collection of words displayed in large letters on a classroom wall or bulletin board). While word walls traditionally include words students supposedly encounter frequently in their reading and writing ("high-frequency words") as well as words they frequently misspell, this approach allows for the word wall to serve as a celebration of what students know—building on their strengths—as opposed to being a display of what students do not know and positioning them in terms of deficits.

In addition to word walls, an authentic and useful resource Jessica used in her 2nd-grade classroom was an alphabet chart with large photos of each student labeled with each student's writing of his own full name in black marker. Eileen did this in kindergarten, having students write their first names. This allowed the children not only to see themselves in the classroom, but as a resource to relate to, highlighting letters, chunks, and connecting words they knew to new words. Jessica used both the word wall and the alphabet chart as resources as she engaged in think-alouds—in whole-class, small-group, and one-on-one settings.

Instead of teaching letter-sound correspondence (*graphophonics*, commonly referred to as *phonics*) as a discrete and decontextualized skill,[7] we have found it more productive to teach phonics through meaningful analogies and comparisons, as a way for children to confirm their predictions based primarily on their prior knowledge and on contextual information. For example, in an inclusive kindergarten classroom in New York City, teachers Eileen Blanco and Carmen Llerena used the song "Down by the Bay," already familiar to the students, as a way to teach them how to use words they already knew to read and create new words. In Mariana's 1st-grade classroom in Georgia, she used her students' names and environmental print familiar to the children to make analogies, unveiling the connections between familiar words and new words. Jessica used a similar strategy in her New York City 2nd-grade classroom, highlighting Spanish and English graphophonic differences, even when the same letter was written. For example, the names Juan and Julie have the same first two letters graphically, but they have different sounds, differing phonologically. As Jessica pointed out, the *J* in *Juan* had the sound of the English *H*. Children became aware of letters and sounds in meaningful contexts—and saw language variation as the norm as opposed to seeing one language as being right and another as being wrong.

Teachers Donna Bell and Donna Jarvis (2002) proposed that as teachers of young children we need to let go of the practice of the letter of the week (a practice commonly employed in kindergarten that teaches a letter per week) and instead engage children in *literacy digs*, like archaeologists. They invite us to think about valuing our students' literacies by engaging them in a dig in the world around them. Here's why.

Young children see print everywhere—in authentic ways. Yet when we narrowly define reading, we dismiss children's knowledge that allows them to distinguish the shampoo bottle from the body wash, a soup can from a can of vegetables. *Literacy digs* recognize all symbols that help children get along and get by in the world—such as the example in Chapter 2, where in *On Our Way to School, an ABC Book of Community Images,* children identified that the letter *M* is for *MetroCard* (see Figure 2.1). Literacy digs value what children already know, while asking them to focus on the label, on the print, making clear connections between literacy in their homes and communities and literacy in school.

Letter of the week (or word/s of the week, often employed in 1st and 2nd grades to teach high-frequency words) frames students as not knowing and as needing remediation, and affords little transfer between knowing the letter or the word(s) of the week and reading the letter or word(s) within a

---

7. When letter-sound correspondence is employed in the K–2 classroom in decontextualized and standardized ways, it may serve to exclude children's prior experiences and funds of knowledge, resulting in educational practices that are not inclusive of children's diversities. Regrettably, such standardized notions are not only privileged in standardized curriculum, but in teacher licensure tests as well.

text. Literacy digs allow the learning environment to be *re-mediated* (Gutiérrez et al., 2009), so that students' ways of knowing are valued in the classroom. Instead of focusing on the acquisition of "the basics" (Dyson, 2013), which are seen as problems of the individual child who needs to be re-mediated, re-mediation requires reorganizing learning opportunities and environments (Gutiérrez et al., 2009) and "rewriting the basics" (Dyson, 2013).

In Jessica's 2nd-grade literacy dig, the children gathered environmental print, capturing pictures and words through digital photography. Then they studied ABC books and found mentor texts, which offered ideas and possibilities for organizing their finds. One group of children coauthored an alphabet book modeled after Yuyi Morales's *Just in Case: A Trickster Tale and Spanish Alphabet Book* (2008), creating a story that included the letters of the alphabet and utilizing the pictures they discovered in reading their worlds. This led to a story that was rich in meaning, portrayed a complex storyline, employed irony as a rhetorical device, and was full of high-frequency words.

UNDERSTANDING EARLY LITERACY AND YOUNG CHILDREN'S READING

To recognize children's full literacy potential, it is important to know that literacy development begins in the very early stages of childhood. Early behaviors such as reading from pictures and writing scribbles are examples of emergent literacy and are important parts of children's literacy development. With the support of family and community members, caregivers, teachers, and peers, as well as through exposure to and engagement in literacy-rich environments, children often progress from emergent to conventional reading—albeit on their own timelines (Genishi & Dyson, 2009). At times, this process seems to take forever. Other times, it seems magical, as captured by a teacher: "It just clicked; he began reading," which ignores emergent reading behaviors children display well before they start reading conventionally.

Independent reading practice and authentic exploration of multiple texts are essential to young children's development as proficient and fluent readers (Cappellini, 2005; Routman, 2003). Children learn best when learning is meaningful, interesting, and functional—when they can make their own choices. In play, young children can develop positive relationships with books and experience book-handling behaviors in an authentic manner, scaffolding their successful literacy development. For example, books and other printed materials can be available in play areas; menus and cookbooks can be used by children who are engaged in playing restaurant. When children are allowed to explore books in unstructured situations and see themselves in the books they read, they may develop emergent and early reading behaviors sooner than expected.

The Reading Process

What do readers do when they read? How do young children start developing conventional reading skills and making meaning of symbols on a page? Does it just "click"? No! Although young children develop as readers in multiple ways and in varying timelines, their background knowledge (schema) about how written language works affects their ability to make sense of the symbols, squiggles, and marks on a page. Children use both their knowledge of literacy and life to help them decode and make sense of texts. That is, they draw on their knowledge of how written texts work within a particular language and on their experiences regarding the context and content of the story. Thus, an essential part of reading words is to read worlds. Through multiple texts and contexts, representing varying perspectives and points of view, reading is developed and learning is broadened. For example, if children's conception of a family (their schema for families) is broadened to include all family compositions, including two-parent families, one-parent families, and same-sex parent families, their learning will be broadened.

Young children's prior experiences with written texts and their linguistic contexts impact their reading development. Children who have not experienced how pages are turned from right to left in reading books in English may not display book-handling behaviors often associated with emergent reading in U.S. classrooms. Children who have experiences with print in a language that features a directionality that is different from English—such as Japanese—may not display "appropriate" directionality in reading English language books.

A child's understanding of how print works in a particular language (for example, directionality, one-to-one correspondence, letter-sound correspondence, and sentence structure in dominant American English) impacts his skills in reading books in that language. Whereas some children come to our classrooms with such an understanding of how written English and books in English work, others do not. Such experiences are not indicative of a child's potential or ability to develop as a reader, but merely signal that the child may have been exposed to oral language or written texts in English. Often, when children do not display such familiarity with how print works in English, they are seen as having been deprived of practices such as bedtime reading. Yet, here we see them as having language and literacy practices that simply differ from the ones overprivileged in U.S. schools. This is an important consideration, as socialization in book reading behaviors and in how written English works (in terms of directionality, for example) do not indicate intellect or ability.

Viewing Reading as Orchestrating and Balancing Cues

Reading is a process of orchestrating cues or signals. There are semantic or meaning cues (often related to the question: Does it make sense?), syntactic or structural cues (often related to the question: Does it sound right?), and graphophonic or visual cues (often related to graphic-sound correspondence: Does it look right?). Paulo Freire (1970) proposed that such questions can be applied not only to *reading words,* but to *reading worlds* as well—using them to problematize injustices. In reading printed texts, whereas semantic or meaning cues emanate from one's life experiences, syntactic or structural cues stem from one's knowledge about a particular language and how it works, and graphophonic or visual cues come from one's experiences with written language, requiring an understanding that sounds can be represented by symbols (such as letters) and that letter-sound correspondences are specific to the context of a particular language.

Both Marie Clay and Ken Goodman proposed that when children come to a word they don't know, they orchestrate these cues in order to decode it. For words they already know, they may rely on their memory, on what the word looks like. While Goodman (1965, 1970, 1996) used the nomenclature cue systems, classifying cues as semantic, syntactic, and graphophonic, Marie Clay labeled them as meaning (M), structure (S), and visual (V) errors. Both systems are briefly explained in Figure 5.1.

When reading, children orchestrate and balance semantic/meaning cues, syntactic/structural cues, and graphophonic/visual cues (phonics). Although Ken Goodman (1996) proposed semantic-pragmatic cues, in reality pragmatics are often forgotten in reading programs and assessments for young children (such as the Fountas & Pinnell Benchmark Assessment System). Yet pragmatics are very important; understanding whether something makes sense (semantics) is based on one's cultural experiences and practices, varying according to context (pragmatics). In reading, whether or not something "sounds right" is largely dependent on one's communicative practices, and whether something "looks right" has to do with one's prior linguistic experiences as well as one's experiences with print. Pragmatic cues are important in linking the other three cue systems to context, in processing language.

Through their own life experiences, some learners may internalize a balanced use of cue systems in a particular language. Other learners may need explicit strategy instruction and demonstration in the context of whole, meaningful, joyous reading experiences. It is important for us teachers to realize that these cues are specific to particular languages. That is, the way that letters and sounds correspond in different languages is different. Sentence structures vary across languages. So do the meanings of specific actions and behaviors. Thus, instead of seeing our multilingual students in terms of what they cannot do in English, it is important for us to document what they *can* do.

Proficient or fluent readers of English, for example, do not sound out every single letter from left to right as commonly believed. Let's read a popular Internet meme that illustrates the point that we do not read every single letter in a word in order to decode and make sense of it:

Figure 5.1. Cue Systems

	Does this make sense within this context?	Does the child:
Semantic Cues Meaning (M)	Children who are familiar with the context of the story are advantaged, as they are able to make connections to their experiences and lives. To get a more accurate understanding of children's reading, it is important to have them read books that are relevant to their experiences or interests, drawing on their experiences and expertise.	• Use the illustrations to make meaning of the text? • Go back to the beginning of the sentence and reread the preceding text, seeking to identify helpful clues? • Skip the word and continue reading the remainder of the sentence, then return to the skipped word with a better understanding of what would make sense? • Draw on her own schema/experiences of reading words and worlds? • Think about the context of the story and what would make sense within that specific context?
	Does this sound right according to the language being used in the book?	Does the child:
Syntactic Cues Structure (S)	It is important to note that language structures differ. For example, the structure of dominant American English, African American Language, and Spanish are different, so what sounds right in one linguistic context will not sound right in another. It is thus important to contextualize syntactic/structural misalignments and not regard them as errors or miscues. In the classroom, acknowledging and teaching syntactic differences across languages, while validating their worth, are necessary practices.	• Use punctuation marks to decode words? • Use the placement of words in the sentence to figure out words? • Use other grammatical features to read words?

Figure 5.1. Cue Systems, *continued*

Grapho-phonic Cues (often shortened and referred to simply as *phonics*)	Does this look right within the linguistic context of the book?	In English, does the child:
	That is, do the letters and sounds match according to the linguistic context of the book? Letter-sound correspondence will vary across languages. For example, /j/ sounds different in English, Spanish, and Portuguese. Also, whereas chunks are the units used for reading English, syllables are the units used for reading words in Portuguese. So the linguistic context will ultimately determine if something looks right and what the typical symbols or symbol clusters are (in English, Spanish, and Portuguese, letters or letter clusters).	• Check the beginning letter or letter cluster first (after thinking about what would make sense)? • Check the ending of the word? • Look for familiar chunks? • Use knowledge of onsets (beginning sound before vowel) and rimes (letters that follow)? For example, for the word *sun, s* would be the onset and *un* the rime. About 500 words can be derived from 37 rimes (Routman, 2003). • Use knowledge of chunks, letters, onsets, and rimes to make analogies to other known words? These questions would have to be rewritten so as to be appropriate to the linguistic context of the book being read.
Visual (V)		

. . . it deosn't mttaer in waht oredr the ltteers in a wrod are, the olny iprmoatnt tihng is taht the frist and lsat ltteer be at the rghit pclae. The rset can be a toatl mses and you can sitll raed it wouthit a porbelm. Tihs is bcuseae the huamn mnid deos not raed ervey lteter by istlef, but the wrod as a wlohe.

This is also the case in other languages, such as Spanish:

. . . no ipmotra el odren en el que las ltears etsan ersciats, la uicna csoa ipormtnate es que la pmrirea y la utlima ltera esten ecsritas en la psiocion cocrrtea. El rsteo peuden estar ttaolmntee mal y aun pordas lerelo sin pobrleams. Etso es pquore no lemeos cada ltera por si msima preo la paalbra cmoo un tdoo.

Additionally, proficient readers employ their knowledge of patterns in the specific language being read and their schemas (about reading and about the world) to make sense of squiggles on a page. For example, read the text in Figure 5.2, decoding its symbols.

Did you give it a try? Or did you avoid the task altogether? What information did you use in order to read the text? Did the illustration provide you with an entry point? Did you use your schema of how the English language works? As you tried to decode the text, did you write in your book—or on another paper? This is similar to how young children start reading notation systems, what Vygotsky (1978) identified as "system[s] of second order symbolism" (p. 110). But—how do we document and learn from children as they read notation systems?

Documenting, Analyzing, and Understanding Children's Use of Reading Cues

Ken Goodman (1965) posited that in reading words, when a spoken utterance does not match its graphic representation, there is a miscue (the misuse of a cue, an error necessary for learning to take place). Marie Clay (1979, 1993) used the word "error," classifying it according to its nature—as being primarily visual, structural, or meaning-based. While recognizing that cues are language-specific, analyzing reading miscues/errors can help teachers gain insights and understand a child's reading processes in a particular language. Goodman and Clay came up with two tools for documenting a child's use of cue systems: *running record* and *miscue analysis.*

Marie Clay (1979) developed running record as a tool, which serves to observe and document a child's use of cue systems and identify entryways for teaching in addition to determining text levels (paying attention to the number of errors made). Ken Goodman (1973) developed reading miscue analysis, another tool to document and analyze children's reading. It focuses on the kinds of miscues made, positioning this information as more important than the number of miscues and recognizing that fluent readers have varying accuracy rates (Goodman, Watson, & Burke, 1987). Miscue analysis seeks to unveil the reasons why miscues were made, which inform teaching (Wilde, 2000).

It is important for teachers to analyze the miscues or errors children make in their reading so that they can understand some of the scaffolds that need to be in place for children to continue growing as readers. When these miscues/errors are consistent, teachers can teach in ways that are responsive to students' needs, so that children become better readers. For example, if a child is consistently omitting words that are longer than two syllables, a lesson on strategies for reading longer words may be helpful. It is most important to know if children's miscues/errors affect their comprehension. This grasp of comprehension is completely lost in schools that adopt levels based solely on accuracy for placing students and for evaluating teachers (neither of which is a pertinent use of miscue analyses or of running records). And children's cultural backgrounds and experiences are often disprivileged in schools that

Figure 5.2. Let's Read! Can You Decode These Words? Can You Make Meaning of This Text?

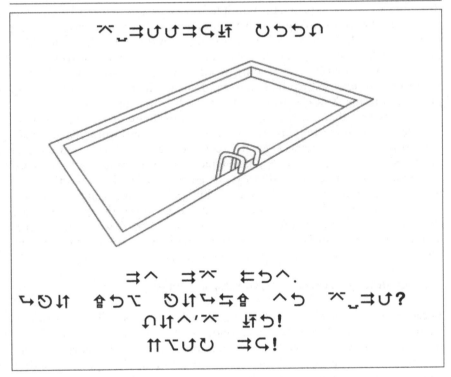

adopt fixed and predetermined books to assess children's reading as they may not be interested or familiar with the information or stories in those books. We acknowledge that such practices are culturally located. We also strive to move beyond the overemphasis on reading words to succeed academically, and propose the necessity of reading worlds—and of rewriting them.

The Cultural Nature of Reading

In recognizing the cultural nature of reading, we invite you to abandon notions that may seem "commonsense," recognizing that they are culturally located. Practices such as reading words from left to right or sounding out each letter vary across languages. As teachers we often expect that as children read, they may think of where they saw particular words before, they may look at the beginning and ending of words and make educated guesses based on the context of the sentence or on the story, or they may look at common chunks within the word (such as *in*, *ip*, *sh*, *an*, *at*). They may also think of other words that sound like the one they are trying to decode. Yet, they will only do so if they are familiar with the way print looks in that particular language. Such practices are filled with cultural assumptions. There are many ways of decoding words on a page and multiple ways in which written language is structured. We must do away with "commonsense" notions, understanding them as cultural, if we are to foster culturally relevant and inclusive teaching practices. We must recognize that reading is a sociocultural endeavor.

Instead of focusing on reading words, therefore positioning children who were not exposed to the language privileged in schools and schooling prior to entering K–2 classrooms (the English language, written language, etc.), we regard them as capable and learn from them, expanding our own knowledge and understanding of how written languages work. Then we are able to make visible connections between children's linguistic and cultural practices and the culture and language typically featured in U.S. schoolbooks.

At the same time, we reaffirm the need to have books in multiple languages, as they allow us to document children's reading behaviors in languages with which they are more familiar and to unveil the ways in which these languages are structured. Then, we can collaborate with our students and their families to make visible how languages vary phonologically and how sentence structures vary, making reading strategies more accessible.

Reading Strategies: On Phonics, Onsets, and Rimes

Because we recognize the situated and diverse nature of children's reading, we do not support decontextualized phonics exercises or the notion of phonics as being a basic skill needing to be mastered in order for children to read. Children need to experience authentic and meaningful language practices while also reading symbols and acquiring graphophonic awareness, or what is commonly referred to as *phonics*, within the context of play and interactions.

Often, children who struggle in reading primarily employ graphophonic cues. Their primary—and often sole—strategy is to sound out letters in words. This is a problem compounded by so many kindergartens that focus on teaching reading solely through decontextualized phonics—via scripted programs such as Fundations. Phonological awareness, the ability to recognize that words are made up of a variety of sound units, develops in authentic engagements with and through language (Moats, 2009). It includes knowing what a word is and tracking words in sentences, playing with language through rhyming and alliteration, recognizing word syllables, manipulating onsets and rimes (explained in the following paragraph), and displaying phonemic awareness (illustrated by Figure 2.1, /m/ is for MetroCard). Phonological awareness includes phonemic awareness, the knowledge of phonemes and how they work, or the understanding of sound units within words. Phonological awareness leads to the understanding that letters and sounds are connected in a particular way in a particular language.

It is thus important to create classrooms where children have multiple opportunities to engage and play with language, and engage in understanding and employing semantic-pragmatic cues: *Does this make sense here?* Children already have semantic knowledge. They know, for example, that it makes sense to pull down their pants in the bathroom but not in the cafeteria. Transferring such knowledge and understandings to reading—instead of relying primarily or solely on sounding out each letter of each word in each sentence on each page of each book—ultimately benefits children.

In English, often, the most important graphophonic cues are at the beginnings of words. So, after teaching children what would make sense and sound right within the given cultural and linguistic context of the text, we often teach them to look at the beginning and then at the end of words for additional information. Finally, children read chunks of letters in words as opposed to sounding out isolated letters. In single-syllable words, these chunks are linguistic units called *onset* (initial consonant or consonant cluster in a word, prior to the vowel) and *rime* (letters that follow the onset; in 3-letter words, often vowel + final consonant) (Goswami & Bryant, 1990; Goswami & Mead, 1992). For example, in the word *rip*, *r-* is the onset and *-ip* is the rime. In the word trip, *tr-* is the onset and *-ip* is the rime. While not all words can be broken into onsets and rimes (and not all words have onsets), this can be a useful strategy, helping children decode new words when reading and spell new words when writing. Onsets and rimes can then be applied to reading longer words by looking at the beginning sound, ending sound, and chunks (such as -an, -ed, -in, -ig, -ight, -ock, and -ake). Such teaching often takes place in *word work*, a curricular structure common in K–2 classrooms employing the balanced literacy framework. Yet, it is important to recognize that this strategy may not be helpful for children learning to read in English by noticing and noting the graphophonic differences and similarities between English and Spanish. In the following sections, we explore a number of literacy curricular structures, such as *read-aloud, shared reading*, and *reading workshop*, seeking to make visible the ways in which they can come to life in inclusive and culturally relevant ways.

ENGAGING IN READ-ALOUDS

Read-alouds are essential in kindergarten–2nd grades. We invite you to engage in read-alouds with the whole class many times throughout the day. Read aloud in the morning to start the day by reading a couple of books, as you take students to lunch, and any other opportunities you find. We have found that reading aloud while children are waiting in the hallway for physical education or music class is a good strategy. Make read-alouds a time that students look forward to. It is also important to send the children home thinking of books and stories, so it can easily be the last thing you do before children are dismissed. Here are a few considerations for read-alouds.

Expand Selection of Books

For reading aloud, we encourage you to select books that will serve to enrich and expand children's repertoire of stories. After all, "if we want children to see reading as a joyous adventure, if we want children to read proficiently, passionately, and critically . . . then we must look carefully at the texts we use and the experiences we construct" (Long, 2004, p. 426). This will likely mean that you will have to expand your knowledge of books beyond your favorites. Marian Wright Edelman (2015) wrote: "It's hard to be what you can't see." She continued:

> When we think about what it is to be "connected," we think about memory. We think about history. We think about storytelling. All of these words that we hear—"literacy," "inclusion," "diversity"—those are all words for connection. . . . When I say to people "why do we need to have diverse books?" it's not because necessarily everybody needs to see themselves reflected in every book, but because we need that sense of connection. We need to live in a global sense. (para.1)

Consider the small number of books by and about People of Color; for example, in 2014, of 3,500 children's books published, 292, or 8.3%, were authored by People of Color and 396, or 11.3%, were about People of Color (Cooperative Children's Book Center, 2015). Thus we encourage you to use your read-aloud time to offer mirrors and windows into the lives of People of Color. We invite you to read books by and about People of Color. This is imperative not only for Children of Color but for all children.

A helpful tool we have adapted for selecting books is Teaching Tolerance's *Appendix D: A Tool for Selecting Diverse Texts*. It includes four distinct—but interconnected—considerations: complexity; diversity and representation; critical literacy; and reader and task. It can be found at http://www.tolerance.org/publication/appendix-d. In addition, there are several blogs and lists included in the *We Need Diverse Books* website, under "Where to Find Diverse Books" (http://weneeddiversebooks.org/where-to-find-diverse-books/).

Teach in Meaningful Ways

It is important to think about entryways to teaching from read-alouds (although it is also important not to make every read-aloud into a lesson). This can be done by engaging in think-alouds (making visible your thought process while reading) and talking about connections between the text and yourself, the text and other texts, and the text and the world. Jessica engages in demonstrating these connections by saying, "This makes me think of when I . . . "; "This reminds me of this other book . . . " In doing so, she demonstrates comprehension strategies to the children she teaches. In going from demonstration to guided practice, she asks children about their connections and declares her genuine love for the books she reads: "Well, this is my favorite. I love the way the author . . . " She also highlights the choices made by authors and illustrators while encouraging children to make connections by asking questions such as: "What does this make you think of?"

Read-alouds can serve to teach Concepts About Print in authentic and meaningful ways. Some of the concepts that can be easily taught are the following:

- recognizing book covers, titles, authors, illustrators;
- turning pages right to left;
- identifying words starting or ending like children's names and other words they recognize in print;
- noting words that sound alike and different; and
- introducing words that lead to talk about other words (that start with the same sound, that rhyme with other words).

We have found it helpful to have multiple copies of the books we read aloud (whenever possible) so that children can follow along if they wish with a copy of their own. This may allow children who need supplementary sensory experiences to remain engaged. Additionally, children can engage in the independent reading of books previously read aloud (allowing additional access points as the child will already be familiar with the story). Even when we do not have multiple copies of the book, we give children access to our copy of the book read.

Encourage Critical Discussion

Read-alouds can serve as a way to introduce topics in other content areas, such as social studies, and make the curriculum more inclusive and representative. When reading books aloud, invite children to problematize *what is* by asking critical questions, such as: Who wrote the text? Who is visible? Who is invisible? Whose perspectives are privileged? Why? In doing so, we can encourage children to question inequities and engage with diversities in authentic and integral ways.

For example, in New York City, when 1st-grade Spanish-English dual-language teacher Karina Malik read aloud *Freedom on the Menu: The Greensboro Sit-Ins* by Carole Boston Weatherford (2005), her students immediately problematized segregation and challenged racist assumptions while engaging in critical dialogue. Karina invited her students to question their own assumptions, "reading between the lines and beyond the pages" (Ladson-Billings, 1992b, p. 312). When 1st grader Alejandra said to Karina: "Oh, but you are not Brown, you are tan," Karina responded by saying:

"This is my color. I am not tan. I'm Brown." Alejandra said that it was "bad" to call someone Brown, despite her own Brown skin. As a Mexican immigrant child with Brown skin herself, Alejandra was being colonized by colorist and racist discourses that had communicated to her the inferiority of her Brown skin.

Karina then engaged her 1st graders in critically analyzing skin color and the feelings they associated with different skin colors. They also considered how skin colors and *racial identities* were positioned in society—historically and contemporarily. Together they examined and challenged their own assumptions. They talked and learned from each other. They asked each other: "Where did you hear this?" and "Do you really believe this or did you hear it somewhere?" They problem-solved in ways that led to expanded understandings of racial identities, coming to challenge deficit and inferiority discourses, which framed Brown and Black identities. In doing so, they engaged in transformative action in their own lives. Reading *Freedom on the Menu*, along with the world that they inhabit, resulted in a powerful learning journey; it resulted in students rewriting themselves and coming to (re)envision their racial identities more positively.

SHARING SHARED READING

Often when children start to read, they are not decoding words but relying on their memory of the text and pictures to read. This is visible, for example, in observing very young children reading Bill Martin Jr. and Eric Carle's (1992) *Brown Bear, Brown Bear, What Do You See?* They may start saying "I see a" and turn the page to peek at the red bird before they complete the sentence with "red bird looking at me." In this case, in addition to illustrations, repetition and language patterns also aid young children in their reading of the text. We call this *reading* because the children are making sense and making meaning, even if they are not sounding out the letters and decoding the words.

K–2 teachers can make the connection between spoken and written words through shared reading. Shared reading is short for "shared read-alouds." It takes place with big books, short texts written on chart paper, or other large text, so that all the children can read the text. Often the teacher demonstrates fluency and expression while reading, helping students see the connections between spoken and written words. Recognizing that they already know what is written down, students join in the reading of the text. Shared reading offers explicit opportunities for demonstration in a low-risk meaningful context. Texts that have repetition and rhyme are particularly well suited for shared reading in the early grades.

"Shared reading is an ideal context for guided participation (that is, while the teacher is demonstrating, students are encouraged to participate without any fear of failure)" (Routman, 2003, p. 131). In shared reading, teachers (or students) may use a pointer, making visible one-to-one correspondence between spoken and written words and engaging in explicit and direct teaching, but also resulting in incidental learning. Teachers may start by inviting students to read with their eyes at first, demonstrating the reading of a text. "Through teacher modeling and encouragement, students join with their peers to read a text collaboratively" (p. 131).

In K–2nd grades, shared reading often focuses on reading and rereading texts selected by the teacher, such as poems, chants, and even pieces written by children in the class. We like to think of shared reading as singing along with a really popular song in a concert, when everyone is singing. If you do not know the words, you can mouth along or sing *la-la-la* and not be ostracized for it. Eventually, after hearing the song many times (and trying to sing it), you come to realize what the words are and sing the lyrics as they were written. The same applies here.

To further support this process while making it more culturally relevant, New York City kindergarten teachers Carmen and Eileen engaged in sharing the process of shared reading (reconceptualizing the practice first proposed by Holdaway, 1979). That is, instead of deciding on one of the many texts commonly used for shared reading, such as Sandra Boynton's (1993) *Barnyard Dance*, the teachers asked students about chants, songs, and rhymes that they commonly heard at home. After all, shared reading is a shared learning event, when students connect through shared feelings and experiences (Holdaway, 1972).

While acknowledging the importance of shared reading, Eileen and Carmen ensured that children's expertise and experiences were being valued as they engaged in teaching practices culturally relevant to the young children they taught (such as the Mexican folk song "Bate Bate Chocolate"). Then they wrote the words to chants, songs, and rhymes well known to the children they taught on chart paper and had the children engage in shared readings. This not only positioned children's home language and literacy practices as worthy, but allowed for one child to teach the others about the text, after which the children engaged in shared reading, a high-support and low-risk literacy practice.

RE-ENVISIONING READING WORKSHOP

Reading workshop is a time in which children work on their reading practices, engage in reading, acquire strategies, and develop as readers. It often includes independent reading and partner reading, reading conferences, minilessons, and small strategy groups (which are often called guided reading). Here we explain each of these components in practice and make visible how they can foster in culturally relevant and sustaining reading engagements.

Independent Reading and Partner Reading

For students in K–2 classrooms, reading is often an adventure. Many of our young students have listened to adults (teachers, librarians, family, and community members) read aloud numerous times. They may already have developed a love of listening to great stories. Others have been told stories orally, coming to develop an understanding of how stories are told and how they are structured. However, giving students the opportunity to explore stories and other texts (oral, performative, or written) and to read independently daily allows them to go on a solo adventure. They often relish the opportunity to go on adventures with their peers/classmates, asking questions, negotiating roles and storylines. The absence of a teacher guiding or facilitating the process can lead them to take more risks, test hypotheses, develop strategies, and negotiate learning partnerships. So, independent reading is an important time, when children can interact with books and other texts in the classroom at their own pace—alone or with peers!

Essential Understandings. Choice is key! As explained in Chapter 3, it is important to make sure your library is stocked with books that not only interest students but will also serve as mirrors and windows (Bishop, 1990). Be certain to have books in all languages that students speak or read, even if you cannot read these books. Note that you can find several popular books translated into many languages (so you may be familiar with the story) and bilingual books (written in two languages). We have found it helpful to ask family and/or community members to record themselves reading books in multiple languages, making them available for all children to listen to on an iPod or computer with headphones. This expands students' knowledge of how languages work. In the age of smartphones, when audio files can be easily emailed, this is a simple yet powerful practice. Children love to listen to their family members read, and they love to listen to the families of their classmates read books in a number of languages. So that more than one student can listen simultaneously, we recommend purchasing headphone splitters for students to use and enjoy listening together.

Independent reading does not have to be silent. We believe there shouldn't be silence in the classroom, especially when it is imposed by the teacher. It should be a time for critical thinking and for critical talk (Laman, 2006). There should always be a "learning buzz," since children make sense of their lives and learning through talk, by interacting with one another, and by making connections. It does not have to be separate from play and interactions. As we constantly negotiate and renegotiate a more expansive definition of reading, based on the practices the children develop themselves, we are better able to value and build on children's multiple literacy practices and ways with words. Examples of such practices include reading a Minecraft manual, a Pokémon character book, or the instructions on how to play the new Hot Wheels virtual game (putting the knowledge into action while reading).

Role of the Teacher. During independent reading, what are we, the teachers, doing? It may be helpful at first for you to demonstrate independent reading. Too often, children do not see their teachers as readers. Of course you will need to keep an eye on the book and an eye on the class if you are the only teacher. If there are two (or more) teachers in your classroom, consider taking turns as readers. If you are not reading, this is not a time to make copies, mark attendance, or organize the classroom. During this time you can also engage children in small-group strategy lessons or in reading conferences (discussed later in this section).

"If you are going to rally your children to love reading and to compose richly literate lives for themselves, then it is terribly important that you are invested in reading right alongside your kids" (Calkins & Tolan, 2010, p. 6). After all, young children need teachers who demonstrate what it means to lead literate lives—to be excited about an author, to have a favorite book. Sharing the joy of reading is essential (Routman, 2003). It is important to share what you are reading and what you will read next—creating a culture of readers in your classroom.

Explain how you go about selecting books to read, and invite other adults to do so as well, so that children learn that there are multiple ways of selecting books. And create spaces for children to be able to select a book themselves—books that they are excited to read independently. If you are part (or have been part) of a book club, explain its purpose and how it works. This may inspire children to establish book clubs in your classroom, fostering authentic and meaningful peer-learning opportunities. Finally, share how you keep track of the books you read, if you do so. Then, invite the children as a community to develop ways of documenting their reading lives instead of imposing a commonly used template listing title and number of pages read, organized according to date, to be signed by a family member or guardian. Make reading joyful, not an obligation. Communicate to your students that reading should not be quantified and valuated in relation to the number of pages read.

Reading Conferences

While a child is reading, lean in and ask the child to read to you, so that you can get a sense of her reading. This is the time in which we teachers take on the role of researchers (Morrell, 2012), finding out who our students are and what they are doing as readers.

In reading conferences, we first draw attention to what the child is doing well by complimenting her. We strive to use specific terms as opposed to the nonspecific "Great job!" As Peter Johnston (2004) explained, our language choices as teachers (and how specific we are) have an impact on children's learning. To highlight fluency in reading, we may say, "I love how you are reading just like you talk!" or "You are changing your tone when the meaning changes and pausing between ideas." This allows the child to recognize what she is doing well.

Then, we ask the child about her strategies. For example, "How did you figure out this word?" This allows us to informally assess the child's orchestration of cue systems. Instead of jumping in to say what we want the child to work on, we make the point of asking the child what she wants to work on to become an even better reader. After that, we choose one or two things (at most) to teach the child, offering possible strategies to further reading growth.

We determine the focus of a reading conference by our observations of the child's reading. At times, our reading conferences will focus on fluency—specifically on reading punctuation, reading dialogue, phrasing, rereading, automaticity, expression, and inflection. We firmly believe that reading conferences are not for correcting accents or linguistic variation (there is never a time for such practices in the culturally relevant classroom), but to expand students' repertoires of reading strategies and to enhance their reading lives.

It is important for us to help *all* children select books featuring language variation, so they do not come to believe that the only fluency that matters—and the only way to read correctly—is achieved when reading books by and about people who are White and speak dominant American English. We have invited Spanish-dominant and English-dominant children to read bilingual books together so that they can learn from and with each other, seeing themselves and their peers as capable. We have highlighted books showcasing features of African American language—such as *Tickle Tickle* by Dakari Hru, *Gettin' through Thursday* by Melrose Cooper, *Goin' Someplace Special* by Patricia McKissack, and *Last Stop on Market Street* by Matt de la Peña. We have also encouraged children to read books such as *I Ain't Gonna Paint No More!* by Karen Beaumont, so that our students can understand that White people employ features of African American Language in their talk too, and that White authors may enrich their writing by employing features of AAL. While some teachers believe that this confuses children, we have found it to significantly expand their language repertoires and to foster a better understanding of languages and how they work—especially with regard to grammar, in authentic ways.

After teaching a strategy, we invite the child to employ that strategy in his reading. After all, we want to go from demonstration to guided practice, and eventually to independent practice (all while recognizing that the process is not lockstep or linear). We write down the specific strategy, so that we can remind the child of it in future interactions. This is what some refer to as keeping children accountable. We like to think of it as making a record of our conversation with the child. The same way that it may take us multiple reminders to actually get something done, the same is true for children. We should treat them humanely, recognizing that at first they may depend on us for strategies, but eventually they will develop independence uniquely—as long as we support this transition with plenty of opportunities for meaningful practice.

Minilessons for Reading

A minilesson is a demonstration. It comes to life as a whole-class or small-group lesson on reading. Many times, it takes place prior to independent reading time. Through minilessons teachers can demonstrate strategies. Minilessons are typically short, and focused on one or two things that the teacher wants to invite students to engage in that day during independent reading.

Minilessons may include components outlined by Calkins and Tolan (2010), such as:

1. *Connecting* today's teaching to students' work as readers and to prior lessons; connecting to observations and anecdotes from the classroom to focus children's attention;
2. *Teaching* how readers can employ the strategy being taught—by using a book the children already know, one that has been read aloud to foreground the strategy as opposed to the story;
3. *Engaging* children by giving them an opportunity to participate in guided practice prior to going off for independent work (at times using clipboards or lap boards); and
4. *Linking* what has been taught to what students already know or are already doing—making visible the usefulness and purpose of the strategy.

To make minilessons relevant, it is important to connect what is being taught to students' interests and lives. The selection of materials must honor children's cultural experiences and linguistic backgrounds.

A minilesson may be as simple as the teacher opening a book and turning the pages while picture reading (at times labeled "picture walks") or as sophisticated as writing critical questions to the author on Post-it notes. By showing how a strategy is used in their own writing, teachers can invite children to listen, observe, engage, and learn. Minilessons often conclude with invitations for children to consider the strategy demonstrated in their own independent practice (Routman, 2003).

In some reading workshops, teachers have a *mid-workshop teaching point* (Calkins & Tolan, 2010). We found that instead of setting up a mid-workshop teaching point, approaching workshops as a conversation and having a fluid structure in mind was helpful. For example, children often engaged in talk about books, making connections and engaging in deepening comprehension strategies. We recognize that reading workshop is like a dance hall,

> where teachers and children adapt to each other. . . . The teacher responds, leads, and sometimes lets go to observe more carefully the rhythms of children in motion. Then teachers and children come together and . . . spread their skilled, responsive movement across times and spaces, dancing their way into the future. (Genishi & Dyson, 2012, p. 20)

Guided Reading as Small-Group Strategy Lessons

Instead of repeating a particular strategy in a series of individual reading conferences, we teachers can group students who would benefit from learning about the same strategy from small-group strategy lessons. Thus membership in a group is not fixed. The sizes of groups vary according to need, but in our experience range from three to six children. We suggest waiting to have groups larger than four until you feel comfortable with small-group strategy lessons. This is an alternative to guided reading (student practice with teacher support).

Guided Reading. Traditionally, guided reading is an approach to teaching reading in which a teacher works with a small group of children who are similar with regard to their reading levels and behaviors. Within the traditional guided reading structure, the teacher selects texts appropriate to students' reading levels, one title per group. Guided reading is a common literacy curricular structure in K–2 classrooms, often implemented as a time for children to practice reading books at their instructional reading levels under close guidance of the teacher (commonly at a kidney-shaped table). While traditional guided reading groups are organized according to reading levels, students in small-group strategy lessons are often reading different texts, which vary by topic and complexity.

Small-Group Strategy Lessons. Strategy groups are flexible (students might even be in multiple groups) and shorter in duration than the traditional guided reading group. There is a clear purpose in small-group strategy lessons, and they can be a valuable component of reading workshop without reifying the notion of levels and of "good" vs. "bad" readers in the classroom. So, we invite you to rethink your guided reading practice, transforming it into small-group strategy teaching opportunities that regard children as capable, and not constraining them to reading levels.

Strategy lessons are similar to minilessons, but would not be relevant to the entire class, so they are conducted in a small-group setting. In such a setting, the teacher briefly engages in shared demonstration (by leading, negotiating, suggesting, supporting, explaining) and focuses on guided practice, which is marked by students taking charge and practicing, applying their learning (Routman, 2003). In this setting, you can provide children with more individual attention and opportunities for guided practice—allowing ample time for children to practice the strategy and for you, the teacher, to observe, lean in, and teach.

We have found strategy lessons to work best when children bring the books they are already reading as opposed to introducing and reading a common (and often leveled) book. Small-group strategy lessons do not happen every day but according to need. We often identified such needs by looking at our observational notes and other forms of ongoing authentic assessments. Small-group strategy lessons allow us teachers to provide the scaffolding necessary for children to grow as readers. Such groups can serve as pedagogical zones of proximal development (Vygotsky, 1978), allowing the child to advance beyond what he can do independently with adult assistance—and/or with the assistance of peers.

On the Complexity of Reading

Young readers integrate pragmatic-semantic, syntactic, and graphophonic cues with a variety of reading strategies to make meaning. Some of them are sampling, inferring, predicting, disconfirming, and correcting. According to Ken Goodman (1994), what distinguishes more proficient readers is how well they orchestrate (bring together) these multiple cues. The more interesting and authentic the text, the more likely it is that young children will be able to develop as proficient readers.

While orchestrating cues is key to reading proficiently, children are rarely taught about the reading process or about orchestrating cues. This can be confusing, especially for children whose home languages and literacy practices do not align with those privileged in schools. As teachers, we can make this process visible, through demonstrations and invitations within the context of our classrooms, clearly articulating what Heath (1982) called *distinctions in discourse strategies and structures* (p. 72). In doing so, we can help children become more intentional and access an array of strategies for reading.

ASSESSMENT AS DOCUMENTING CHILDREN'S LITERACY PRACTICES

It has been widely documented that effective teaching is based on observations and ongoing assessment. After all, assessment is: "An ongoing, complex process in which we aim to discover and document what children are learning over time in many situations and across multiple symbol systems, so that we can help them learn more" (Genishi & Dyson, 2009, p. 116). To meet each child's needs and negotiate imposed academic standards, it is imperative that we teachers learn how to systematically and formatively assess children's learning, using observation as the foundation (Genishi & Dyson, 2009). We document our observations with notes on Post-its, longer narratives on index cards or note pads, retellings through audio notes, and through the creation of picture portraitures.

Then, after observing and documenting, we engage in analysis—asking, for example: What stories can I see? What are the patterns? We answer these questions by looking at observation records across time and space and taking them apart. After analyzing our observations, we ask ourselves: Knowing what I now know, how can I better support this child's learning? By looking closely and listening carefully to the children we teach (Mills, O'Keefe, & Jennings, 2004), we can better understand who they are as learners and as human beings. This is never simple, but has the potential to help us transform our teaching practices. In addition to analyzing our ongoing observations and documentation, we also assess children with regard to interest and motivation, strategies and skills, comprehension, and development of literacy concepts, all of which are central to early reading.

Interest and Motivation

To assess children's interests and motivation, we embrace the practice of interviewing as assessment, learning from and with the children we teach. We design our own questions and adapt according to the responses we receive. We have used both interviews about reading processes and interviews with questions related to books (assessing comprehension). Across time and space, we have used formal and informal interviews as ways of learning from the children we teach, from their families, and from their communities. The *Burke Reading Interview* (Goodman, Watson, & Burke, 1987) is one example of such an interview.

The Burke Reading Interview can give us teachers insights into our students' beliefs about reading and about how they see themselves as readers. We can use this information to design strategy lessons and to plan literacy engagements. It includes "questions that probe students' beliefs of what reading is, how it works, and who they are as readers" (Martens, 2015). It includes the following questions:

1. When you're reading and you come to something you don't know, what do you do? Do you ever do anything else?
2. Who is a good reader you know?
3. What makes _____ a good reader?
4. Do you think _____ ever comes to something he/she doesn't know?

5. "Yes": When ____does come to something he/she doesn't know, what do you think he/she does? "No": Suppose ____comes to something he/she doesn't know. [What would he/she do?]
6. If you knew someone was having trouble reading, how would you help that person?
7. What would a/your teacher do to help that person?
8. How did you learn to read?
9. What would you like to do better as a reader?
10. Do you think you are a good reader? Why?

(Goodman, Watson, & Burke, 1987, pp. 135–136)

As with any other tool, we adapt this list of questions according to context, rather than following it strictly—always remembering that the child should be the focus, not the tool.

Based on the information from observations and interviews, we are better able to identify books that the children we teach might be interested in. In doing so, we help them use their imaginations and create interpretations of stories through their knowledge of characters, for example. Most of all, we have found that interviews (whether formal or informal) can serve as a tool for positioning children as worthy, capable, and knowledgeable individuals with specific interests and motivators (Lindfors, 2008). They remind us that no formula to teach reading will apply to all.

Strategies and Skills

To informally assess cue use, we have found it helpful to sit with a student and a pile of books selected according to his interests and funds of knowledge, asking the child to read to us. We explain that we are learning about how readers figure out new words as they read and so we are going to take notes. We see it as essential for the child to select the book to be read, as interest, experience, and motivation are likely to affect reading. When the child comes to a new word, we watch what he does to figure it out.

- Does the child rely heavily on sounding it out as a first or sole strategy?
- Does the child use illustrations in order to make predictions?
- Does the child go back to the beginning of the sentence and start again?
- Does the child skip the word and look for clues in the rest of the sentence?
- Does the child make analogies to other known words?
- Does the child draw on his own experiences (about life and literacy) to help make sense of the text?

- Does the child think about what would make sense or rely more heavily on sounding out?
- What other strategies does the child use? What do these strategies tell you about the child as a reader?

When the child attempts to read a new word—whether inaccurately or accurately—we ask what he did to figure it out. We write down notes about the cue systems the child seems to use. This provides us with valuable information about the child's use of cue systems. For a formal assessment, we use either a running record analysis or a reading miscue inventory. (See Figure 5.3 for a description of how to use a running record; see also Clay [2003] for running record, and Goodman, Watson, & Burke [1987] or Wilde [2000] for miscue analysis.)

In many schools, formal assessments are selected by the district or by the administrator. If this is the case, you can (and should) still engage in informal assessments as well, while understanding that these assessments should inform teaching and learning and do not serve as formal or summative evaluations of who your students are as readers (or of teacher quality).

Comprehension: Diverse Reading Response Strategies

A variety of literature response strategies can be used by students in the K–2 classroom. Note that any time children engage in talk about a book, when they connect the story to their lives, to other books, and to situations in the world, they are also engaging in comprehension strategies. Examples of such practices can be found throughout this book. One strategy that does not primarily depend on oral or written words is sketch-to-stretch (developed by Harste, Short, & Burke, 1988).

Sketch-to-Stretch. After reading a book aloud, we teachers can ask children to sketch what the story means to them—through graphics, symbols, words—encouraging them to make connections. Then we can ask children to share their representations with peers before talking about their intended meaning. This strategy can serve to discuss reading as a transactional act, since the intended and perceived meaning may not match. As children engage in sketch-to-stretch, we can engage in interpretive probing, asking children questions in order to discover what they know and why they think the way they do. We propose that it is important to focus on children's processes rather than evaluating the final product.

There are many other ways of responding to literature! In Supplemental Resource 5.2 (at www.tcpress.com) we describe specific strategies for responding to texts that may foster comprehension—from *Creating Classrooms for Authors and Inquirers* by Short and Harste (1996)—to illustrate how no one way is the right way. Each strategy has been tried in K–2 settings. We encourage you to reinvent these strategies and create new ones.

Figure 5.3. Miscues, Reading Errors, and Approximations

Miscues are often documented through running records and/or miscue analyses. Running records (Clay, 1979, 2003) seek to capture children's oral reading though a written record so that we teachers can analyze a child's reading process and progress, identifying patterns and using the information to facilitate the child's learning. Running records are often conducted with running record forms (Clay, 1979, 1993, 2003), but can be done on blank sheets of paper. Some teachers prefer to have a typed-up version of the text being read by the child on which to record miscues. Although we have found that using typed versions of texts may constrain the texts available for children to read.

While we acknowledge that Marie Clay used the term *error* in running records, here we choose to use the term *miscue* instead of *error*. *Error* may signify something negative. Typical miscues include additions (added words), substitutions (substituting one word with another), and omissions (skipping over a word altogether). All of these impact accuracy. When a child makes a miscue and then returns to the text repeating and fixing the miscue initially made, we have a self-correction. Self-corrections null miscues. For example, if a child reads "Goodnight mom" and then rereads and corrects the miscue with "Goodnight moon," while reading the well-known book by Margaret Wise Brown, the child has made one miscue and one self-correction. Thus, 1 (miscue) − 1 (self-correction) = 0 (no miscues), and no miscue is recorded. There are other kinds of miscues that children make. For teachers wanting to learn more about this, we recommend reading *Running Records for Classroom Teachers* by Marie Clay (2003). Please note that while certain commercial kits include packets including specific books for running records, a running record can be done with any book.

The reading accuracy rate can be calculated by dividing the number of words read correctly by the total number of words read. For example, if a child reads 84 words correctly out of a passage of 100 words, the child's accuracy rate is 84%. Marie Clay (2000) posited that if a child has lower than a 90% accuracy rate on a book, the book is too hard to be read independently. If the accuracy rate is 95% or above, the book is too easy. Accuracy rates between 91% and 94% are indicative of books that are "just right" for the child. Here, we note that while this information may be helpful, reading varies across languages, contexts, and domains. As Sandra Wilde (2000) explained, many fluent readers skip words, substitute words, mispronounce words, and still make meaning of a text. Also, a child who is bilingual in Spanish and English may be reading a much more complex text in Spanish at a higher accuracy rate than she does in English. It is important to access and assess the child's full linguistic repertoire; otherwise, we teachers are prone to have an incomplete portrait of a child's literacy practices. As teachers, we have only used these percentages as parameters, not as impositions. *(continued on next page)*

Developing Literacy Concepts

One of the well-known assessments of literacy concepts is the *Concepts About Print* discussed in Chapter 2 (Clay, 2000). Additionally, you may engage in an "informal observation of book knowledge" (Owocki & Goodman, 2002, p. 104), documenting book handling, print knowledge, and interpretive knowledge. You can create checklists, listing concepts and observed behaviors such as the ones shown in Figure 5.4 (from Owocki & Goodman, 2002,

Figure 5.3. Miscues, Reading Errors, and Approximations, *continued*

In addition to accuracy, running records include assessments of fluency—assessing whether a child reads just like she talks or in a choppy manner (mostly 1–2 word phrases) and her rate of reading (how many words per minute). Finally, it includes an assessment of the child's understanding or comprehension of the book—recalling some key information, seeking to make connections between the book and prior experiences, and displaying awareness of the resources employed by the author to enhance understanding. For immigrant children and children whose backgrounds and identities do not match the so-called norm, or the language and cultural practices portrayed in the book being read, it is important to be aware of how they may be dis/advantaged by their contextual knowledge. The more interest and prior knowledge children have about the topic of a book, the more likely they are to use their prior knowledge to make sense of the scribbles on the page (that is, the text).

We have found that a child may be reading aloud with a 90% accuracy level, but understanding the story and reading with great fluency. This may be an appropriate instructional book for the child if, for example, all the miscues are due to using Spanish language rules to read English language texts—possibly adding a vowel at the end of a word or inverting nouns and adjectives. It is also essential to note that counting language transfer and accents as miscues will result in inaccurate depictions of the child as a reader.

We recognize that a child's home language may not reflect a "standard" or privileged notion of Spanish or English, but the miscues and variations may not take away from the child's comprehension. For example, there are different pronunciations and cultural ways of saying words, such as dropping of the *d* at the end of words in Spanish and adding *l*, like for *pared* (saying *parel*) or pronouncing the *r* as /h/. So, while at first glance reading *pahel* instead of *pared* may be recorded as a miscue, this may comprise a culturally located pronunciation. This happens in English and other languages as well. With English, children may drop the *g* when reading *ing* endings, which is not a miscue, but the knowledgeable and sophisticated transfer of linguistic rules. The more we teachers can learn about children's linguistic practices, the better able we will be to build bridges between their home and community language and literacy practices and the language and literacy practices privileged in schools and schooling.

Also, if we consider learning to read a process of approximations and recognize that adults seldom read aloud when they are reading to themselves, asking children to read aloud may yield an inaccurate portrait of their reading. Reading aloud may cause performance anxiety. Consider the following questions: Have you ever been afraid to read something in front of a group of individuals your age? Or have you been evaluated on such an occasion? You may be prone to stumble, be less fluent, and make miscues as you read an unfamiliar text under such conditions. This is something to keep in mind as we teachers seek to support children's language and literacies in more holistic ways.

Figure 5.4. Literacy Concepts

Literacy Concepts	Observed behavior displayed by child, who . . .
Book Handling	• Holds book upright • Understands that print proceeds from left to right and top to bottom in languages such as English and Spanish • Turns pages right to left—in books written in languages such as Spanish and English • Reads print on left page before right page—in books written in languages such as Spanish and English • Uses book title and cover illustration to make predictions • Articulates understanding that a book contains an author's message • Demonstrates knowledge of the role of an illustrator, someone who creates the visuals for a book
Print Knowledge	• Understands that pictures are viewed and print is read • Knows what a letter and what a word are (in languages such as English and Spanish) • Participates in reading when the language is predictable • Attempts to match voice with print (one-on-one correspondence) • Reads some words conventionally
Interpretive Knowledge	• Eagerly selects a book to read alone or to someone else • Knows that books contain stories as well as other kinds of information • Labels pictures while looking through the pages of a book • Uses pictures to make up a connected story or sequence of events • Discusses/retells stories, referring to character, setting, problems, plot episodes, resolution, theme • Retells in a logical sequence • Makes personal connections with books • Makes connections between and among books

Note. Adapted from Owocki & Goodman, 2002, p. 104.

p. 104), so as to document children's book handling, print knowledge, and interpretive knowledge informally as you observe, document, and learn from your students and their literacy practices.

Assessment Informs Teaching

Most important, assessment must inform teaching. It should be a way of documenting children's development as readers. Assessment should be about "kidwatching" (O'Keefe, 1997), about documenting children's literacy development as unique and worthy, as a way of understanding who each child is and who you can be as a teacher. After all, the

> most telling assessment strategies and most compelling curricular decisions emerge from classroom conversations and authentic classroom data. Even the best assessment tools reveal certain things and conceal others. Thoughtful teachers use these tools, they aren't used by them. (Mills, 2005, p. 2)

REFLECTING ON READING AND LOOKING AHEAD . . .

In Chapter 5 we explored the diverse ways in which young children read worlds and words. We invited you to fully cultivate young children's literacy potential, recognizing the ways in which they make sense of a variety of symbols within varied social and cultural contexts—long before entering kindergarten. In doing so, we considered diverse possibilities, perspectives, and points of view in K–2 classrooms. Through examples from diverse classrooms, we explored how teachers can support young children's reading development while honoring their experiences and expertise. For example, we made visible how read-alouds can be ways of expanding the curriculum while valuing multiple voices and languages from a critical perspective. Further, we invited you to reimagine traditional literacy curricular structures as you read about reimaginings in real K–2 classrooms. In doing so, we invited you to bring reading workshop to life in ways that honor children's strengths and diversities.

In Chapter 6, we rework the traditional writing workshop, which often presumes that all children engage in a similar, uniform, regimented, and standardized writing process. We focus on writing diverse words and worlds, inviting you to write a curriculum that honors the brilliance of diverse children.

On Writing Diverse Words and Worlds

Writing a Curriculum That Honors the Brilliance of Diverse Children

> No matter what, just let them write every day. Even if you're not sure what to teach, just let them write. They'll do fine. (Ray, 2004, p. ix)

In this chapter we invite you to learn from diverse children as authors as you let them write—learning from them as writers and positioning yourself as a critical researcher (Morrell, 2012). To illustrate this process, we share ways of honoring children's reasons for writing as well as their families' and communities' funds of knowledge, (re)positioning them centrally in our own classrooms. We propose revising interactive and shared writing in ways that are authentic for children and do not presume procedural control by the teacher. We emphasize that writing develops as reading does—that is, one does not precede the other; they develop together and inform each other.

As we honor diversities, we invite you to re-envision writing workshop, to consider and create multiple ways to engage in the teaching of writing. Writing workshop is an approach to teaching writing first established by Donald Graves (1983). Primarily it focuses on writing as a process instead of focusing on evaluating the product. "Authenticity is the heart and soul of writing workshop. Children write to carry out their communication purposes; write to be published; they write to be read" (Lindfors, 2008, p. 30). While some classrooms employ a very structured writing workshop process or list, from our perspective this is far from what Donald Graves proposed. We encourage you to move away from rigid (and timed) minilessons, which place great stress on teachers and exclude many students.

As we enter K–2 classrooms, in this chapter we share ways in which writing conferences are reframed—from fixing mistakes to building on the strengths of diverse children. In such settings, sharing becomes a true celebration of the diversities in children's work as opposed to merely illustrating what teachers initially envisioned or planned to teach. Examples from K–2 classrooms highlight alternative resources and tools for enriching the writing experiences of young children. After all, writing does not happen in a lock-step, linear process. Using writing workshop effectively involves trusting students but also creating spaces for them to grow as writers and develop their own ways of writing . . . in an ever-evolving workshop, which honors a variety of processes and timelines.

Again and again, we focus on the process of writing—as opposed to focusing on what was produced as a result. As we share examples of the work of diverse children in kindergarten–2nd grade, from the perspectives of practicing teachers, we address questions such as Why? When? How?

EARLY WRITING

To develop a positive image of themselves as capable writers, children must understand what written language is used for. Often, in the hurry to teach the hows, we may neglect the whys. This is a mistake, as children need to know why they should learn how to write and develop as writers. To do so, they must understand the following:

- The function of language (what written language is for—to document and communicate);
- Its possible formats (how written language is organized—such as narrative and informational text);
- How to write their words on paper (the relationship between orthography—how language looks—and phonology—how language sounds); and
- How they might go about conveying meaning (through punctuation: spacing, capitalization, periods, etc.).

Coming to understand writing is not a linear process.

Although in their early writing young children have not yet discovered conventional letterforms, they approximate the way print looks through squiggles on a page. And even though "children's early forms of cursive and print aren't readable to adults, and aren't even readable to the writers soon after they're written, we call this *writing* because it is intended to communicate meaning" (Owocki & Goodman, 2002, pp. 81–82).

Children present and represent meaning through multiple symbols. They are "symbol weavers," as Anne Haas Dyson (1990) documented. Dyson (1990) posited that young children use symbols to represent their experienced world and to construct imagined worlds, emphasizing the critical role of art and play in children's growth as symbol makers. In fact, "play is a particular symbol system especially relevant to young children's literacy development" (Whitmore et al., 2005, p. 297). In this chapter, while acknowledging children's movement toward more conventional practices, we honor any effort that is intended to convey meaning, regarding it as *writing*.

Children must develop a positive sense of themselves as writers in order to develop as writers. They can do so only if we value their attempts and honor their approximations. We must remember that children in K–2 classrooms are writers, but they are 4-, 5-, 6-, 7-, or 8-year-olds at the same time (Ray & Glover, 2008). Thus, we cannot expect their writing to look like ours.

In fostering a rich writing environment filled with culturally relevant and inclusive practices, it is important to recognize that young children are individuals and will have specific interests and motivations (Lindfors, 2008). They should be encouraged to experiment with a wide range of writing—poetry, music, digital movies, historical books, comics, jokes, labels, ads, collages, (auto)biographies, and more—for multiple purposes (Avery, 2002; Ray, 2006). As teachers, our responsibility "is to allow for meaningful opportunities for writing that draw from their social and cultural experiences and to help them explore new possibilities" (Owocki & Goodman, 2002, p. 93).

WRITING WITH PURPOSE

Children learn to write because it serves a purpose: to communicate! Yet while young children's writings may have letters and words, they may also rely on other symbol systems as they create meaningful messages (Dyson, 1989). For example, drawings may be more accessible to classmates than writing and may serve more of a purpose in communicating, resulting in more engagements and responses (Graves, 1983). As children develop as writers of words, they should not be discouraged from drawing, but rather encouraged to use drawing more deliberately, as illustrated by Figure 6.1.

In their kindergarten, teachers Eileen and Carmen observed that children who drew pictures with rich details were better able to author richer stories. Drawing served to capture meaning. Without drawing, children's entire stories often became reduced to a single word or a simple sentence composed of a few words.

Writing What We Know

When children feel that they have the power to write in ways that reflect their multiple areas of expertise—social, cultural, and linguistic—they are more likely to show us a fuller picture of what they know about language, literacy, and the world. Play and their very childhoods should be present in their writing (Dyson, 2001). For example, in play, young children may write an invitation or write themselves into a story, establishing or capturing friendships. We teachers may also offer writer's notebooks to students, so that they can take notes, record observations, and capture their experiences and interests through art notes, words, and other symbols. A writer's notebook should be a child-centered, no-pressure resource. It is a place to start thinking and can serve to initiate conversations, investigations, and play. It should reflect who the child is.

Figure 6.1. Employing Multiple Symbol Systems

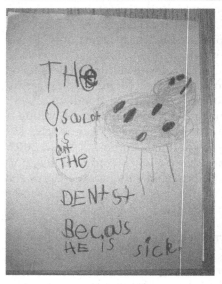

Valuing what children noticed about their immediate environment, teachers Carmen and Eileen played with language as they invited their kindergarteners to play *I Spy* with words and symbols in the classroom, school, home, and community—a variation of the *Literacy Dig* activity explained in Chapter 5. Their students took digital photos and made alphabet books with them. Some children labeled the prints—for example, a child labeled a garbage can with "g" while another wrote the letter and a sentence to go along with it. Figure 6.2 shows the sentence for F: "I found a friend." You will notice that the child used lines to separate the words. She wrote "I" conventionally; "f" for found, indicating an awareness of beginning sounds; "a" conventionally; and "fan" for friend. She also used punctuation (a period) at the end of her sentence.

Carmen and Eileen also engaged the children in making big books for interactive read-alouds that documented what children heard when they got home from school and what they heard at bedtime, initially recorded in their writer's notebooks, which had been taken home to record observations. Interactive read-alouds can foster gains in vocabulary and enhance story schemas (McGee & Schickedanz, 2007). Through the creation of big books grounded in children's lives, being culturally and linguistically relevant, these teachers were able to engage the children in reading what they knew, in whatever languages they were fluent. For example, one of the pages of the book *When I Go to Bed* reads: "When I go to bed, I hear *buenas noches mi amor, dulces sueños!*" while another reads: "When I go to bed, I hear *I love you a bushel and a peck and a hug around the neck.*"

Figure 6.2. "I found a friend": Writing about What We Spy in Our School

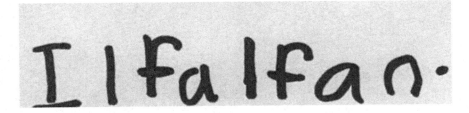

Honoring Children's Experiences and Expertise in Writing

> We operate from a core belief that children do not need to "get ready" to be readers and writers; instead, we believe they are already readers and writers—albeit on their own terms—as they live and learn inside literate communities. (Ray & Glover, 2008, p. xvii)

While we wholeheartedly share this belief, children often see themselves from deficit perspectives and often cannot think of anything worthy of writing. In our teaching, we honor children's experiences and expertise. We ask questions such as: Where are you from? What is your history? We invite children to write about their names and stories (refer to the examples in Chapter 2). Yet, to have them write about such personal topics, we need to communicate the value of such topics in our classrooms. From this perspective, writing workshops can serve as spaces where young children develop capable identities as writers. Writing workshop can be a space where children share their experiences, fully engage their linguistic expertise, negotiate social relationships, and author imagined worlds. To foster writing workshop as a generative space, we suggest starting with an exploration of the school neighborhood or community that brings reading, writing, and talk together. (See Supplemental Resource 6.1 at www.tcpress.com for a few of our suggested books and ideas for getting started or for expanding your teaching practices.)

In the inclusive kindergarten classroom taught by Eileen and Carmen, the children went on neighborhood walks, documenting what they saw through digital photos and picture drawing; and then they wrote about their walk. Some engaged in informational writing, others in narrative writing. To supplement the photos taken, the children searched for pictures in digital (websites) and printed sources (promotional leaflets, newspapers). For example, Nevaeh (an African American kindergartner) engaged in mapping and labeling her neighborhood. Benji, a bilingual kindergartener whose first language is Mandarin, narrated his journey to school (see Figure 6.3).

In the kindergarten classroom in which Nevaeh and Benji were students, teachers engaged students in reading their neighborhood, their worlds. This

Figure 6.3. A Narrative of Going to School

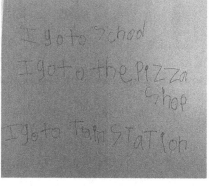

precedes reading words. After all, a picture or image of a place, person, or object signifies meaning in a more concrete way than a word. After capturing neighborhood images, the teachers asked students to focus on image details, to Think-Pair-Share what they saw, heard, smelled, felt, and thought, and then decide which image or word would express what they were going to write about. Think-Pair-Share is important, because "students often need to talk out what they plan to write before beginning to write" (Tompkins, 1990, p. 135).

INTERACTIVE WRITING

Interactive writing provides students with a high-support and low-risk setting to develop and become confident in their writing. Working with a peer or teacher offers students the opportunity to learn from and with their writing partner(s). Interactive writing can incorporate demonstration, shared demonstration, guided practice, and independent practice (Routman, 2003).

If a teacher and one or more students are writing together, they may decide on a topic for writing and plan the writing together, making the process visible and accessible. It is helpful for us teachers to engage in think-alouds so that students are privy to our intentions and processes. They share the marker/pen/pencil and take turns writing. We may then support students by reminding them what they wanted to write.

In interactive writing, learning builds on what children already know—on the existing schemas, the knowledge, experiences, and languages with which they enter the classroom. This allows them to develop an understanding of themselves as capable writers. Teachers can build and expand on students' funds of knowledge by incorporating their interests and expertise into interactive writing activities. In doing so, they communicate to students that their lives are rich and filled with worthy topics. Interactive writing also helps students develop:

- print awareness;
- orthographic knowledge;
- syntactic knowledge;
- comprehension skills;
- alphabetic knowledge;
- vocabulary; and
- understanding of conventions.

There are many ways of bringing interactive writing opportunities to life in the K–2 classroom, including (but not limited to):

- written conversations;
- morning messages;
- letters or memos;
- invitations;
- stories; and
- instructions ("How to").

Many of these can be brought to life as whole-class, small-group, or one-to-one activities. In the next sections we focus on three of these interactive activities.

Written Conversations

Written conversations are conversations or communicative exchanges in the form of writing. They can happen between two students (working akin to passing notes or texting in class) or between a student and a teacher. They can happen asynchronously (like e-mails) or synchronously (like text messages and Internet chats), in dialogue journals, on Post-its, or sheets of paper (large or small). The way that written conversations work is simple. One person writes a question, the other answers, and a conversation is started. Sound simple? It is! And young children are often excited to engage in written conversations with their teachers and friends. Written conversations can happen before children are writing in conventional ways. For example, in Phillip Baumgarner's preschool classroom in Athens, GA, children engaged in written conversations through art notes, using mailboxes and writing correspondence, delivered daily by one of the children (see Figure 6.4).

Through written conversations, children learn from other writers, as demonstrations happen in authentic exchanges about different styles and ways of communicating through writing, as well as spelling, syntax, vocabulary, and print concepts. At times, children engage in written conversations with teachers; thus a written conversation becomes a "zone of proximal development" for writing (Vygotsky, 1978), an authentic opportunity for apprenticeship (Lindfors, 2008). At other times, they learn from and with their peers. They write regularly, fluently, and authentically. And they often want to follow conventions, because they want to be understood (Daniels & Daniels, 2013).

Written conversations are great opportunities for children to experiment with what they are learning about letters, sounds, written communication, vocabulary, and print concepts in the company of other (at times more experienced) writers. Written conversations "invite students to talk about what they know and to inquire about what they don't" (Van Sluys & Laman, 2006, p. 231) and not only afford writers an immediate response, but also give them reason to shape their texts in ways their readers will understand. Through written conversations, knowledge construction happens as children develop and test a never-ending series of hypotheses, or ideas, about the ways in which a particular language works. Young writers hypothesize that what they write, although it may be squiggly lines, has meaning.

Written conversations also allow us teachers to get to know our students better—and often make visible the role of interests and experiences in writing. For example, Figure 6.5 shows a written conversation where a 5-year-old child in kindergarten spelled the word GAMEBOY conventionally, while drawing an elephant and spelling *centers* as SNCRS. (Please note that for the benefit of our readers, we wrote what the child read as his responses; however, making such transcripts is *not* a practice we embrace.)

Morning Messages

Morning messages are common in K–2 classrooms and welcome students each morning. They communicate meaning and can often serve to teach writing. A morning message is a short message (written like a letter) displayed in the classroom—typically on chart paper, an easel, or a SMART Board. At times morning messages may be printed and left at students' tables/desks. Morning messages should contain authentic and relevant communication so that students are anxious to read the message each morning as they enter the classroom. They can serve to bring together reading, writing, and word study into a daily lesson. Morning messages are a well-known and widely used component of a balanced literacy framework.

The practice of morning messages requires teachers' purposeful planning and thoughtful consideration. In 2nd grade, Jessica slowly transitions from

Figure 6.4. Written Conversations in Preschool

writing morning messages herself to having students take turns writing them on the SMART Board. In doing so, she goes from demonstrating how to write a short letter to the class, to shared writing, to independent practice. Because Jessica teaches in a dual-language classroom, and the school where she teaches employs a rollercoaster model (alternating languages by school day), her morning messages alternate between English and Spanish.

Figure 6.5. A Written Conversation in Kindergarten

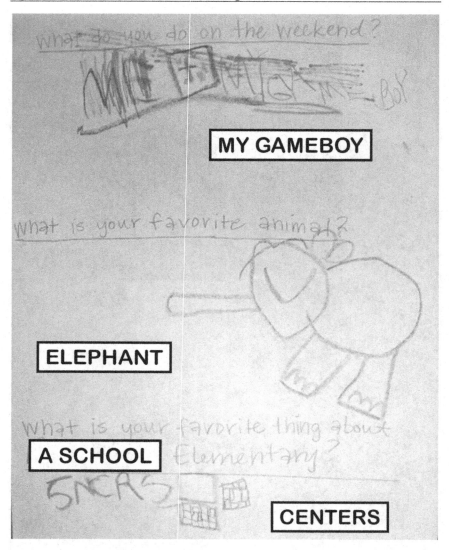

Writing a morning message can be a process of generating a classroom text, helping students to see themselves as powerful and capable writers. Literacy strategies that can be enacted by morning messages include (but are not limited to):

- shared reading/interactive reading;
- shared writing/interactive writing;

- concepts about print;
- word work;
- comprehension; and
- syntax.

A common practice associated with morning messages is shared reading, which models and demonstrates multiple aspects of reading, from fluency to comprehension. For example, we teachers can demonstrate the use of strategies to inform reading and writing, such as self-monitoring and self-correcting (Routman, 2003). Finally, morning messages can be used to invite students to share their lives, welcoming students' multiple cultural backgrounds and promoting an inclusive classroom community.

Interactive Story Writing

Because children may feel that their interests aren't worthy and don't belong in school, they may be resistant or reluctant writers at first. We teachers may need to provide encouragement and support for children to believe in themselves as writers and engage in authoring from their lives. Here is what happened when teacher Erin Chong used a minilesson to engage 2nd-grader Caleb in a "six-room" image writing activity (Heard, 1999; see Figure 6.6 for explanation of this technique).

When Erin asked Caleb, a student with an identified disability, to respond to the six questions in the activity, he wrote "nothing" six times, once in each box or "room." Yet Erin knew about and valued his knowledge of Minecraft and his interest in gargoyles (resulting from a neighborhood architecture study in which his class had engaged). Thus she was able to engage Caleb in co-authoring an interactive story (see Figure 6.7).

Although he was initially resistant, once Caleb realized that his knowledge of Minecraft was valued, he engaged in the activity with a new attitude. He recorded that he was feeling "very awesome." From there, he was able to write about what he knew and was interested in: Minecraft. Caleb went on to draw and write about a Minecraft character (see Figure 6.8). When children write about what they know, when they write about their lives, they are more likely to be interested and engaged in the task.

MAKING WRITING WORKSHOP RELEVANT FOR YOUR SETTING

The writing workshop envisioned by Donald Graves (1983) has been interpreted by many—including Lucy Calkins (1986), Randy Bomer (1995), Katie Wood Ray (2001), Carol Avery (2002), and Tasha Tropp Laman (2013). Carol Avery interpreted writing workshop for early childhood settings in particular. Randy Bomer proposed that writers keep a notebook documenting

Figure 6.6. Six-Room Image Writing

Six-room image writing is a strategy whereby students can learn and practice the craft of poetry, "making it easier to express what they feel in their hearts" (Heard, 1999, p. 64), or engage in authoring narratives and descriptive pieces. This strategy makes the authoring process more accessible by breaking it into six parts, offering multiple means of representation and engagement, and by encouraging students to write about what they know—drawing on their experiences, expertise, and funds of knowledge.

Here's how it works: Teachers may foster a common experience, such as a neighborhood walk, invite students to draw on memories, or select a topic they've explored before (as evident in their previous work, in play, or in their writer's notebook). For example, after engaging in demonstration and shared practice (with students, providing scaffolding), you may invite students to look closely at a photo they took during a neighborhood walk (or imagine the picture or place they will be writing about). Alternatively, you may invite them to bring photos, drawings, or artifacts from home. Ask them to close their eyes and take themselves back to that moment or memory. On a sheet of paper divided into six boxes (representing six rooms), students consider each of the following questions, as they reflect on the experience or memory, capturing their answers (with words and/or pictures) in each of the boxes:

1. **What do you see?** similes or metaphors to describe the image or moment
2. **What is the quality of light?** shining, sparkling, red, blue
3. **What do you hear?** rustling of leaves? sound of rain?
4. **What do you wonder—or want to know more about?** questions you have about the image or moment
5. **What do you feel about it?** write down any feelings you have about the image or moment
6. **What is a word or phrase that seems to capture the experience?** write that word or phrase down, copying it three times (pp. 69–70)

Then, students are invited to use the phrases, words, or images that they wrote down in each box to begin to draft a narrative or poem that describes this moment or memory. The boxes can be rearranged as the students create a poem, which may be nonrhyming, or serve to author a piece in another genre (such as descriptive writing or narrative writing, whether real or imagined).

Students can revise and edit their pieces as they meet in authors' circles to read their writing and invite responses. They may engage in peer conversations or writing conferences, using insights offered to revise their pieces. Their friends may even write themselves into their poem or narrative. This may also be a time in which teachers may lean in and teach in writing conferences, inviting students to consider revisions, which may include conventions such as capitalization, spelling, and punctuation. This process is akin to those experienced by authors—seeking peer review, revising, attending to conventions—and moves students closer to publishing their work.

The younger the children, the more fluid this process is likely to be. It is important to remember that the published piece will still be filled with approximations and may not have many words, as young children make meaning through a variety of symbols. After all, a published piece in kindergarten, 1st grade, or 2nd grade will look very different from a published piece by professional authors who are adults. In K–2, publishing means that the piece is ready to be shared with a wider audience.

Figure 6.6. Six-Room Image Writing, *continued*

Extending the activity. You can add questions, depending on the age of the children, their needs, and experiences, such as:

- **What would it taste like?** sweet, tart, sour, salty
- **What might the image feel like if you touched it?** use your imagination and make it up if necessary
- **How does it smell?** flowery, musty
- **If your image could speak, what would it say?** welcome!, hungry?, come here!
- **What would it sound like?** fizz, peep, slam, swoosh, tick-tock

We hope that you will adapt this strategy and make it relevant for your own setting!

Adapted from *Awakening the Heart* by Georgia Heard (1999; pp. 67–74)

Figure 6.7. From Six-Room Image Writing to Interactive Writing

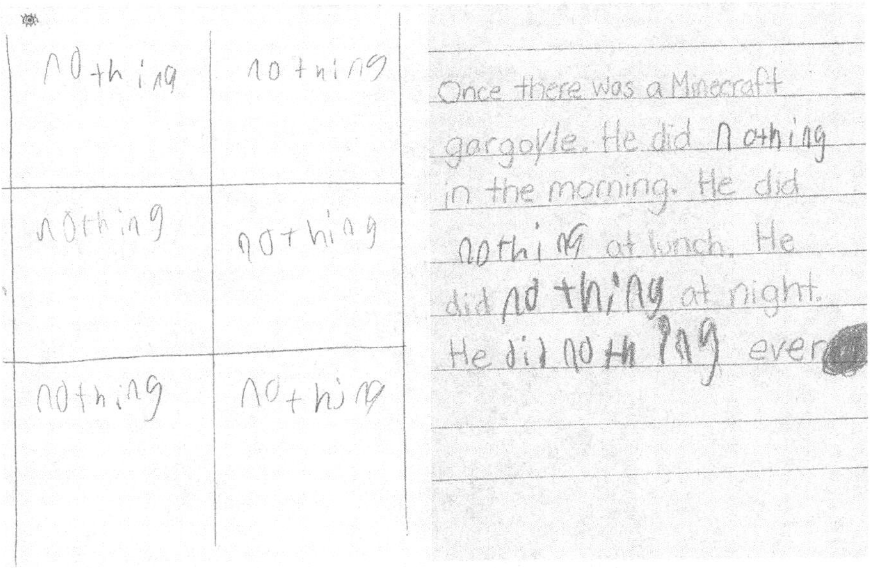

their lives and then get ideas for writing from these writers' notebooks. Then after researching more about the topic, writers engage in drafting, revising, editing, publishing, and reflecting on the process—recursively. Lucy Calkins (2003) proposed that units of study (a series of closely related minilessons) be covered at each grade level, having developed a yearlong curriculum with units of study and minilessons that align with learning standards. Katie Wood Ray urged us to honor developmentally appropriate writing—and proposed that no matter what happens, writing workshop time is sacred.

We recognize that while ideas for minilessons may be helpful, a lock-step, linear process is unlikely to work for every child. Rather, such a process

Figure 6.8. Student authoring of Minecraft character

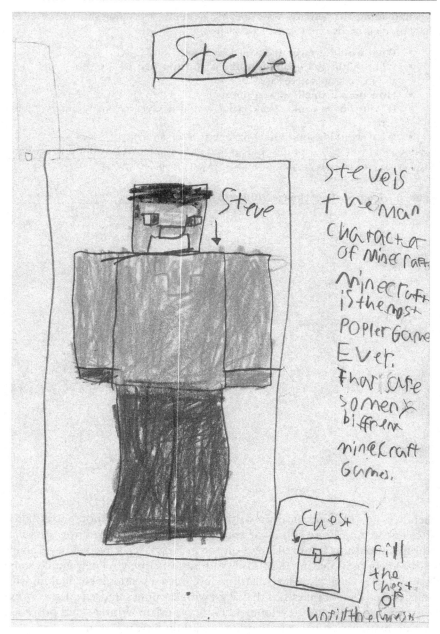

Steve is the main character of Minecraft. Minecraft is the most popular game ever. There are so many different Minecraft games.

may communicate that writing demands going uniformly through multiple sequential steps of selecting a topic, drafting, revising, editing, and publishing. We urge you to think of what is culturally relevant for the children you teach as you engage them in writing workshop, while recognizing that our own writing processes are as unique as we are. Why would we impose a standardized process onto children, especially those with diverse cultural and linguistic practices?

Tasha Laman (2013) invited us to reinvent writing workshop as a framework for multilingual writers, outlining ways for building a community of writers, engaging in teaching that is inclusive of all writers, and sharing and celebrating multilingual writing. She suggested we start building writing communities in our classrooms by having "a meeting area where everyone can sit together to learn new strategies for writing and to read their work aloud" (p. 12). She urged us to recognize that child writers:

- "often work independently but sometimes collaborate to get someone else's expertise";
- "follow a process and use tools of the craft" (p. 12), such as charts, dictionaries, books, and a variety of materials for writing;
- must have their interests, histories, and experiences honored and validated within the context of the classroom; and
- can write in dominant American English and/or in any of their home languages.

Here we invite you to reclaim writing workshop as a time to honor diversities in writers and writing, to engage in writing as a process. We invite you to reinterpret and reinvent it in your own setting—honoring your students and who they are. Writers develop their own processes individually, making sure it works for them. This is what should happen in writing workshop and is especially important for bilingual and multilingual learners.

There are three well-known parts of writing workshop: minilessons, independent writing, and sharing (Avery, 2002; Lindfors, 2008; Laman, 2013). We briefly explain each of them below.

Minilessons

Minilessons for writing were first envisioned by Lucy Calkins (1986), who wrote that a "ritual of beginning every writing workshop with a whole-group gathering brings form and unity to the workshop" (p. 168). Minilessons often communicate to children that writing workshop is starting. Minilessons are to be simple and brief. The choice of what to focus on in minilessons should be based on observations of children's authoring processes. Minilessons "are invitations, not mandates" (Avery, 2002, p. 111).

Minilessons are focused lessons lasting generally no more than 10 minutes, although, as Carol Avery (2002) underscored, at times they end up being really short and other times really long. "I say that a minilesson for writing is no longer than five to eight minutes and then I present one in thirty seconds and another takes twenty minutes. This kind of tension is inherent in teaching" (p. 6). They are meant to be meaningful lessons about something that children may employ in their own writing.

Minilessons can serve "to teach content about writing processes (collecting, nurturing, drafting, revising, editing, publishing), or about craft (genre lessons, reading like writers, beginnings, etc.), or something that you notice many of your students need help with (final punctuation)" (Laman, 2013, p. 7). Topics for minilessons should emanate from teachers' observations of students' writing interests and processes. For example, observing that her 2nd-grade students were sharing their first drafts as if they were finished, Jessica Martell demonstrated how she edits and revises her own writing to clarify meaning and clearly communicate her message. In a series of minilessons, she demonstrated ways of clarifying ideas, adding descriptive words and phrases, considering and reconsidering word choice, and rearranging the text for clarity. Then, she invited students to share how they were editing and revising their own writing, making multiple processes visible and accessible. If her students were experiencing difficulties developing their storylines, she may have chosen to demonstrate the use of graphic organizers for story mapping. As Avery (2002) shared about her own planning of minilessons: "I'll determine tomorrow's minilesson by the way today's workshop goes" (p. 35), emergently and generatively.

We have found it beneficial to start with minilessons about community and classroom procedures. In the bilingual and multilingual classroom, there should also be some minilessons that pertain to language(s)—to differences across languages, affordances of languages, etc. Regardless of the topic, minilessons should be focused and short; this is why they are called *mini*. This acknowledges the fact that young children will not (and should not) sit for long. We propose that minilessons be conducted by teachers alone or in collaboration with children, who share their processes, strategies, understandings, and skills.

For minilessons, children usually convene in an area where the entire classroom community can be accommodated. In Jessica's 2nd grade and in Eileen and Carmen's kindergarten, it is a meeting area near an easel and the SMART Board. So that children will be engaged in shared demonstrations, some teachers use clipboards with paper and writing tools (pens, pencils) or lap dry-erase boards with markers. This allows children to practice with support before they engage in independent practice.

While it can seem daunting to plan according to students' changing needs and learning as opposed to having plans done ahead of time (all aligned to learning standards which must be met), it is important to honor who young children are as individuals and build on their unique learning pathways. This can foster cultural competence and high academic expectations (Ladson-

Billings, 1995a). We propose that centering the teaching of writing on students' lives and interests can foster their development as writers.

In her classroom, Jessica is always assessing through observations (written on Post-it notes and index cards) and analysis of children's work. Intentionally and purposefully she lets her students show her what they know and are interested in. Then, she observes and documents their writing practices and questions, focusing on the process. She brings these together as she seeks to meet learning standards for second grade and beyond in child-centered, inclusive, and culturally relevant ways. This is how she determines minilessons to be taught.

In general terms, there are five broad categories of content for minilessons identified by Katie Wood Ray (2004):

- techniques (word choice, sentence structure),
- strategies (the process of writing),
- understandings (writers get ideas for writing from their lives and experiences),
- conventions (capitalization, punctuation, and spelling), and
- questions (children question themselves as they write).

Techniques and Strategies: Reading Like a Writer. Students are often instructed to read like a writer (Ray, 2006)—to study the craft of writing. By having children read a book they are interested in or that reflects diverse characters in diverse contexts employing diverse languages, we teachers can help them use their imaginations and create interpretations of the story through their knowledge and experiences. For example, in reading the book *First Animal Encyclopedia* by Penelope Arlon (2002), 5-year-old Lorenzo (a lover of animals) learned to organize the pages of his book according to category (*reptiles* and *amphibians and things in the water*), as shown in Figure 6.9. Note that he used bold letters to label each category and each example. Larger letters were used for the page title, and smaller letters were used for the labeling of specific animals that belong to each category. These were strategies and techniques displayed in the mentor text he had read.

Strategy: Planning One's Writing. One of the strategies commonly employed by writers is to select a topic and plan the writing. While not everyone plans her writing graphically, many writers do, so teaching this strategy within a meaningful context may be helpful. Figure 6.10 displays two examples of planning. Second-grader Elvira drew and labeled the parts of her home (left), the setting where her story would take place. Kindergartner Nevaeh used a graphic organizer (right) to plot her journey from home to school. Notice that each student had a different way of planning her story. Nevertheless, both found graphic planning to be helpful in developing their writing.

Figure 6.9. Reptiles and Amphibians

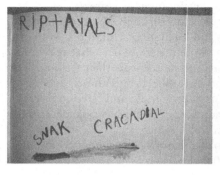

Figure 6.10. Planning

   Minilessons serve as demonstrations. "When we *show* students, rather than just telling them, they are able to observe our thinking in action and to connect it to a visual" (Laman, 2013, p. 47), developing a more concrete understanding. Then they get to work and may apply helpful techniques and strategies they learned to their own authoring processes. Minilessons are often followed by independent writing time, the heart of writing workshop.

Independent Writing

In kindergarten–2nd grades independent writing is typically a period of time when children are working on their own writing. During this time it is important to provide a variety of materials and tools so that students can select what to use. Students should have choices—what to write about, in what language, on what paper, for what purpose, in what format.

Even though the work is often independent, it is not individual. Children often talk with one another during this time. They may act out stories as they envision story plots and interact with each other. They may decide to write together. The teacher walks around the room, paying close attention to and documenting students' processes, and conducting writing conferences with individual students, honoring diversities in their writing processes.

Independent Writing in Kindergarten. It was May in Eileen and Carmen's inclusive kindergarten and children were invited to select one aspect of their neighborhood to write about. Nevaeh chose to write about one of her favorite things in her neighborhood: the ice cream truck! Figure 6.11 shows how Nevaeh went from planning her story using the six-room image writing strategy (refer to Figure 6.6; Heard, 1999) to drafting her story, which was then edited, revised, and published. Her teachers honored her writing approximations as she authored and published *Ice Cream* (Figure 6.11). Below is a transcription of Nevaeh reading her published piece combined with the spacing and punctuation she employed in her published piece for your benefit as a reader (again, transcribing children's words is not an instructional practice we embrace or recommend; we employ it here so that you can access Navaeh's authoring):

I really feel hot!

It is hot because the

sun was

hot like

fire!!

ICE CREAM!!!

I hear a truck, rummm rummmm

I think ice cream. Cold!!!

I get money to get ice cream!

I am happy! I love ice cream!

Writing Conferences. Writing conferences happen within the context of independent writing. We like to think of writing conferences as a time to build on the strengths of each child. Writing conferences are conversations about a student's writing—conversations between writers (Calkins, 1986). Their focus is not on "correcting" a specific writing or even making it better. It is about cultivating growth in the writer through talk—developing effective techniques, helpful strategies, and critical questions. Conferences can be one-on-one or happen in small groups with flexible membership, focusing on specific strategies—depending on students' processes and practices.

In writing conferences, first we ask the student to tell us about her writing, so as to avoid imposing our own understandings and interpretations onto the student's writing. We listen, learn, take notes, and ask clarification

Figure 6.11. Mapping, Drafting, and Publishing

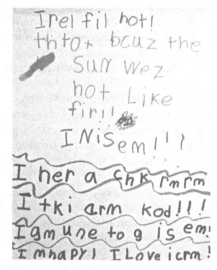

questions. This information becomes the foundation for writing conferences.

Laman (2013) suggested that our first response as teachers should be to listen carefully and actively, recording our observations—focusing on content, understanding, and learning, not on correction. "This kind of listening helps us teach to a student's intentions and consider one thing that may move the writer along, something that is just within this writer's grasp" (p. 92). After this, she suggested teaching from students' strengths. This can be done by using strategies such as noticing and naming (Johnston, 2004), making visible to the student what she is already doing, or making connections to other texts (written by students or by published authors). After which, we can conclude the writing conference with something that will invite and inspire the student to return to her writing by highlighting the importance of the topic or the surprising plot twists.

But as we listen to children, we find that there are so many things we could teach them. How do we decide what to focus on? We suggest thinking of what might be most beneficial for the child's writing life and deciding on one thing to focus on; otherwise we might shut the child down, even if we have the best intentions. For example, we can focus on apprenticeship (Lindfors, 2008; Rogoff, 2003), on teaching something that the child will hopefully be able to do independently in the future. According to Ray (2004), conferences should help children to:

- identify and grow ideas to write about;
- draw or write words and signs on a page, learning to signify;

- plan and engage in prewriting activities, such as planning (refer to Figure 6.10);
- imagine additional crafting possibilities that enhance the text;
- move toward employing conventional writing; and
- set writing agendas.

Conferences should not always be facilitated by the teacher; peer conferences can be very helpful as well. We can use minilessons to teach students about ways to engage in writer-to-writer conversations with their peers, asking questions, encouraging, and noticing. As noted earlier, writing does not have to be isolated; isolation excludes many community-based composing processes. Consider call-and-response in African American communities, interactions "between speaker and listener in which all of the statements ('calls') are punctuated by expressions ('responses') from the listener," which lead to coauthored narratives (Smitherman, 1977, p. 104). Such processes have long been known to be effective in teaching speakers of African American Language. For example, Piestrup (1973) documented how African American Language–speaking students taught with African American discourse strategies, including call-and-response, made greater academic gains and were better able to switch between African American Language and dominant American English (the so-called Standard English) according to context.

Writing conferences can be thought of as conversations through which teachers learn about their students' language practices and support their writing development in culturally relevant ways, fostering cultural and linguistic competence and holding high expectations. Conferences are also about fostering emotional connections, communicating the value of students' home literacies and community resources, and cultivating the belief in the writer's capacity, potential, and worthiness. In conferences that are writer-to-writer conversations, teachers and students learn from and with each other.

Sharing

Sharing is a commonly used procedure that may close the writing workshop—just as minilessons may serve as openings. During this time students can perform their writing, engage with a real audience, answer their peers' questions, and teach and learn from their peers. It is not a time for teachers to address skills, although observations gathered during sharing may inform a subsequent minilesson. Foundational to sharing is the reminder that thinking about writing is essential and that others are interested in what has been written. In addition to this common sharing time, children may share with peers throughout writing workshop and engage in peer conferences.

At the end of writing projects in Jessica's 2nd grade there are publishing celebrations in which family members and peers learn about and review published work. Such celebrations can happen throughout the year in a variety of ways. Some can be in-class celebrations, when students read each other's work and offer feedback. Some can take place across grades, by inviting another class in to read, review, and celebrate the work. Others may include families.

In Jessica's class, publishing celebrations often involve families and community members. In addition to families, Jessica invites the principal, assistant principals, student teachers, specials teachers, counselors, parent coordinators, school aides, previous grade teachers, speech therapists, older siblings (who attend the school), and security guards to celebrate children as authors. Anyone who knows the students is invited to learn about, review, and celebrate their work.

Each year, the children in Jessica's 2nd grade make invitations for family and community members as they prepare for each publishing celebration. As family and community members line up outside the classroom door, the children stand by tables where their work is displayed. Post-it notes and pencils are distributed for reviews, questions, insights, connections, and comments. Jessica explains to her students, "You know, it's been a long time since your family members have been in 2nd grade, so you may have to help them read 2nd-grade writing." Then, she goes outside the classroom and explains to the waiting family and community members that the writing they are about to see would not be "adult-perfect" but is "2nd-grade perfect," because the authors are 2nd graders. She asks them to celebrate children's approximations and to leave a comment on Post-its for their own child(ren) and for at least three other writers—in the language of their choice. After all, as she explains to family members, "You are part of the 2nd-grade family. We are all family." She asks the family members to leave specific comments—not just "great job!" She shows them a few examples (in English and in Spanish), such as explaining how an illustration helped bring the text to life. She then offers to write down their words if they prefer (accommodating those who may feel uncomfortable writing). After the families finish viewing the writing, the children celebrate each other's writing and write comments and notes on Post-its regarding each other's writings. Their writing is reviewed by an authentic and interested audience. It has an authentic purpose and meaning.

TEACHING SPELLING: WHEN? HOW? WHY?

Children spell by remembering how words and chunks of words look. If they rely on phonology more than on visual strategies, they are more likely to misspell words (Goswami & Bryant, 1990). A strategy commonly used for spelling is to make analogies to similar words, focusing on spelling patterns for chunks or words (Hodges, 1991). According to researchers (cf. Flood, Jensen, Lapp, and Squire, 1991), children who are good readers but poor spellers appear to make excellent use of meaning-based strategies, but not strategies that require them to look at words in detail, recognizing recurring patterns of chunks within words.

Teaching about spelling within the meaningful context of words is commonly referred to as *word work*. To spell, it is necessary to understand that written meaning is primarily represented through words, which are made up of chunks (syllables in languages such as Spanish and Portuguese), which often represent familiar and recurring patterns. Although patterns are common and may be helpful in spelling, not all words follow patterns, so a child will have to remember exceptions (words that do not follow patterns). Because chunks and patterns are language-specific, we must not equate a child's ability to identify them with "smartness" as it is likely that children familiar with a language will experience advantages in word work and spelling in that language. That is, children who speak dominant American English at home may be able to identify chunks and write words conventionally in dominant American English. While this may signal that a child is "advanced," it is important to consider how the linguistic context of each child's home language mis/aligns with the language of schooling.

Development of Conventional Spelling

Children construct knowledge about written language as they read and write in meaningful and authentic contexts. Conventional spelling usually develops through a number of approximations. Typically children begin with drawings and scribbles, indicating they understand that writing communicates something. Then, in languages such as English and Spanish, they develop an understanding that print proceeds from left to right, top to bottom. They also come to realize that letters can be and are put together to signify something—even if they don't yet grasp letter-sound correspondence or the understanding that letters and combinations of letters (graphemes) represent the smallest units of sound (phonemes). This is often instantiated by children making strings of unrelated letters to create intended meaning without yet displaying the understanding of units such as chunks and words. These strings have no set numbers of letters from one word to another. Children may even fill an entire page with letters in order to write a single word (Bird, Goodman, & Goodman, 1994). They are developing the *alphabetic principle*, the understanding that words are made of letters and that letters and letter patterns represent sounds.

As they become familiar with words, young children start writing strings of letters for each word—typically three to six (Bird et al., 1994). Early phonemic spelling may appear next. This is when children start using letters to represent beginning and maybe ending sounds of words (e.g., P or PK for *park*) and start employing letter-name spelling, writing at least three sounds in a word, employing vowels and consonants; *park* may now be spelled *pak*.

As children engage in meaningful opportunities for writing, they may start using visual strategies over phonological ones. While some may start writing consonants, such as prk for *park*, they develop a system approaching conventional spelling, using letter-sound correspondence and employing both consonants and vowels. Finally, students develop conventional spelling, relying on their memories of what words look like, their knowledge of word chunks, and making analogies to known words. This is when they may be spelling most words conventionally. The process of approximations is visible, for example, in Nevaeh's writing of the word *because*, which had multiple iterations over time in kindergarten before she came to spell it conventionally: *b » bk » bkz » bckuz » bcauz » becuz » because*.

Spelling develops from word work, but also from many interactions with written language, through reading and being read to, paying attention to environmental print, writing, and demonstrations made by teachers, which model and teach strategies within the context of real reading and writing. It also develops from writing, from observing peers write, and from having conversations about writing. Spelling should not be taught separately—it should be taught within the context of reading and writing. Like Carol Avery (2002), we too "discovered that conventional spelling develops when children write every day in a classroom filled with language" (p. 361).

Strategies for Spelling

In teaching diverse children, it is important to recognize that convention is contextually dependent—for example, "b4" is the conventional spelling of "before" within a texting context and "ain't" is the conventional spelling of "am not" in many interactions. With this in mind, some strategies that may be helpful for young children (identified by Laminack & Ray, 1996) include:

- thinking about how the word looks;
- visualizing if it is a short word or long word;
- making connections to other known words;
- looking to see if the word is printed nearby (word wall, book, etc.); and
- thinking about what sounds are heard in stretching the word (although this is the least efficient way to generate the conventional spelling of a word).

Strategies for spelling may vary during the phases of drafting and editing. During drafting, children often use one or more of these strategies (Shanklin, 1993):

- making predictions;
- writing down the sounds they hear;

- marking words that don't look right;
- looking around the room to see if the word is visible;
- looking for the word in a book other than a dictionary;
- thinking about the parts or chunks of the word; and
- thinking of other words and making analogies.

During the editing phase, children may be encouraged to try one or more of these strategies (Shanklin, 1993):

- trying to spell the words in multiple ways, picking the one that looks right;
- consulting a dictionary;
- asking a peer or a teacher; and
- adding the word to their personal word list (especially if they believe they will be using it again).

Language Variation and Spelling

If children say "aks" instead of ask, they may write the word as ax, acs, or aks. It is essential to validate the child's approximation, while explaining that the conventional spelling privileges dominant American English. Also, if children employ their phonological knowledge of another language (such as Spanish) to write words in English, they will experience a graphophonic misalignment. Teachers should acknowledge such efforts while making the misalignment visible in respectful and positive ways. Teachers can create multiple opportunities for children to write translinguistically (across linguistic codes), while also giving children access to the language of power or the language of those who have power (Delpit, 1988). To honor children's multiple linguistic practices and ways with words, there should be room for children to write in ways that are linguistically relevant to them; only then will such linguistic identities be sustained and cultural competence cultivated.

MOTIVATING AND INSPIRING WRITERS

We teachers need to have numerous strategies to motivate our students to develop as writers. Over time and with the help of our colleagues and of professional resources, we have found a number of ways to motivate and inspire our students, including the following:

- using published texts to support children in writing;
- using your own writing to make points during minilessons;
- helping children develop meaningful topics about which they are experts—such as their family funds of knowledge as well as their own;

- inviting children to share meaningful stories that connect to their lives;
- offering strategies such as Georgia Heard's (1999) six-room image poem to help children capture the event or memory about which they are writing (refer to Figure 6.6); and
- introducing children to authors through author studies and interviews.

In the following sections we explore three ways of inspiring and motivating young writers: author studies, mentor texts, and sharing your own writing.

Author Studies

Seeking not only to study an author's craft but to provide a counter-narrative to the single story of authors being White, monolingual English-speakers, each year Jessica invites her 2nd graders to contact an Author of Color and invite him or her to visit their classroom. This happens either through emails or letters, written by the 2nd graders (refer to Figure 3.3, for example).

Author Visits. Before each author's visit, Jessica engages her class in an in-depth study of the author's books. The students delve deeply into learning about the author's life, writing, and body of work. They have the opportunity to inquire into an author's themes, characters, and writing style. Author visits not only afford the children information about the authoring process but affirm their own worthiness as authors. These author visits include a reading and time for dialogue (for which children prepare questions ahead of time). They also include a signing session, so that each child has a signed copy of one of the author's books. As described in Chapter 3, the visit by award-winning African American author Jacqueline Woodson inspired the children in Jessica's class to recognize that they all had stories to tell. They learned that they could tell their stories whether or not they could spell all words correctly.

Another year, Greg Foley, a children's Author of Color, visited the classroom and inspired many of Jessica's more reluctant writers (many of them Boys of Color) to see themselves capably, as authors. Below, we share students' reactions to Greg Foley's visit, which lasted only a couple of hours, but impacted students' lives long after.

The Impact of Greg Foley's Visit. Greg Foley is the author of many children's books, including *Purple Little Bird, Make a Wish Bear,* and the 2008 Charlotte Zolotow Award–winning *Thank You Bear!*, which has been translated into many languages. The day of Greg Foley's visit to Jessica's classroom was a day of much excitement. The children had never met a "real" author. And they were about to meet a children's Author of Color. They had made a welcome poster for him, displaying drawings of characters in his books. They had read all of his children's books multiple times and studied his craft.

Figure 6.12. Example of Writing After Greg Foley's Visit

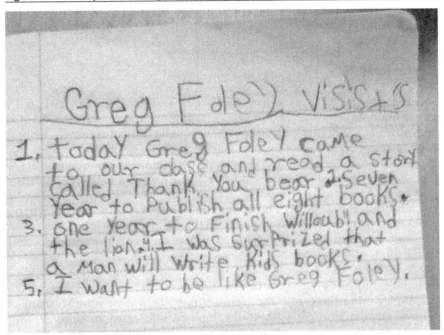

When he arrived in Jessica's classroom, he read one of his books and then answered children's questions. The children asked if he had deliberately written all of his books about relationships, how long it took him to write his first book, how he got ideas for his books, when he started writing, and what his favorite books were when he was their age. They wanted to better understand how one becomes an author. After a long and intense discussion, Foley signed books for each of the children. Then he said goodbye. He became their image of a children's author.

Following Foley's visit, students engaged in learning about and applying the very things he had shared about his writing process. In fact, as soon as Foley left, the children asked Jessica if they could write. And write they did (see Figure 6.12)—especially the Boys of Color who had been more reluctant writers. They wrote and wrote and wrote some more. They wanted to be authors. "I didn't know I could be an author before," one of them said.

Greg Foley's visit provided impetus and motivation for the children to write. It also served as a situated representation of a possible future. It served as a mentor text for their very futures. As a Mexican American boy, Miguel, voiced in Spanish: *"Cuando yo crezca quiero ser un autor, como Greg Foley"* [When I grow up, I want to become an author like Greg Foley]. Miguel carried his signed book as a prized possession in his backpack each and every day through the end of the school year. He read it to his little sister. He read it by himself. He authored himself as a reader. When he went to 3rd grade he made sure to stop by and show us his book, still a prized possession in his backpack. Foley's book served as a reminder to Miguel—of his present and future as an author.

Mentor Texts

Mentor texts are "any texts that you can learn from" (Fletcher, 2011). To honor multiple languages, identities, and cultural practices, we select mentor texts that feature multiple diversities. For example, a mentor text for writing about a common household object may be a picture book that features language, racial, and cultural diversities while describing an important object—such as Carmen Tafolla's bilingual book *What Can You do with a Rebozo?/ Que puedes hacer con un rebozo?*, Yoshiko Uchida's *The Bracelet*, or Jacqueline Woodson's *This is the Rope*. These books can serve as mentor texts for young children to write about known objects. In this way we teachers are able to use mentor texts to build meaningful bridges between school expectations and family funds of knowledge.

It is important to make multiple kinds of mentor texts available—including, but not limited to, books, websites, and song lyrics. For example, after visiting the *Life at the Limits* exhibit at the American Museum of Natural History, 2nd-grader Antonio employed the six-room image writing strategy (explained in Figure 6.6). He used the website for the exhibit as a mentor text to author a sophisticated text (filled with details) about his visit (Figure 6.13). During a writing conference, taking a positive view of his writing, his teacher Elizabeth Rollins made visible the importance of spacing between words (conventions) to writing a text. Yet, instead of having him rewrite the text, she suggested that he perform a "story surgery," by cutting and pasting his words akin to the function of a word processor. In doing so, she taught him an important point while valuing diversities in children's writing and celebrating approximations. We have found such a strategy to be particularly helpful for children with language-processing disorders, dyspraxia, and specfic learning disabilities that affect a child's fine motor skills and handwriting.

Sharing Our Own Writing

As we seek to inspire and motivate writers, it is essential that we share our writerly lives with the children we teach—both in more formal settings (such as minilessons) as well as informally. If you are not an avid writer yourself, get started! After all, we can only ask children to take that step and share their work if we do so ourselves. And enjoy! After all, "the modeling by people that we love is what changes us" (Routman, 2003, p. 11). And what better way to teach young writers to ask questions of their own writing than to ask questions of ours?

Figure 6.13. Expansive Mentor Texts for Writing

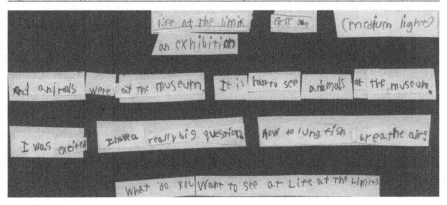

DOCUMENTING GROWTH

We document children's growth in writing by taking detailed notes about their processes and keeping copies of images of products—at multiple points in time. We do not write on children's writing, either adding captions, corrections, or conventional writing to their original texts. Although we know it will not be error-free, it will be "kindergarten-, 1st-grade-, or 2nd-grade perfect," as Jessica explains to family members who come to publishing celebrations. We document the functions of writing, the formats and genres being employed, and the conventions of writing (orthography, phonology, punctuation). But we also document children's understandings, strategies, techniques, and questions across time and space, always asking ourselves how we may be able to transform our teaching in order to honor children's learning processes.

What to document? Here are a few questions we have used to guide us, adapted from Bird, Goodman, and Goodman's *Scale of Writing Development* (1994, p. 95):

- Does the child attempt to write in scribbles or draw? Are there patterns in the scribbles? Patterns in the drawings? Directionality? Is a communicative purpose apparent?
- Is the child writing alphabet and pretend letters throughout the page? Do these letters have meaning?
- Does the child copy words from environmental print and books?
- Is the child writing what look like words in lines across the page? Alphabet letter strings? Separating words with a space or marker (as in Figure 6.2)?
- Does the child communicate the meaning of the message she wrote consistently across time?
- Is the child using letters that match sounds?

- Is the child engaged in writing for a variety of functions employing a variety of formats? Which ones?
- Is the child inventing spellings? (We document the child's spelling of words, seeking to understand patterns and documenting growth.)
- Does the child write a story that is understandable? Is the story made up of sentences? Does the story have a beginning, middle, and end?
- Is the child engaging in revision and editing of his story? Are there details, dialogue? Is he employing punctuation? How? When?

As we ask these and other questions, we must remember that young children's processes of learning to write comprise "not so much learning skills as figuring out how to participate in the socially organized world of school" (Dyson, 2013, p. 164). To document learning, we can look closely at pieces of writing, watch and listen as children are engaged in the writing process, capture the stories they author through improvisations and interactions, and ask children questions about their writing and work over time. After all, "learning to write involves learning how to manipulate symbols to participate in varied kinds of composing practices and in the larger world of values and beliefs" (Dyson, 2013, p. 165).

REFLECTING ON WRITING AND LOOKING AHEAD . . .

In this chapter we encouraged you to (re)write a curriculum that honors the brilliance of diverse children, by re-envisioning writing workshop and moving away from presuming that all children engage in a similar, uniform, regimented, and standardized writing process. We shared how we seek to make writing relevant to our students. In exploring possibilities, we learned from young children who write with purpose, who write what they know. We learned from these young authors and sought to devise ways to honor children's reasons for writing as well as their families' and communities' funds of knowledge in our classroom.

In the Conclusion, we urge you to transform the way you teach by using the strategies and tools presented throughout this book—and in the Internet-based Supplemental Resources. To do so, we invite you to challenge and transform the way the children you teach are seen in schools and in society. We invite you not only to regard each and every one of them as capable and worthy, recognizing that all children learn to make meaning—to read, write, and talk—in unique ways, but to *actively challenge*, through your actions and words, the misalignment between diverse children and uniform school practices, which have historically and contemporarily positioned diversities as deficits. After all, "If you are not for social justice then you are for social injustice" (Morrell, 2015, p. 310).

Negotiating Beliefs, Standards, and Practices to Create Classrooms Where Diverse Learners Are Valued

Throughout this book we have invited you into a number of K–2 classrooms to demonstrate how the concepts we discussed are put into practice to teach reading, writing, and talk in culturally relevant and sustaining ways. The tools and strategies provided are intended to be helpful and relevant, but we encourage you to reinvent them in your own setting, making them contextually meaningful.

In inviting you to listen to and value the stories young children, families, and communities tell, the questions they ask, and the expertise they have, we showed you ways to (re)position children's names, histories, traditions, and funds of knowledge centrally in your curriculum and teaching. All of these can come to life within the context of high academic expectations. After all, fostering culturally relevant teaching requires that we teachers build solid pedagogical bridges between our students' homes and school lives, negotiating "pedagogical third spaces" (Souto-Manning, 2010b), while still meeting (if not surpassing) the expectations of district and state curricular standards, albeit in child-centered, inclusive, and meaningful ways.

Although we encourage you to negotiate ways of putting into practice your belief that every child is capable, we recognize that no one teacher can do everything—especially not everything at once. Nevertheless, we believe that all teachers can all take on one or two ideas shared in this book to begin implementing in their classrooms tomorrow or next week. In Supplemental Resource 7.1 (at www.tcpress.com), we offer some resources for teaching reading, writing, and talk in culturally relevant ways, connecting culturally relevant resources to inclusive ways of supporting diverse children's reading, writing, and talk in K–2 classrooms.

But even before starting to implement strategies and pedagogical practices, we can start by rejecting deficit notions of the children we teach (often so pervasive for Children of Color, low/no-income, and other minoritized identities). In doing so, we can move toward transforming the way the children we teach are seen in our classrooms and schools. We have also found it essential to critically problematize and challenge our own beliefs. For example, if we do not see specific children as able to succeed, it is unlikely that they will succeed in our classroom. We must consider whether we treat everyone equitably—and see every child as having "infinite capacity" (Delpit, 2012) to learn and succeed. If not, why not? Does it have anything to do with how society sees his or her race, ethnicity, language, socioeconomic background, family composition, or gender? To problematize such assumptions (often built on single stories about a group of people; Adichie, 2009) from the perspective that "there is no achievement gap at birth" (Delpit, 2012, p. 3), we suggest starting with an *assets inventory* of each child, raising expectations for *all* children while recognizing that "all humans are capable of learning" (p. 29).

Can all students learn? Of course! After all, learning is defined as changing participation in a community of practice (Rogoff, 2003). Often we do not take time to celebrate students' learning journeys. Instead of valuing learning destinations, it is important to treasure learning journeys. It is up to us to create the conditions whereby all children can embark on meaningful learning journeys, especially including Children of Color, children from low- or no-income families, children who are "emergent bilinguals" (García & Kleifgen, 2010), and children who represent diversities that have historically been seen in terms of deficits. If we do not believe in our students and care about and for them, they are likely not to succeed in our classrooms. We must believe in them, care for them, and genuinely love them. "Without human caring, the best science is minimally effective" (Routman, 2003, p. 221).

As teachers committed to equity in education, we keep in mind that standards do not necessitate standardization. This is especially important during a time in which such a belief is propagated by publishers who seek to profit from education. Instead of teaching from boxes, we need to teach from our students' lives. We need to teach in ways that honor and sustain the cultures, languages, and histories of the students we have—while creating the conditions for them to experience success academically. Doing so, Gloria Ladson-Billings (1995a) posited, is "just good teaching" (p. 159).

We have no time to waste as we seek to engage in culturally relevant and culturally sustaining literacy teaching and learning. "We teachers need to continue to evaluate how we use our time. First and foremost, we must do whatever we can to ensure that our students love learning" (Routman, 2003, p. 218). At the same time, we must ensure that we are not imposing our own timelines and deadlines, knowledge and experiences, normatively onto young children's learning (Genishi & Dyson, 2009).

Because schooling has historically failed students from diverse minoritized backgrounds, we must teach with a deliberate sense of urgency for racial, social, and linguistic justice. We intentionally make the most out of the time we have with our students. We teach, learn, and assess in ways that will foster students' seeing themselves as competent, capable, and powerful in school and in society. How? We genuinely believe in them and in their potential. We teach in ways that demonstrate such a belief. Because we realize that our time is valuable and that we must focus on our students, we reduce interruptions. We use transitions as opportunities for teaching and learning. Most of all, we make the time to learn about our students as unique human beings. We get to know their families and learn from them. As we seek to continue developing as teachers, we engage in professional learning that helps us continue to see the promise and possibility of our students. And we build in time to reflect, to re-assess, and to critically re-evaluate what we are doing. We teach with a sense of urgency while placing students, their lives, experiences, and interests centrally.

We reject ideas of standardization as the solution to our diverse class-rooms and affirm that all children cannot be expected to learn the same way. This would be possible only if we lived in a homogenous society of clones, and we are not convinced that such societies exist—anywhere! When we ex-pect all our students to learn the same way, we honor certain children over others, often those who have been historically privileged; we engage in privi-leging certain ways of speaking, being, and experiencing the world; we create and reify inequities.

The notion of "best" in terms of teaching practices needs to be prob-lematized. Who determines how students learn best? They do! As teachers, we facilitate their learning journeys. But we have to begin with them. We must meet them where they are, acknowledging and learning about all of the richness they bring to school each day, but we can't stay there. We must embark on the learning journey together, blurring the roles of teacher and learner. We must build bridges between what the students know, what their experiences and funds of knowledge are, and the academic expectations set for them. We must do this all while making sure they look forward to read-ing, writing, and talk, and that they see themselves as capable authors, read-ers, and communicators.

Our hope is that as you put into practice concepts presented in this book and reinvent the practices we shared in your own setting, you advocate, edu-cate, and engage. Advocate for your belief that every child is capable and has "infinite capacity" (Delpit, 2012), taking a stand against notions that keep such capacities from being realized. Educate colleagues, families, and the larger community about the possibilities (and power) of bringing together students' languages, cultures, and experiences with high expectations and standards for learning. One does not negate the other. Engage your students in learning—in ways that help them envision the many exciting possibilities ahead of them; in ways that make them feel proud of their identities, of their families, of their communities; in ways that lead them to question inequities in schools and society.

Our hope is that you will take a stance against inequities perpetuated in schools each and every day, by honoring the multiple ways to learn inherent in the children you teach. Design your curriculum and teaching universally and inclusively, in ways that honor children's diversities. Our greatest hope is that you can engage diverse young children in language and literacy practices that will help them change their worlds—while also transforming ours!

Children's Book List

Adoff, A. (1973). *Black is brown is tan*. New York, NY: Amistad.

Arlon, P. (2002). *First animal encyclopedia: A reference guide to the animals of the world*. New York, NY: DK Publishing.

Beaumont, K. (2005). *I ain't gonna paint no more!* New York, NY: Scholastic.

Boynton, S. (1993). *Barnyard dance*. New York, NY: Workman Publishing Company.

Bracegirdle, P. J. (2012). *The dead family Diaz*. New York, NY: Dial Books for Young Readers.

Bradby, M. (2000). *Momma where are you from?* New York, NY: Orchard Books.

Brown, M. (2011). *Marisol McDonald doesn't match/Marisol McDonald no combina*. New York, NY: Lee & Low Books.

Brown, M. W. (1947). *Goodnight moon*. New York, NY: Harper & Row.

Choi, Y. (2001). *The name jar*. New York, NY: Dell Dragonfly Books.

Cooper, M. (1998) *Gettin' through Thursday*. New York, NY: Lee & Low Books.

de la Peña, M. (2015). *Last stop on Market Street*. New York, NY: G.P. Putnam's Sons.

Diggs, T. (2011). *Chocolate me!* New York, NY: Feiwel and Friends.

Dobeck, M., Fountas, I., & Pinnell, G. S. (2008). *Trucks*. Portsmouth, NH: Heinemann.

Ewald, W. (2002). *The best part of me*. Mount Pocono, PA: Little, Brown Books for Young Readers.

Foley, G. (2007). *Thank you, bear!* New York, NY: Viking Books for Young Readers.

Foley, G. (2011). *Purple little bird*. New York, NY: HarperCollins, Balzer + Bray.

Foley, G. (2013). *Make a wish bear*. New York, NY: Viking.

Frasier, D. (1991). *On the day you were born*. New York, NY: Harcourt Children's Books.

Hru, D. (2002). *Tickle tickle*. Brookfield, CT: Roaring Brook Press.

Hughes, L. (2009). *My people*. New York, NY: Atheneum Books for Young Readers.

Kates, B. (1992). *We're different, we're the same, and we're all wonderful!* New York, NY: Random House Books for Young Readers.

Laínez, R. C. (2005). *I am René, the boy/Soy René, el niño*. Houston, TX: Arte Público Press.

Laínez, R. C. (2009). *René has two last names/René tiene dos apellidos*. Houston, TX: Piñata Books.

Lester, J. (2005). *Let's talk about race*. New York, NY: Amistad.

Martin Jr., B., & Carle, E. (1992). *Brown bear, brown bear, what do you see?* New York, NY: Henry Holt and Company.

McKissack, P. (2001). *Goin' someplace special*. New York, NY: Atheneum Books for Young Readers.

Medina, J. (1999). *My name is Jorge: On both sides of the river*. Honesdale, PA: Wordsong.

Morales, Y. (2008). *Just in case: A trickster tale and Spanish alphabet book*. New York, NY: Roaring Brook Press.

Morales, Y. (2014). *Viva Frida*. New York, NY: Roaring Brook Press.

Myers, W. D. (2009). *Looking like me*. New York, NY: Egmont.

Parr, T. (2003). *The family book*. New York, NY: Little, Brown and Company.

Parr, T. (2009). *It's okay to be different*. New York, NY: Little, Brown and Company.

Recorvits, H. (2003). *My name is Yoon*. New York, NY: Frances Foster Books.

Richardson, J., & Parnell, P. (2005). *And Tango makes three*. New York, NY: Little Simon.

Ringgold, F. (1991). *Tar beach*. New York, NY: Crown.

Santora, M. C. (2011). *The day the towers fell*. Grapevine, TX: SEGR Publishing.

Soto, G. (1996). *Too many tamales*. New York, NY: G. P. Putnam's Sons.

Tafolla, C. (2008). *What can you do with a rebozo?/¿Que puedes hacer con un rebozo?* Berkeley, CA: Tricycle Press.

Tonatiuh, D. (2015). *Funny bones: Posada and his day of the dead calaveras*. New York, NY: Harry N. Abrams.

Trujillo, R. E. (2009). *La última ola de Marianela*. New York, NY: Big Head Fish.

Turner, A. W., & Himler, R. (1987). *Nettie's trip South*. New York, NY: Macmillan

Ushida, Y. (1996). *The bracelet*. New York, NY: Putnam & Grosset.

Weatherford, C. B. (2005). *Freedom on the menu: The Greensboro sit-ins*. New York, NY: Dial Books for Young Readers.

Woodson, J. (1997). *We had a picnic this Sunday past*. New York, NY: Hyperion Books for Children.

Woodson, J. (2001). *The other side*. New York, NY: G. P. Putnam's Sons.

Woodson, J. (2002). *Each kindness*. New York, NY: Nancy Paulsen Books.

Woodson, J. (2002). *Visiting day*. New York, NY: Scholastic.

Woodson, J. (2005). *Show way*. New York, NY: G. P. Putnam's Sons.

Woodson, J. (2013). *This is the rope: A story from the great migration*. New York, NY: Nancy Paulsen Books.

Woodson, J. (2014). *Brown girl dreaming*. New York, NY: Nancy Paulsen Books.

References

Adichie, C. (2009). *The danger of a single story*. Retrieved from http://www.ted.com/talks/chimamanda_adichie_the_danger_of_a_single_story.html

Alexander, M. (2010). *The new Jim Crow: Mass incarceration in the age of colorblindness*. New York, NY: The New Press.

Allen, J. (2010). *Literacy in the welcoming classroom: Creating family-school partnerships that support student learning*. New York, NY: Teachers College Press.

American Speech-Language-Hearing Association (ASHA). (2015). *Social language use (pragmatics)*. Retrieved from http://www.asha.org/public/speech/development/Pragmatics/

Anisfeld, M. (1991). Neonatal imitation. *Developmental Review, 11*(1), 60–97.

Au, W. (Ed.). (2014). *Rethinking multicultural education: Teaching for racial and cultural justice* (2nd ed.). Milwaukee, WI: Rethinking Schools.

Avery, C. (2002). *. . . And with a light touch: Learning about reading, writing and teaching with first graders* (2nd ed.). Portsmouth, NH: Heinemann.

Baker, C. (2014). *A parents' and teachers' guide to bilingualism* (4th ed.). Tonawanda, NY: Multilingual Matters.

Bakhtin, M. (1981). Discourse in the novel. In M. Holquist (Ed.), *The dialogic imagination* (pp. 259–422). Austin, TX: University of Texas Press.

Bell, D., & Jarvis, D. (2002). Letting go of "letter of the week." *Primary Voices, 11*(2), 10–24.

Bhattacharjee, Y. (2012, March 17). Why bilinguals are smarter. *The New York Times*. Retrieved from http://www.nytimes.com/2012/03/18/opinion/sunday/the-benefits-of-bilingualism.html?_r=0

Bird, L. B, Goodman, K. S., & Goodman, Y. M. (1994). *The whole language catalog: Forms for authentic assessment*. Santa Rosa, CA: American School Publishers.

Bishop, R. S. (1990). Mirrors, windows, and sliding glass doors. *Perspectives: Choosing and Using Books for the Classroom, 6*(3), ix–xi.

Bomer, R. (1995). *Time for meaning: Crafting literate lives in middle and high school*. Portsmouth, NH: Heinemann.

Bronson, P., & Merryman, A. (2009, September 5). Even babies discriminate. *Newsweek*. Retrieved from http://www.newsweek.com/2009/09/04/see-baby-discriminate.html

Cahnmann, M. (2006). Reading, living, and writing bilingual poetry as scholARTistry in the language arts classroom. *Language Arts, 83*(4), 341–351.

Calkins, L. (1986). *The art of teaching writing*. Portsmouth, NH: Heinemann.

Calkins, L. (1991). *Living between the lines*. Portsmouth, NH: Heinemann.

Calkins, L. (2003) *Units of study for primary writing: A yearlong curriculum*. Portsmouth, NH: Heinemann.

Calkins, L., & Tolan, K. (2010). *A guide to reading workshop*. Portsmouth, NH: Heinemann.

Canagarajah, A. S. (2013). *Literacy as translingual practice: Between communities and classrooms.* New York, NY: Routledge.

Cappellini, M. (2005). *Balancing reading and language learning: A resource for teaching English language learners, K-5.* Portsmouth, NH: Heinemann.

Cazden, C. (2001). *Classroom discourse: The language of teaching and learning.* Portsmouth, NH: Heinemann.

City of New York. (2012). *What we know about the health effects of 9/11.* Retrieved from http://www.nyc.gov/html/doh/wtc/html/know/know.shtml

Clark, K. B., & Clark, M. K. (1939). The development of consciousness of self in the emergence of racial identification in Negro pre-school children. *Journal of Social Psychology, 10,* 591–597.

Clark, K. B., & Clark, M. K. (1947). Racial identification and preference in Negro children. In T. M. Newcombe & E. C. Hartley (Eds.), *Readings in social psychology* (pp. 169–178). New York, NY: Holt.

Clark, K. B., & Clark, M. K. (1950). Emotional factors in racial identification and preference in Negro children. *Journal of Negro Education, 19*(3), 341–350.

Clay, M. M. (1979). *The early detection of reading difficulties: A diagnostic survey with recovery procedures.* Portsmouth, NH: Heinemann.

Clay, M. M. (1993). *An observation survey of early literacy achievement.* Portsmouth, NH: Heinemann.

Clay, M. M. (2000). *Concepts about print: What have children learned about printed language?* Portsmouth, NH: Heinemann.

Clay, M. M. (2003). *Running records for classroom teachers.* Portsmouth, NH: Heinemann.

Cohen, C. C., Deterding, N., & Clewell, B. C. (2005). *Who's left behind?: Immigrant children in high and low LEP schools.* Washington, DC: The Urban Institute.

Common Core State Standards. (2011). *The standards » English language arts standards.* Retrieved from http://www.corestandards.org/the-standards/english-language-arts-standards

Common Core State Standards Initiative. (2016). *English language arts standards » Reading: Foundational skills » kindergarten.* Retrieved from http://www.corestandards.org/ELA-Literacy/RF/K/

Compton-Lilly, C. (2003). *Reading families: The literate lives of urban children.* New York, NY: Teachers College Press.

Cooperative Children's Book Center. (2015). *Children's books by and about people of color and first/native nations published in the United States.* Retrieved from https://ccbc.education.wisc.edu/books/pcstats.asp

Core Knowledge Foundation. (2013). *Kings and queens: Tell it again! Read-aloud supplemental guide* (New York ed.). Mountain View, CA: Creative Commons Licensing.

Daniels, H., & Daniels, E. (2013). *The best-kept teaching secret: How written conversations engage kids, activate learning, and grow fluent writers, K–12.* Thousand Oaks, CA; Corwin.

Delpit, L. (1988). The silenced dialogue: Power and pedagogy in educating other people's children. *Harvard Educational Review, 58*(3), 280–299.

Delpit, L. (2012). *Multiplication is for white people: Raising expectations for other people's children.* New York, NY: The New Press.

Derman-Sparks, L., & Ramsey, P. (2011). *What if all the kids are White?: Anti-bias multicultural education with young children and families* (2nd ed.). New York, NY: Teachers College Press.

Dewey, J. (1938). *Experience and education.* Indianapolis, IN: Kappa Delta Pi.

Diaz, J. (2009). Author Junot Diaz's New Jersey. *Ledger Live.* Retrieved from http://www.nj.com/ledgerlive/index.ssf/2009/10/junot_diazs_new_jersey.html

Dyson, A. Haas, & Genishi, C. (2005). *On the case: Approaches to language and literacy research.* New York, NY: Teachers College Press.

Dyson, A. Haas. (1983). The role of oral language in early writing processes. *Research in the Teaching of English, 17*(1), 1–30.

Dyson, A. Haas. (1989). *Multiple worlds of child writers: Friends learning to write.* New York, NY: Teachers College Press.

Dyson, A. Haas. (1990). Symbol makers, symbol weavers: How children link play, pictures and print. *Young Children, 45*(2), 50–57.

Dyson, A. Haas. (2001). Where are the childhoods in childhood literacy? An exploration in outer (school) space. *Journal of Early Childhood Literacy, 1*(1), 9–39.

Dyson, A. Haas. (2003). *The brothers and sisters learn to write: Popular literacies in childhood and school cultures.* New York, NY: Teachers College Press.

Dyson, A. Haas. (2013). *Rewriting the basics: Literacy learning in children's cultures.* New York, NY: Teachers College Press.

Earick, M. (2009). *Racially equitable teaching: Beyond the Whiteness of professional development for early childhood educators.* New York, NY: Peter Lang.

Edelman, M. W. (2015, August 21). It's hard to be what you can't see. *Huffington Post.* Retrieved from http://www.huffingtonpost.com/marian-wright-edelman/its-hard-to-be-what-you-c_b_8022776.html

Elliott, S. (2011, August 31). Honoring Sept. 11, with care. *The New York Times.* Retrieved from http://www.nytimes.com/2011/09/01/business/media/marketers-honoring-sept-11-with-care.html?_r=1&pagewanted=all

Every Student Succeeds Act of 2015, Pub. L. No. 114–95.

Faltis, C. (1997). *Joinfostering: Adapting teaching for the multilingual classroom.* Upper Saddle River, NJ: Merrill.

Fassler, R. (2003). *Room for talk: Teaching and learning in a multilingual kindergarten.* New York, NY: Teachers College Press.

Fletcher, R. (2011). Ralph Fletcher on mentor texts [Audio podcast]. *Choice Literacy.* Retrieved from https://www.choiceliteracy.com/articles-detail-view.php?id=994

Flood, J., Jensen, J., Lapp, D., & Squire, J. (Eds.). (1991). *Handbook of research on teaching the English language arts.* New York, NY: Macmillan.

Fountas, I., & Pinnell, G. (2011). *Fountas and Pinnell benchmark assessment system 1 and 2* (2nd ed.). Portsmouth, NH: Heinemann.

Freire, P. (1970). *Pedagogy of the oppressed.* New York, NY: Continuum.

Freire, P. (1985). Reading the world and reading the word: An interview with Paulo Freire. *Language Arts, 62*(1), 15–21.

Freire, P. (1998). *Teachers as cultural workers: Letters to those who dare teach.* Boulder, CO: Westview Press.

Freire, P. (2000). *Pedagogy of the oppressed* (30th anniversary ed.). New York, NY: Bloomsbury.

García, E. E., & García, E. H. (2012). *Understanding the language development and early education of Hispanic children.* New York, NY: Teachers College Press.

García, O., & Kleifgen, J. (2010). *Educating emergent bilinguals. Policies, programs and practices for English language learners.* New York, NY: Teachers College Press.

Gee, J. P. (2005). *An introduction to discourse analysis: Theory and method* (2nd ed.). New York, NY: Routledge.

Genishi, C. (1976). *Rules for code-switching in young Spanish-English speakers: An exploratory study of language socialization* (Unpublished doctoral dissertation). University of California, Berkeley.

Genishi, C. (1998). *Young children's oral language development.* Urbana, IL: ERIC Digest (ED301361). Retrieved from http://files.eric.ed.gov/fulltext/ED301361.pdf

Genishi, C., & Dyson, A. Haas. (1984). *Language assessment in the early years.* Norwood, NJ: Ablex Publishing Corporation.

Genishi, C., & Dyson, A. Haas. (2009). *Children, language, and literacy: Diverse learners in diverse times.* New York, NY, and Washington, DC: Teachers College Press and National Association for the Education of Young Children.

Genishi, C., & Dyson, A. Haas. (2012). Racing to the top: Who's accounting for the children? *Bank Street Occasional Papers, 27,* 18–20.

Goodman, K. S. (1965). A linguistic study of cues and miscues in reading. *Elementary English, 42*(6), 639–643.

Goodman, K. S. (1970). Psycholinguistic universals in the reading process. *Journal of Typographic Research, 4*(2), 103–110.

Goodman, K. S. (1973). *Miscue analysis: Applications to reading instruction.* Urbana, IL: NCTE. Retrieved from http://files.eric.ed.gov/fulltext/ED080973.pdf

Goodman, K. S. (1994). Reading, writing, and written text: A transactional sociopsycholinguistic view. In R. B. Ruddell, M. R. Ruddell, & H. Singer (Eds.), *Theoretical models and processes of reading* (4th ed.) (pp. 1220–1244). Newark, DE: International Reading Association.

Goodman, K. S. (1996). *On reading: A common-sense look at the nature of language and the science of reading.* Portsmouth, NH: Heinemann.

Goodman, Y. M., Watson, D. J., & Burke, C. (1987). *Reading miscue inventory: Alternative procedures.* New York, NY: Richard C. Owen.

Goodwin, A. L., Cheruvu, R., & Genishi, C. (2008). Responding to multiple diversities in early childhood education: How far have we come? In C. Genishi & A. L. Goodwin (Eds.), *Diversities in early childhood education: Rethinking and doing* (pp. 3–10). New York, NY: Routledge.

Goswami, U., & Bryant, P. (1990). *Phonological skills and learning to read.* East Sussex, UK: Psychology Press.

Goswami, U., & Mead, F. (1992). Onset and rime awareness and analogies in reading. *Reading Research Quarterly, 27*(2), 152–162.

Graves, D. (1983). *Writing: Teachers and children at work.* Portsmouth, NH: Heinemann.

Graves, D. (2004). *Teaching day by day: 180 stories to help you along the way.* Portsmouth, NH: Heinemann.

Gregory, E., Long, S., & Volk, D. (2004). Syncretic literacy studies: Starting points. In E. Gregory, S. Long, & D. Volk (Eds.), *Many pathways to literacy: Young children learning with siblings, peers, grandparents, and communities* (pp. 1–5). London, UK: RoutledgeFalmer.

Gutiérrez, K. (2008). Developing a sociocritical literacy in the third space. *Reading Research Quarterly, 43*(2), 148–164.

Gutiérrez, K., Morales, P., & Martínez, D. (2009). Re-mediating literacy: Culture, difference, and learning for students from nondominant communities. *Review of Research in Education, 33,* 212–245.

Halliday, M. A. K. (1993). Towards a language-based theory of learning. *Linguistics and Education, 5,* 93–116.

Harste, J., Burke, C., & Woodward, V. (1981). *Children, their language and world: Initial encounters with print.* Washington, DC: National Institute of Education.

Harste, J., Short, K., & Burke, C. (1988). *Creating classrooms for authors: The reading-writing connection.* Portsmouth, NH: Heinemann.

Heard, G. (1999). *Awakening the heart: Exploring poetry in elementary and middle school.* Portsmouth, NH: Heinemann.

Heath, S. B. (1982). What no bedtime story means: Narrative skills at home and at school. *Language and Society, 11*(2), 49–76.

Heath, S. B. (1983). *Ways with words: Language, life, and work in communities and classrooms.* New York, NY: Cambridge University Press.

Heath, S. B. (2012, May). *Two four-letter words: Love and care.* 2012 Teachers College, Columbia University Medalist Dinner. New York, NY.

Hilliard, A. (2014). What do we need to know now? In W. Au (Ed.), *Rethinking multicultural education: Teaching for racial and culture justice* (2nd ed., pp. 25–38). Milwaukee, WI: Rethinking Schools.

Hodges, R. (1991). The conventions of writing. In J. Flood, J. M. Jensen, D. Lapp, & J. R. Squire (Eds.), *Handbook of research on teaching the English language arts* (pp. 775–786). New York, NY: Macmillan.

Holdaway, D. (1972). *Independence in reading: A handbook on individualized procedures*. New York, NY: Scholastic.

Holdaway, D. (1979). *The foundations of literacy*. New York, NY: Scholastic.

Hughes, L. (1951). Harlem [2]. In A. Rampersad (Ed.), (1994), *The collected poems of Langston Hughes* (p. 426). New York, NY: Vintage Books.

Johnston, P. (2004). *Choice words: How our language affects children's learning*. Portland, ME: Stenhouse.

Ladson-Billings, G. (1992a). Liberatory consequences of literacy: A case of culturally relevant instruction for African American students. *Journal of Negro Education, 61*(3), 378–391.

Ladson-Billings, G. (1992b). Reading between the lines and beyond the pages: A culturally relevant approach to literacy teaching. *Theory into Practice, 31*(4), 312–320.

Ladson-Billings, G. (1994). *Dreamkeepers: Successful teachers of African American children*. San Francisco, CA: Jossey-Bass.

Ladson-Billings, G. (1995a). But that's just good teaching! The case for culturally relevant pedagogy. *Theory into practice 34*(3), 159–165.

Ladson-Billings, G. (1995b). Toward a theory of culturally relevant pedagogy. *American Educational Research Journal, 32*(3), 465–491.

Ladson-Billings, G. (2006). From the achievement gap to the education debt: Understanding achievement in U.S. schools. *Educational Researcher, 35*(7), 3–12.

Ladson-Billings, G. (2011). Boyz to men?: Teaching to restore Black boys' childhood. *Race Ethnicity and Education, 14*(1), 7–15.

Ladson-Billings, G. (2014). Culturally relevant pedagogy 2.0: a.k.a the remix. *Harvard Educational Review, 84*(1), 74–84.

Laman, T. T. (2006). Changing our minds/changing the world: The power of a question. *Language Arts, 83*(3), 203–214.

Laman, T. T. (2013). *From ideas to words: Writing strategies for English language learners*. Portsmouth, NH: Heinemann.

Laminack, L., & Ray. K. W. (1996). *Spelling in use: Looking closely at spelling in whole language classrooms*. Urbana, IL: NCTE.

Lindfors, J. (2008). *Children's language: Connecting reading, writing, and talk*. New York, NY: Teachers College Press.

Long, S. (2004). Passionless text and phonics first: Through a child's eyes. *Language Arts, 81*(5), 417–426.

Long, S. (2011). *Supporting students in a time of core standards: English language arts grades preK–2*. Urbana, IL: NCTE.

Long, S. (2014). *Exquisite names: Name stories from Mrs. Martell's second grade!* (unpublished course material). New York, NY: Teachers College, Columbia University.

Long, S., Volk, D., Baines, J., & Tisdale, C. (2013). "We've been doing it your way long enough": Syncretism as a critical process. *Journal of Early Childhood Literacy, 13*(3), 418–439.

Martens, P. (2015). *Learning about readers through the Burke reading interview*. Retrieved from https://retrospectivemiscue.wordpress.com/2015/08/17/learning-about-readers-through-the-burke-reading-interview/

Maxwell, L. A. (2014, August 19). U.S. school enrollment hits majority-minority milestone. *Education Week*. Retrieved from http://www.edweek.org/ew/articles/2014/08/20/01demographics.h34.html

McGee, L., & Schickedanz, J. (2007). Repeated interactive read-alouds in preschool and kindergarten. *The Reading Teacher, 60*(8), 742–751.

McIntosh, P. (1990). Interactive phases of curricular and personal re-vision with regard to race. (Report No. 219). Center for Research on Women, Wellesley College, Wellesley, MA.

Mills, H. (2005). It's all about looking closely and listening carefully. *School Talk, 11*(1), 1–2.

Mills, H., O'Keefe, T., & Jennings, L. B. (2004). *Looking closely and listening carefully: Teaching literacy through inquiry.* Urbana, IL: NCTE.

Moats, L. (2009). *The speech sounds of English: Phonetics, phonology, and phoneme awareness* (2nd ed.). Boston, MA: Sopris West.

Moll, L., & Greenberg, J. (1990). Creating zones of possibilities: Combining social contexts for instruction. In L. Moll (Ed.), *Vygotsky and education: Instructional implications and applications of sociohistorical psychology* (pp. 319–348). Cambridge, UK: Cambridge University Press.

Moll, L., Amanti, C., Neff, D., & Gonzalez, N. (1992). Funds of knowledge for teaching: Using a qualitative approach to connect homes and classrooms. *Theory Into Practice, 31*(2), 132–141.

Morrell, E. (2012). Teachers as critical researchers: An empowering model for urban education. In G. Cannella & S. Steinberg (Eds.), *The critical qualitative research reader* (pp. 364–379). New York, NY: Peter Lang.

Morrell, E. (2015). Powerful English at NCTE yesterday, today, and tomorrow: Toward the next movement. *Research in the Teaching of English, 49*(3), 307–327.

New, R. S., & Mallory, B. L. (1994). Introduction: The ethics of inclusion. In B. Mallory and R. New (Eds.), *Diversity and developmentally appropriate practices: Challenges for early childhood curriculum* (pp. 1–13). New York, NY: Teachers College Press.

Nieto, S. (2000). Placing equity front and center: Some thoughts on transforming teacher education for a new century. *Journal of Teacher Education, 51*(3), 180–187.

Nieto, S. (2010). *The light in their eyes: Creating multicultural learning communities* (10th anniversary ed.). New York, NY: Teachers College Press.

No Child Left Behind Act of 2001, Pub. L. No. 107–110.

O'Keefe, T. (1997). The habit of kidwatching. *School Talk, 3*(2), 4–5.

Owocki, G. (1999). *Literacy through play.* Portsmouth, NH: Heinemann.

Owocki, G. (2001). *Make way for literacy: Teaching the way young children learn.* Portsmouth, NH: Heinemann.

Owocki, G., & Goodman, Y. M. (2002). *Kidwatching: Documenting children's literacy development.* Portsmouth, NH: Heinemann.

Paley, V. G. (1986). On listening to what children say. *Harvard Educational Review, 56*(2), 122–132.

Paley, V. G. (1988). *Bad guys don't have birthdays: Fantasy play at four.* Chicago, IL: The University of Chicago Press.

Paley, V. G. (1990). *The boy who would be a helicopter: The uses of storytelling in the classroom.* Cambridge, MA: Harvard University Press.

Paley, V. G. (1992). *You can't say you can't play.* Cambridge, MA: Harvard University Press.

Paley, V. G. (2000). *White teacher* (2nd ed.). Cambridge, MA: Harvard University Press.

Paley, V. G. (2007). Goldilocks and her sister: An anecdotal guide to the doll corner. *Harvard Educational Review, 77*(2), 144–151.

Paris, D. (2009). "They're in my culture, they speak the same way": African American Language in multiethnic high schools. *Harvard Educational Review, 79*(3), 428–447.

Paris, D. (2012). Culturally sustaining pedagogy: A needed change in stance, terminology, and practice. *Educational Researcher, 41*(3), 93–97.

Piestrup, A. M. (1973). *Black dialect interference and accommodation of reading instruction in the first grade.* Berkeley, CA: University of California, Language Behavior Research Lab.

Ray, K. W. (2001). *The writing workshop: Working through the hard parts (and they're all hard parts).* Urbana, IL: NCTE.

Ray, K. W. (2004). *About the authors: Writing workshop with our youngest writers.* Portsmouth, NH: Heinemann.

Ray, K. W. (2006). *Study driven: A framework for planning units of study in the writing workshop.* Portsmouth, NH: Heinemann.

Ray, K. W., & Glover, M. (2008). *Already ready: Nurturing writers in preschool and kindergarten.* Portsmouth, NH: Heinemann.

Rogoff, B. (2003). *The cultural nature of human development.* Oxford, UK: Oxford University Press.

Rogoff, B., Matusov, B., & White, S. (1996). Models of teaching and learning: Participation in a community of learners. In D. Olson & N. Torrance (Eds.), *The handbook of cognition and human development* (pp. 388–414). Oxford, UK: Blackwell.

Rosenblatt, L. (1978). *The reader, the text, the poem: The transactional theory of the literary work.* Carbondale, IL: Southern Illinois University Press.

Rosenblatt, L. (1988). *Writing and reading: The transactional theory* (Technical Report No. 416). Champaign, IL: Center for the Study of Reading. Retrieved from https://www.ideals.illinois.edu/bitstream/handle/2142/18044/ctrstreadtechrepv01988i00416_opt.pdf

Routman, R. (2003). *Reading essentials: The specifics you need to teach reading well.* Portsmouth, NH: Heinemann.

Shanklin, N. (1993). My strategies for spelling. In L. Rhodes (Ed.), *Literacy assessment: A handbook of instruments* (p. 90). Portsmouth, NH: Heinemann.

Short, K. (1997). *Literature as a way of knowing.* York, MN: Stenhouse.

Short, K., & Harste, J. (1996). *Creating classrooms for authors and inquirers* (2nd ed.). Portsmouth, NH: Heinemann.

Siegel, M. (1984). *Reading as signification* (Unpublished doctoral dissertation). Indiana University, Bloomington, IN.

Simon, C. A. (2015). *Using the think-pair-share technique.* Retrieved from http://www.readwritethink.org/resources/resource-print.html?id=30626&tab=1

Smitherman, G. (1977). *Talkin and testifyin: The language of Black America.* Detroit, MI: Wayne State University Press.

Smitherman, G. (1996). *African-American English: From the hood to the amen corner.* Minneapolis, MN: University of Minnesota. Retrieved from http://writing.umn.edu/lrs/assets/pdf/speakerpubs/Smitherman.pdf

Souto-Manning, M. (2007). Honoring children's names and, therefore, their identities. *School Talk, 12*(3), 1–2.

Souto-Manning, M. (2009). Acting out and talking back: Negotiating discourses in American early educational settings. *Early Child Development and Care, 179*(8), 1083–1094.

Souto-Manning, M. (2010a). *Freire, teaching, and learning: Culture circles across contexts.* New York, NY: Peter Lang.

Souto-Manning, M. (2010b). Teaching English learners: Building on cultural and linguistic strengths. *English Education, 42*(3), 249–263.

Souto-Manning, M. (2010c). Challenging ethnocentric literacy practices: (Re)Positioning home literacies in a Head Start classroom. *Research in the Teaching of English, 45*(2), 150–178.

Souto-Manning, M. (2013a). Competence as linguistic alignment: Linguistic diversities, affinity groups, and the politics of educational success. *Linguistics and Education, 24*(3), 305–315.

Souto-Manning, M. (2013b). *Multicultural teaching in the early childhood classroom: Approaches, strategies and tools, preschool-2nd grade*. New York, NY and Washington, DC: Teachers College Press and Association for Childhood Education International.

Souto-Manning, M. (2013c). On children as syncretic natives: Disrupting and moving beyond normative binaries. *Journal of Early Childhood Literacy, 13*(3), 368–391.

Souto-Manning, M., & Cheruvu, R. (2015). Multiculturally sustaining pedagogy in early childhood teacher education. In L. Couse & S. Recchia (Eds.), *Handbook of early childhood teacher education* (pp. 288–303). New York, NY: Routledge.

Sterponi, L. (2007). Clandestine interactional reading: Intertextuality and double-voicing under the desk. *Linguistics and Education, 18*(1), 1–23.

Stires, S., & C. Genishi. (2008). Learning English in school: Rethinking curriculum, relationships, and time. In C. Genishi & A. L. Goodwin (Eds.), *Diversities in early childhood education: Rethinking and doing* (pp. 49–66). New York, NY: Routledge.

Swadener, B., & Lubeck, S. (Eds.). (1995). *Children and families "at promise": Deconstructing the discourse of risk*. Albany, NY: State University of New York Press.

Tompkins, G. (1990). *Teaching writing: Balancing process and product*. Upper Saddle River, NJ: Pearson.

Twine, F. W. (2004). A white side of black Britain: The concept of racial literacy. *Ethnic and Racial Studies, 27*(6), 878–907.

UNESCO. (2003). *Education in a multilingual world*. Retrieved from http://unesdoc.unesco.org/images/0012/001297/129728e.pdf

Valdés, G. (1996). *Con respeto: Bridging the distances between culturally diverse families and schools*. New York, NY: Teachers College Press.

Valenzuela, A. (1999). *Subtractive schooling: U.S.-Mexican youth and the politics of caring*. Albany, NY: SUNY Press.

Van Sluys, K., & Laman, T. T. (2006). Learning about language: Written conversations with elementary language learners. *The Reading Teacher, 60*(3), 222–233.

Vygotsky, L. S. (1978). *Mind in society: The development of higher psychological processes*. Cambridge, MA: Harvard University Press.

Vygotsky, L. S. (1981). The genesis of higher mental functions. In J. V. Wertsch (Ed.), *The concept of activity in Soviet psychology* (pp. 144–188). Armonk, NY: Sharpe.

Whitmore, K., Martens, P., Goodman, Y., & Owocki, G. (2005). Remembering critical lessons in early literacy research: A transactional perspective. *Language Arts, 82*(5), 296–307.

Wilde, S. (2000). *Miscue analysis made easy: Building on student strengths*. Portsmouth, NH: Heinemann.

World Bank. (1995). *Priorities and strategies for education*. Washington, DC: The International Bank for Reconstruction and Development.

Index

NAMES

Adichie, C., 2, 41, 78, 81–82, 142
Adoff, Arnold, 36
Alexander, M., 25
Allen, J., 40
Amanti, C., 10, 23
Anisfeld, M., 28
Arlon, Penelope, 127
Au, W., 21
Avery, Carol, 113, 121, 123, 125, 126, 134

Baines, Janice, 37–38, 46–47, 61
Baker, C., 5
Bakhtin, M., 16
Baumgarner, Phillip (teacher), 118
Beaumont, Karen, 100
Bell, Donna (teacher), 46–47, 83, 84
Bentley, Dana Frantz (teacher), 45–46
Bhattacharjee, Y., 5–6
Bird, L. B., 133, 139–140
Bishop, Rudine Sims, 31, 41, 42, 78, 98
Blanco, Eileen (teacher), 33–34, 80, 84, 97, 113–114, 126, 129
Bomer, Randy, 121, 123
Boynton, Sandra, 97
Bracegirdle, P. J., 31
Bradby, Marie, 34–35
Bronson, P., 35
Brown, Margaret Wise, 107
Brown, Monica, 34
Bryant, P., 93, 132
Burke, C., 40, 57–58, 90, 104–106

Cahnmann, M., 35
Calkins, Lucy, 31–32, 99, 101–102, 121, 123, 125, 129
Canagarajah, A. S., 4
Cappellini, M., 81, 85
Carle, Eric, 32, 96
Cazden, C., 26–27, 62
Cheruvu, R., 4–5, 14, 16, 20, 23
Choi, Yangsook, 34
Chong, Erin (teacher), 121
Clark, K. B., 35–36
Clark, M. K., 35–36
Clay, Marie M., 6, 18, 24, 28–29, 87–90, 106–107
Clewell, B. C., 5
Cohen, C. C., 5
Compton-Lilly, C., 28
Cooper, Melrose, 100

Daniels, E., 118
Daniels, H., 118
de la Peña, Matt, 1–2, 41–42, 100
Delpit, L., 44, 135, 142, 143
Derman-Sparks, L., 5, 14, 15
Dernikos, Bessie, 24–25
Deterding, N., 5
Dewey, J., 82
Diaz, Junot, 41–42
Diggs, Taye, 36–37
Dobek, Maryann, 31
Dyson, Anne Haas, 2, 5–7, 13, 15–17, 28, 30, 66, 67, 72, 79, 85, 102, 103, 112, 113, 140, 142

Earick, Mary, 40, 41, 43
Edelman, Marian Wright, 94
Elliott, S., 8
Ewald, Wendy, 37

Faltis, C., 19
Fassler, R., 18, 71

Fletcher, R., 138
Flood, J., 132
Foley, Greg, 136–137
Fountas, I., 31, 48–49, 87
Frasier, Debra, 64
Freire, Paulo, 15, 16, 18, 39, 40, 45–46, 64, 81, 82, 87

García, E. E., 23
García, E. H., 23
García, O., 142
Garner, Eric, 75, 79
Gee, J. P., 13
Genishi, Celia, 2, 4–7, 14, 15, 17, 20, 23, 26, 28, 54, 60–61, 66, 85, 102, 103, 142
Glover, M., 113, 115
Gonzalez, N., 10, 23
Goodman, Ken S., 87–90, 103, 133, 139–140
Goodman, Y. M., 17, 20, 26–27, 28–29, 40, 66, 72, 74, 83, 90, 104–108, 112, 113, 133, 139–140
Goodwin, A. L., 4–5, 14, 20, 23
Goswami, U., 93, 132
Graves, Donald, 55, 111, 113, 121
Greenberg, J., 18, 23
Gregory, E., 21, 22
Gutiérrez, K., 16, 17, 21, 22, 84–85

Halliday, M. A. K., 71
Harste, J., 57–58, 106
Heard, Georgia, 121–123, 129, 135–136
Heath, Shirley Brice, 6, 9, 12, 13, 15, 18, 20, 28–29, 39, 61, 62, 103
Hilliard, A., 19

Hodges, R., 132
Holdaway, D., 97
Hru, Dakari, 100
Hughes, Langston, 7, 36

Jarvis, D., 46–47, 83, 84
Jay-Z, x
Jennings, L. B., 104
Jensen, J., 132
Johnston, Peter, 99–100, 130

Kates, Bobbi, 37
King, Martin Luther, Jr., x, 43
Kleifgen, J., 142

Ladson-Billings, Gloria, ix–xi,
    2, 3, 7, 12, 15, 21–22, 59,
    61, 67, 76, 77, 83, 95,
    126–127, 142
Laínez, René Colato, 34
Laman, Tasha Tropp, 98, 118,
    121, 125–128, 130
Laminack, L., 134
Lapp, D., 132
Lester, Julius, 35, 36
Lindfors, J., 27, 40, 67, 105,
    111, 113, 118, 125, 130
Llerena, Carmen (teacher),
    33–34, 80, 84, 97, 113–
    114, 126, 129
Long, S., 21, 22, 37–38, 40,
    94
Long, Susi, 33n
Lubeck, S., 48

Malik, Karina, 95–96
Mallory, B. L., 5
Martell, Jessica (teacher), xiii–
    xv, 31–34, 47–58, 62–72,
    75–80, 83–85, 94–95,
    119, 126–127, 131–132,
    136–139
Martens, P., 83, 104, 112
Martin, Bill, Jr., 32, 96
Martínez, D., 16, 22, 84–85
Martínez-Martínez, Victoria,
    32n
Martin, Trayvon, 75

Matusov, B., 22
Maxwell, L. A., 5, 6
McGee, L., 114
McIntosh, Peggy, 43
McKissack, Patricia, 100
Mead, F., 93
Medina, Jane, 34
Merryman, A., 35
Mills, H., 104, 109–110
Moats, L., 92
Moll, L., 10, 18, 23
Morales, P., 16, 22, 84–85
Morales, Yuyi, 36, 85
Morrell, E., 99, 111, 140
Moscoso, Gabriela, 24–25
Myers, Walter Dean, 36

Neff, D., 10, 23
New, R. S., 5
Nieto, S., 14, 56–57

O'Keefe, T., 104, 109
Owocki, G., 17, 20, 26–29,
    57–58, 66–68, 72, 74, 83,
    106–108, 112, 113

Paley, Vivian G., 4, 13, 14, 26,
    30, 40, 59, 67, 69, 75
Paris, D., 2n, 3, 83
Parks, Rosa, 43
Parnell, P., 66
Parr, Todd, 37, 66
Piestrup, A. M., 131
Pinnell, G., 31, 48–49, 87

Ramsey, P., 5, 14, 15
Ray, Katie Wood, 111, 113,
    121, 123, 127, 130–131,
    134
Recorvits, Helen, 34
Richardson, J., 66
Ringgold, Faith, 35
Rogoff, B., 5, 22, 130, 142
Rollins, Elizabeth (teacher),
    138
Rosenblatt, L., 82
Routman, R., 30, 39, 41, 85,
    96–97, 99, 101–103, 116,

121, 138, 142

Santora, M. C., 9, 14
Schickedanz, J., 114
Shanklin, N., 134–135
Short, K., 42, 106
Siegel, M., 30
Simon, C. A., 36
Smitherman, G., 7n, 131
Soto, Gary, 49, 50
Soulja Boy, 37
Souto-Manning, Mariana, 7,
    8, 12–14, 16, 18, 25n, 27,
    32, 37, 41, 46, 60, 61, 81,
    84, 141
Squire, J., 132
Sterponi, L., 13
Stires, S., 5, 6
Swadener, B., 48

Tafolla, Carmen, 138
Tisdale, C., 37–38
Tolan, K., 99, 101–102
Tompkins, G., 116
Tonatiuh, Duncan, 31
Trujillo, Rafael, 77–78
Turner, Ann, x
Twine, F. W., 35

Uchida, Yoshiko, 138

Valdés, G., 14, 20, 23
Valenzuela, A., 61
Van Sluys, K., 118
Volk, D., 21, 22, 37–38
Vygotsky, L. S., 22, 23, 67,
    69–72, 90, 103, 118

Watson, D. J., 40, 90,
    104–106
Weatherford, Carole Boston,
    75, 95
White, S., 22
Whitmore, K., 83, 112
Wilde, Sandra, 90, 106, 107
Woodson, Jacqueline, 24–25,
    35, 55–57, 75, 136, 138
Woodward, V., 57–58

SUBJECTS

ABC books, xv, 24–25, 84–85
Adoptive families, 66
African American Language (AAL), 7, 7n,
    10–12, 18–19, 21, 27, 100, 131
"All About" books, 21
Alphabet books, xv, 24–25, 84–85
Alphabet charts, 83
Alphabetic principle, 133
American Museum of Natural History, 138
American Speech-Language-Hearing Association
    (ASHA), 19
And Tango Makes Three (Richardson & Parnell),
    66
Apprenticeship, 130–131
Appropriateness, as term, 3, 5, 20, 23, 37, 60
Assessment, 103–110
    of comprehension, 106
    of cue use, 105–106
    of interest and motivation, 104–105
    of literacy concepts, 106–109
    of reading level, 12
    role in informing teaching, 109–110
    of writing development, 138–140
Assets inventory, 142
Authenticity, in writing, 111, 118
Authoring, 29–30
Author studies, 55–57, 77–78, 136–137
Awakening the Heart (Heard), 122, 123

Banking approach (Freire), 45–46
Barnyard Dance (Boynton), 97
Best Part of Me, The (Ewald), 37
Bible, 28
Big books, 46–47, 114–115
Bilingualism, x, 5–6, 48–54, 71, 77–78, 98
Black is Brown is Tan (Adoff), 36
Black Lives Matter, 75–76
Books, concepts about print (Clay), 6, 18,
    28–29, 85, 86, 95, 106–109
Bracelet, The (Uchida), 138
Brown Bear, Brown Bear, What Do You See?
    (Martin & Carle), 32, 96
Brown Girl Dreaming (Woodson), 55, 57
Burke Reading Interview (Goodman et al.), 40,
    104

Call-and-response interactions, 131
La Casa Azul (East Harlem bookstore), 72
Chocolate Me! (Diggs), 36–37
Chunks, 132, 133
City of New York, 8
Classroom environment, 40–43
    examining classroom talk, 73–74
    inventory of, 40–41
    library, 41–42
    Nuestro Tiempo (Our Time), 57–58, 68–73
    room arrangement, 42–43

Common Core State Standards Initiative, 12,
    20–21, 24–26, 33–34, 37, 48, 50–51,
    64–68
Communities of practice. *See* Learning
    communities
Community literacies, 20–21
Comprehension, 106
Concepts About Print (Clay), 6, 18, 28–29, 85,
    86, 95, 106–109
Cooperative Children's Book Center, 61, 94
Core Knowledge Foundation, 44
Creating Classrooms for Authors and Inquirers
    (Short & Harste), 106
Critical dialogue, 25, 95–96, 98
Cue systems, 10, 30–31, 60, 61, 84, 86–91,
    100, 103, 105–106
Culturally relevant teaching and learning
    diverse classrooms and, 2–3
    histories of children, 34–35, 43–44, 62–67,
        78–80
    home and community connections in, 23–25,
        28
    learning communities in. *See* Learning
        communities
    listening to children and, 7, 10–15, 16, 21,
        40, 48–54
    names of children, 32–34, 84
    oral language and, 77–79
    racial identities of children, 35–37, 41–42, 96
    reading and, 82–83, 91–103
    sociocultural approach and, 22–25
    voices of children, 37–38
Curriculum, racially equitable teaching, 43–44

Day the Towers Fell, The (Santora), 9, 14
Dead Family Diaz, The (Bracegirdle), 31
Deficit discourses, x, 2–5, 10, 13, 18–20, 115,
    141–142
Developmentally appropriate practice (DAP), 3,
    5, 20, 23, 37
Día de los Muertos (Day of the Dead), 23–24, 31
Directionality, 18, 29, 81, 86
Diversity, 17–38, 71–73. *See also* Culturally
    relevant teaching and learning
    books portraying, 31
    at center of teaching, 21–22
    deficit perceptions, x, 2–5, 10, 13, 18–20,
        115, 141–142
    family and community funds of knowledge,
        10, 18, 20, 23, 24, 47, 48–54, 62–67, 77,
        79–80, 82, 84n, 105, 111, 117, 122, 135,
        138, 140, 141
    honoring diversities, 2–3
    language homogeneity versus, 4–6
    mainstream American English and, 6
    nature of, in K-2 classrooms, 1–4
    as the new "normal," 2

reading, writing, and talk, in diverse
    classrooms, 2–4, 31–32, 54–57
    standardization of teaching versus, 5, 6–7
Dominant American English
    defined, 6
    home language versus, 108
    kindergarten "readiness" and, 6–7
    language variation and, 100
    multilingualism and, 10–12
    as norm, 7
    spelling and, 133, 134
    switching between African American
        Language (AAL) and, 131
    teaching English language learners, 15–16
    use in school, 18–19
"Down by the Bay" (song), 84
Dreamkeepers, teachers as (Ladson-Billings), 7

Each Kindness (Woodson), 55
Early fluent reading, 81
Early reading, 81
Early writing, 112–113
East Asian languages, 29, 86
Ebonics. See African American Language (AAL)
Emergent reading, 81, 85
Environmental print (Clay), 24, 27–28, 46,
    47–48, 75–76, 84, 85, 92, 134, 139
Eurocentrism, 61
Every Student Succeeds Act of 2015, 5
Existence proofs (Souto-Manning), x

Faces of Ground Zero–10 Years Later (exhibit in
    New York City), 8–10
Fairness, 13–14, 26, 59, 67, 75–76
Family Book, The (Parr), 66
Family involvement, 47–54
    cultural knowledge, 48–54
    The History of Us (oral history project),
        62–67, 79–80
    technical knowledge, 47–48
Fantasy play, 13–14, 26, 30, 35–36, 40, 57–58,
    59, 67–73, 75–76
First Animal Encyclopedia (Arlon), 127
Fluent reading, 81
Fountas and Pinnel Benchmark Assessment System
    (Fountas & Pinnell), 31, 48, 87
Freedom on the Menu (Weatherford), 75, 95–96
Friendship, 13–14, 26, 59, 67, 75–76
Fundations, 92
Funds of knowledge (Moll et al.), 10, 18, 20,
    23–24, 47, 48–54, 62–67, 77, 79–80, 82,
    84n, 105, 111, 117, 122, 135, 138, 140,
    141
Funny Bones (Tonatiuh), 31

Generative themes, 24–25
George (student), 27
Gettin' through Thursday (Cooper), 100
Goin' Someplace Special (McKissack), 100

Google Translate, 71
Graphemes, 133
Graphic organizers, 126
Graphic-sound correspondence, 87
Graphophonics, 30–31, 84, 86–87, 89, 92–93,
    103, 135
Guided reading, 44, 48–54, 102

Histories of children, 34–35, 43–44, 62–67,
    78–80
History of Us, The (oral history project), 62–67,
    79–80
Homogeneity, 4–7

I Ain't Gonna Paint No More! (Beaumont), 100
"I Am From" activity, 34–35
I am René, the Boy/Soy René, el Niño (Laínez),
    34
"I Can Read Swag" (Long), 37–38
Independent reading, 30–31, 44, 85, 98–99
Independent writing, 128–131
India, 22
Infinite capacity (Delpit), 142, 143
Interactive writing, 44, 116–121, 122
Interpretive knowledge, 29, 107, 109
I Spy activity, 114
It's Okay To Be Different (Parr), 37

Japanese language, 29, 86
Juan (student), 7, 8–15, 16
Just In Case (Morales), 85

Large-group talk, 62
Last Stop on Market Street (de la Peña), 1–2, 100
Learning communities, 39–58, 142
    authenticity, interest, and play in, 40, 54–58
    classroom environment, 40–43
    curriculum, 43–44
    family involvement in, 47–54
    The History of Us (oral history project),
        62–67, 79–80
    teaching strategies, 44–45
    valuing literacy of children, 18, 31–38, 45–47
Let's Talk About Race (Lester), 35, 36
Letter-sound correspondence, 84n
Letter writing, 55, 72
LGBTQ families, 66
Library, classroom, 41–42
Life at the Limits (exhibit in New York City),
    138
Listening
    importance of, 74
    to student voices, 7, 10–15, 16, 21, 40,
        48–54. See also Learning communities
    valuing stories children tell, 18, 31–38
    in writing conferences, 130
Literacy. See also Oral language; Reading;
    Writing
    concept of, 17

Literacy., *continued*
  as dialogic and social, 23
  observing and documenting children's
    practices, 8–15, 18–22
  teachers as learners, 15–16, 18, 69, 70
Literacy Dig activity, 84–85, 114
Lived experiences, 46
Looking Like Me (Myers), 36

Make a Wish Bear (Foley), 136–137
Marisol McDonald Doesn't Match (Brown), 34
Martín (student), 48–54
Mentor texts, 14, 23–24, 32, 37, 55, 85, 127,
    136–137, 138
Mexicans and Mexican Americans, 23–24,
    48–54
Mid-workshop teaching points, 101–102
Minilessons, 101–102, 123–128, 131
Miscue analysis, 90–91, 107–108
Momma, Where Are You From? (Bradby), 34–35
Monolingualism, 5–6, 71
Morning messages, 118–121
Multiculturalism, 15–16
Multilingualism, x, 4, 5–6, 10–16, 71
My Name is Jorge (Medina), 34
My Name is Yoon (Recorvits), 34
My People (Hughes), 36

Name Jar, The (Choi), 34
Names of children, 32–34, 84
Name Storybooks activity, 32–34
Naming (Freire), 15
National Association for the Education of Young
    Children (NAEYC), 5
Nettie's Trip South (Turner), x
New York City terrorist attacks (2001), xi, 8–15
No Child Left Behind Act of 2001, 5
Nuestro Tiempo (Our Time), 57–58, 68–73

One-on-one talk, 62, 73
On Our Way to School (ABC class book), 24–25,
    84–85
Onset, 93
On the Day You Were Born (Frasier), 64
Oral language, 59–80. *See also* Listening
  components of, 60
  connections with writing, 79–80
  culturally relevant teaching and, 77–79
  documenting and supporting development
    of, 26–27
  examining classroom talk, 73–74
  functions of talk, 74
  The History of Us (oral history project),
    62–67, 79–80
  importance of, 26–27, 59
  linguistic diversity, 71–73
  in moving beyond scripted practices, 14–15
  multilingualism and, 10–16
  nature of, 60–61

storytelling tradition, x, 61–67
and three Fs of childhood (Paley), 13–14, 26,
    30, 40, 57–58, 59, 67, 75–76
valuing, 18, 31–38
Other Side, The (Woodson), 55, 75

Palestinian Americans, 78–79
Partner reading, 98–99
Phonemes, 133
Phonics, 30–31, 84, 86–87, 89, 92–93, 103,
    135
Phonology/phonological awareness, 60, 61, 92,
    132, 133–134, 135
Picture walks, 46, 101
Play. *See* Fantasy play
Portuguese language, 71
Pragmatics/pragmatic knowledge, 10, 18–20,
    60, 61, 87, 103
"Pretty Boy Swag" (Soulja Boy), 37–38
Print knowledge, 6, 18, 27–30, 85, 86, 106–
    109
Procedural writing, 21, 50–54
Purple Little Bird (Foley), 136–137

Questions, in storytelling, 61–62

Racial identities of children, 35–37, 41–42, 96
Read-alouds, 30–31, 35, 42, 44, 53–54, 93–96,
    114–115
Reading, 81–110
  assessment in documenting literacy practices,
    103–110
  assessment of, 12, 103–110
  author studies, 55–57, 77–78, 136–137
  in balanced literacy framework, 30–31
  cue systems, 10, 30–31, 60, 61, 84, 86–91,
    100, 103, 105–106
  culturally relevant, 82–83, 91–103
  cultural nature of, 91–92
  as decoding, 81, 86, 87, 88, 90, 91–93, 96
  early, 81
  early fluent, 81
  emergent, 81, 85
  empowering young children as readers,
    83–85
  environmental print (Clay), 24, 27–28, 46,
    47–48, 75–76, 84, 85, 92, 134, 139
  fiction versus nonfiction, 9, 13–14, 16, 24
  fluent, 81
  guided, 44, 48–54, 102
  independent, 30–31, 44, 85, 98–99
  like a writer, 127
  nature of, 82, 86–90
  official versus clandestine, 13
  reader strategies, 92–93
  understanding early literacy, 81, 85–93
Reading conferences, 99–101
Reading workshop, 97–103
Rime, 93

Running records, 90–91, 106, 107–108
Scaffolded support, 30–31
Scale of Writing Development (Bird et al.), 139–140
Self-talk, 62, 73
Semantics/semantic knowledge, 10, 60, 61, 86–87, 88, 93, 103
September 11, 2001 terrorist attacks, xi, 8–15
Shared reading, 44, 96–97
Shared writing, 131–132, 138
Show Way (Woodson), 35, 55
Sketch-to-stretch, 106
Small-group talk, 62, 102–103
Social nature of learning (Souto-Manning), 11, 12
Sociocultural approach, 22–25
Spanglish, 7, 18–19
Spanish language, 7, 10–12, 18–19
Spelling, 132–135
Standard English. *See* Mainstream American English
Starbraid and the Three Bears (class story), 61
Story mapping, 126
Storytelling, x, 18, 61–67, 121, 122
Subtractive perspective, 61
Symbol weavers (Dyson), 112–113
Syntax/syntactic knowledge, 10, 60, 61, 86–87, 88, 103

Talk. *See* Oral language
Tar Beach (Ringgold), 35
Teachers College Press (tcpress.com), 3, 23, 34, 37, 40, 41, 67, 75, 82–83, 106, 115, 141
Teaching Tolerance, 94
Tell it Again! Read-Aloud (kindergarten unit), 44
Terrorist attacks, September 11, 2001, xi, 8–15
Thank You, Bear! (Foley), 136–137
Think-Pair-Share activity, 36, 116
This is the Rope (Woodson), 35, 55, 138
Three Fs of childhood (Paley), 13–14, 26, 30, 40, 57–58, 59, 67, 75–76
Tickle Tickle (Hru), 100
Today's Schedule, 45
Too Many Tamales (Soto), 49, 50
Transcription, 128, 130
Transformation of participation (Rogoff et al.), 22
Translingualism, x, 4
Trucks (Dobek), 31

La última ola de Marianela (Trujillo), 77–78

UNESCO, 5

Venn diagrams, 37
Visiting Day (Woodson), 24–25, 55
Visual strategies, 132, 133–134
Viva Frida (Morales), 36
Voices of children, 7, 10–15, 16, 21, 37–38, 40, 48–54

Ways with Words (Heath), 20
We Can Read big book, 46–47
We Had a Picnic This Sunday Past (Woodson), 55
We Need Diverse Books (website), 94
We're Different, We're the Same, and We're All Wonderful! (Kates), 37
What Can You Do with a Rebozo?/¿Que Puedes Hacer con un Rebozo? (Tafolla), 138
When I Go To Bed big book, 114–115
White doll-Black doll experiments, 35–36
Whole-group area, 42–43
Whole language, 30–31
Word walls, 46, 83, 134
Word work, 93, 133
World Bank, 5
Writer's notebook, 113–114, 123
Writing, 111–140
    authoring and, 29–30
    author studies, 55–57, 77–78, 136–137
    connections with oral language, 79–80
    documenting growth in, 138–140
    independent, 128–131
    interactive, 44, 116–121, 122
    motivating writers, 135–138
    notation systems, 28, 30, 90
    overprivileging, 10, 13
    planning one's writing, 127–128
    procedural, 21, 50–54
    publishing celebrations, 131–132
    with purpose, 113–116
    reading like a writer, 127
    spelling, 132–135
    understanding early literacy, 112–113
    valuing children's experience and expertise, 115–116
Writing conferences, 111–112, 129–130
Writing workshop, 44, 111, 115–116, 121–132, 140

Zone of proximal development (Vygotsky), 23, 67–70, 103, 118

About the Authors

Mariana Souto-Manning, Ph.D., is Associate Professor and Coordinator of the Early Childhood Education Program at Teachers College, Columbia University. She is a former early childhood teacher and now teaches courses related to early literacy and multicultural education. Souto-Manning is author of five books, including the award-winning *Multicultural Teaching in the Early Childhood Classroom: Approaches, Strategies, and Tools, Preschool–2nd Grade* (Teachers College Press, 2013). From a critical perspective, her research examines the sociocultural and historical foundations of early childhood teacher education, early schooling, language development, and literacy practices in pluralistic settings. Her work can be found in journals such as *Linguistics and Education, Research in the Teaching of English,* and *Teachers College Record.* She is the recipient of a number of research awards, including the AERA (American Educational Research Association) Division K Innovations in Research on Diversity in Teacher Education Award. She has held various appointed and elected positions with professional organizations, currently serving as NCTE (National Council of Teachers of English) Research Foundation Chair and AERA Language and Social Processes Special Interest Group Chair. She lives in New York City with her spouse and children. For more information, visit http://www.tc.columbia.edu/faculty/ms3983/

Jessica Martell is a public school teacher in New York City and an instructor at Teachers College, Columbia University. Jessica holds a master's degree in Bilingual Education from Hunter College, City University of New York (CUNY). She has 18 years of experience teaching dual-language (Spanish/English) and inclusive kindergarten, 1st, and 2nd grades. She is a trustee of the NCTE Research Foundation, a charter member of NCTE's Professional Dyads and Culturally Relevant Teaching program, and a member of the NCTE Task Force on Equity and Early Childhood Education. In 2014, she received NCTE's Early Childhood Educator of the Year Award. She lives in East Harlem, New York, with her spouse and children. This is her first book.